HD
9940
.U6
L453

Cray, Ed.

Levi's

LEVI'S

ED CRAY

Illustrated with Photographs

BOSTON

HOUGHTON MIFFLIN COMPANY

1978

Library of Congress Cataloging in Publication Data

Cray, Ed.
  Levi's.

  Includes bibliographical references and index.
  1. Levi Strauss and Company — History.   I. Title.
HD9940.U6L453   331.7′68′70973   78–19027
ISBN 0–395–26477–4

Printed in the United States of America

V 10 9 8 7 6 5 4 3 2 1

For
Ruth Lauren Adams,
In Memoriam
and
For Frank, Mike and Sam,
Friends

Never, indeed, have I seen a man so badly turned out. Too evidently unshaven since his disappearance, he was gotten up in a faded flannel shirt, open at the neck and without the sign of cravat, a pair of overalls, also faded and quite wretchedly spotty, and boots of the most shocking description. Yet in spite of this dreadful tenue, he greeted me without embarrassment and indeed with a kind of artless pleasure. Truly the man was impossible, and when I observed the placard he had allowed to remain on the waistband of his overalls, boastfully alleging their indestructibility, my sympathies flew back to Mrs. Effie. There was a cartoon emblazoned on this placard, depicting the futile efforts of two teams of stout horses, each attached to a leg of the garment, to wrench it in twain. I mean to say, one might be reduced to overalls, but this blatant emblem was not a thing any gentleman need have retained.

— HARRY LEON WILSON, *Ruggles of Red Gap*

Contents

Illustrations

following page 114

Levi Strauss, about age forty
Jacob W. Davis
Levi Strauss, about 1890
Levi Strauss & Co., 14–16 Battery Street, about 1870
Levi Strauss & Co., 14–16 Battery Street after the earthquake
    of 1906
Engraving of the Donahue Building
The perils of an old-time drummer
A cattle round-up in 1902
A page from a company catalogue
An operator in the Koverall factory
Daniel Koshland
Walter Haas, Sr.
Peter Haas, Sr., and Walter Haas, Jr.

LEVI'S

Chapter I

The Founder

THE THREE MEN sat contented, pleasantly heavy with the evening meal. In the golden aureole of the dining room's gaslights, they puffed on Gunst's finest Havanas and sipped the last of the champagne with which they began and ended their nightly ritual.

No matter the three of them ate at the damask-draped and wood-paneled St. Francis every night, at the same table, with the same waiter, amid the same potted palms. Each dinner was a satisfying celebration of their success in America, *Gott sedank.*

Here, in San Francisco, such things were possible. A Jew from Bavaria, still speaking with an accent, could eat in the finest hotel in the city. And not only eat dinner, but have the other diners acknowledge him with a sober nod or an invitation to join their table for dessert. He understood these gestures of tacit recognition that he was one of them, a leader in the business world.

He could overlook the occasional raised eyebrow or the few who pointedly turned away when they recognized that the millionaire dry-goods merchant Levi Strauss and the wealthy dry-goods merchant Abraham Gunst were dining with their bookmaker. But the bookmaker was their friend — and he ate with them every night, whether he could afford his meal or not. If today he couldn't pay, tomorrow he could pay twice over. Or the day after. Levi Strauss did not turn his back on his friends.

Any sense of outrage the scandalized felt would have been compounded if they knew that the dark-complected dry-goods merchant would soon leave the dining room to visit discreetly a married woman. But some things one did not flout, even in a city as tolerant as San Francisco.

So it was this evening. So it had been in the years since he had established himself. Levi Strauss felt comfortable in the routines of his day. They lent stability to a man's life.

Each morning at nine o'clock he left his home at 317 Powell Street on Union Square, and set off for work. On the way, he might stop to chat at Neustadter Brothers across the street or at David Bachman and Company next door. They were competitors, but friends as well.

At ten o'clock he would stride into the building Levi Strauss and Co. had built in 1866 on Battery Street, four floors of the finest domestic and foreign dry goods, clothing, and household furnishings to be had in the West. Ten salesmen were on the road, and if they complained about the snow blockade of last winter or the reluctance of store owners to place substantial orders, still, business was good. Salesmen always complained. These young men didn't appreciate how much better off they were than he had been when he first came to America. They carried no eighty-, no hundred-pound packs. They *schlepped* no rutted tracks to weather-worn farmhouses in mountain hollows, hoping for a twenty-five-cent sale of needles or duck cloth or handkerchiefs. They didn't tramp ten miles in a day to sell three dollars' worth of goods — and there had been days when he counted himself lucky to sell a dollar's worth.

Once shouldered, the peddler's pack was never forgotten. He was seventeen when he first set out from Lexington, Kentucky, in a straw hat and linen duster to peddle the goods older brothers Jonas and Louis provided from New York. The pack was a shoulder-wracking burden always, but a blessing too, with its supply of New York merchandise. The basket peddlers and trunk carriers with their secondhand clothes and patched pans had little hope of prospering. At least a pack peddler such as he could aspire to become a wagon-baron, like Lazarus and Isidor Straus, and Henry Lehman in Alabama, or Adam Gimbel, and Meyer Guggenheim in Pennsylvania. Beyond the wagon — and it had seemed a majestic ambition at the time — perhaps a dry-goods store. The Seligman brothers had done it, and then become bankers.

The immigrant merchants all shared the dream — if they weren't dispirited by their poverty, their poor English, or their fear of this unfamiliar country with its rough ways.

His salesmen today had an easier life. They gave away no two-for-a-penny spools of thread or packets of pins to thank the gaunt women of the hills who bought their meager goods. He had, for a friend was always a better customer than a stranger. His salesmen didn't even carry their merchandise with them. Instead, they traveled with large sample trunks and catalogues, at company expense, often by railroad. They rented wagons for their wares and stayed in hotels, perhaps not hotels of the quality of the St. Francis, with its Irish-linen tablecloths or its waiters who carefully effaced themselves between courses. But any hotel was better than a barn, or sleeping by the side of roads, huddled in the brush along a creek, wary of strangers who might rob a Jewish peddler of a few cents and his goods while he washed his socks in the stream. Washing their socks every night — *that* the salesmen still did. It was the drummer's legacy, a habit handed down through the generations.

Levi Strauss, however, no longer hung his socks on a bush to dry, or wore them wet, squishing in his shoes the next day. The Strauss family now hired maids, Mexican or Irish girls, to wash, clean the house, iron shirts, even cook.

His older sister Fanny needed the help. Their brother Louis was visiting from New York — six days to cross the entire continent on the Central Pacific. It was a wonder, compared with the three months Levi had spent sailing from New York to San Francisco twenty years earlier.

With Louis staying at the house, there were twelve to care for: Fanny and David Stern; their seven children; brother Jonas's oldest son, Nathan, here from New York to learn the business; and Levi Strauss, at forty-four the acknowledged head of the family.

As the head of the family, perhaps he set a bad example for

Nathan, lately calling himself Nathaniel. Unlike David Stern, Levi Strauss did not take an active part in the temple. He and Louis Sloss contributed the gold medal given each year to the best Sunday School student, but his attendance in *shul* was, well, sporadic.

Of course, Nathan-Nathaniel should be interested in the fancy houses and fancier ladies. He was young, and such diversions were normal. Furthermore, he knew about his uncle. Levi Strauss was a vigorous bachelor, and if he was not the most handsome of men, still there were those ladies who found his dark features and heavy-lidded eyes intriguing. He seemed to be hiding deep secrets, secrets of shrewd business dealings, no doubt. With what else would a man as wealthy as Levi Strauss concern himself? There was also about him an air of independence, of self-confidence. At a time when the Orthodox Jew left his hair uncut and all men of prominence grew wondrous beards, Levi Strauss remained clean-shaven. So Levi Strauss, in black split-tail coat and glistening stovepipe hat of Japanese silk, was considered a prize catch in San Francisco's Jewish community. It would be unthinkable for him to marry outside the faith, even if he did not strictly observe the rituals of his religion. Yet the ambitious mothers of the Jewish neighborhoods along O'Farrell, Geary, and Post no longer set their eyes on the most eligible bachelor in the city, perhaps in the entire West. They had learned to reckon with Fanny Stern.

Each year that Levi remained unmarried, Fanny's resolve grew stronger. At first it was unspoken; then it was hinted. In time it would be openly discussed. Fanny wanted her four sons to inherit Levi Strauss & Co.

Jacob, her oldest, was now twenty-two, a salesclerk on Montgomery Street, learning a business. Sigmund, sixteen, Louis, just become a *bar mitzvah,* and the youngest, Abraham, would follow Jacob's lead. They were devoted to their uncle.

The children of the other partners in Levi Strauss & Co. were not as devoted or had other interests. The sons of his oldest sister, Mary, who had died a few years before, and

William Sahlein, worked at the Battery Street office but talked of opening their own retail business. Louis Strauss had no children. Jonas's son Nathan was a playboy, a swell, a New Yorker. To Fanny it was clear: Who else was more deserving than the four sons of the fifth partner, David Stern, and his wife, Fanny Strauss Stern?

Unless Levi Strauss, the senior partner, took a wife. Then he might have sons of his own, heirs to rend the design Fanny had conceived in the quiet sewing room of the house on Powell Street.

So Fanny looked after her younger brother, made a home for him, and carefully introduced him to women she calculated would occupy his affections. Married women.

For Levi Strauss, it was a comfortable arrangement. Fanny cared for him at home and introduced him to pleasant women whom he might visit from time to time. The women welcomed his attentions — he was, after all, a considerate man — and enjoyed the special favors he provided. Thus he retained his freedom yet could savor the masculine pleasures of married life. He remained single.

The arrangement left his personal life placid, his business routines settled. He entered the Battery Street building at ten each morning, checked the sales figures from the previous day in the office at the rear of the building, then spent the balance of the morning on the floor. He talked with customers, Samuel Marks down from Roseburg, Oregon, on his annual buying trip, or Weinstock and Lubin, buying some linens for their store in Sacramento. Strauss spent time with the fifty stockclerks and bookkeepers employed by his company; there was no better way to learn what was happening in the business than to talk to the people on the floor or in the shipping room. In this way, too, he could seek out the twenty-dollar-a-week clerks who might be advanced in the growing establishment of Levi Strauss & Co. Nephews or no, it was Levi Strauss's staunch belief that advancement should be earned on merit alone.

Initially, the clerks were nervous around him, but when they learned he preferred "Levi" to "Mr. Strauss," they felt more at ease. Leaning against stacks of merchandise or examining bills of lading in the gaslight of the chandeliers — he had spent $25,000 to finish the interior of 14–16 Battery Street — the major figure in this $3-million-a-year company discussed business with his employees and friends.

After lunch he would be off to meetings of the other enterprises in which he had an interest: real estate holdings, the gas company, the succession of businessmen's committees.

Then back to Battery Street and the Italianate building with its cast-iron front, its patented freight elevator, and the multifarious inventory. Late in the afternoon, he finally sat down at the desk in the large office he shared with his confidential bookkeeper and close friend, Philip Fisher. Together they reviewed the books and dealt with the day's correspondence.

At five o'clock he left the building; Fisher would close up an hour later. As always, Barney Schweitzer was waiting; the wool merchant, too, was a man of firm habits. Together they would have a drink and discuss the day's affairs before setting off for home.

Habitually, he walked the eight blocks from Battery to Powell. On pleasant days, when there was no westerly, he would stride the distance, his black hat secure, enjoying the promenade. The men of Levi Strauss's day were stout advocates of brisk walks, weekend outings, and life-restoring spas.

West from Battery he crossed Montgomery Street, his five-foot six-inch figure lost among the many men of substance in identical black broadcloth suits and silk tophats. Beyond the gaslighting of Montgomery Street and its growing clutch of banks and financial offices lay Kearny, with its horse cars and mile of fashionable shops. Ten-foot-tall panes of glass flanking Kearny disintegrated with each earthquake, providing yet more business for the insurance brokers on Montgomery. In the block beyond, Chinese vegetable sellers glided among the black-frocked men and whaleboned women. Dupont Street would soon be renamed Grant, for a general turned President was far more important than a mere naval officer. Thirty thousand Chinese lived along Dupont in no more than twelve square blocks, sleeping in rotation in dank warrens, working for as little as a dollar a day. The dark alleys behind the exotic façades of Chinatown were every bit the equal of Shanghai's worst; police roped off Dupont to protect unwary Caucasians from the highbinder's cleaver when the perennial tong wars erupted.

The Chinese were industrious, willing to accept jobs white laborers disdained. As long as the Celestials remained laundrymen or servants, there was no trouble — but recently they had been taking in piecework, sewing shirts and pants at a fraction of the price that white women demanded. It would lead to trouble sooner or later, for the Chinese and for the business firms that deprived the Irish and Germans of work. That some of the employers were Jews was more troublesome still to the businessmen of Temple Emanu-El.

San Francisco's Israelites or Hebrews — "Jew" was considered opprobrious — had prospered with the city in the twenty years since Levi Strauss had arrived, on March 14, 1853. Fleishhackers, Steinharts, Zellerbachs, Haases, and Sutros were now among the city's most influential citizens. In the boisterous city that was San Francisco during the Gold Rush, "Jew" and "Gentile" were distinctions of no significance. There was no established elite, no acknowledged society. (The city would not have a social Blue Book until 1888.) Those who might have formed a protective, self-serving class of First Citizens — the Indians and Mexicans who had lived on the sand hills before James Marshall's discovery of gold at Sutter's Mill — were swept away by disdainful Forty-Niners.

The most successful of these fortune hunters, either miners or merchants, became California's elite in the 1850s. That so many arrived with murky pasts or dubious futures was best overlooked. In a land where fortunes were built and squandered with startling suddenness, only today's reputation mattered. Yesterday James Flood and W. S. O'Brien were running a restaurant on Montgomery and snatching whispers of financial gossip; today they were the most successful speculators in the Comstock silver mines. Tomorrow they would

----

parlay their millions into the richest bank on the Pacific Coast.

Christendom had never known such a commonweal as San Francisco. A sandy military post for a tattered garrison of Mexican troops was transformed into Babel and Babylon in two years. Swarms of newcomers heaved up the city: wealthy, or at least privileged, men from the Atlantic seaboard; dirt-poor adventurers from the hardscrabble lands west of the Alleghenies and Appalachians; and foreigners, especially Germans and Irish. Jews here had no bitter struggle for self-respect or acceptance from an established society such as they confronted elsewhere; there was no ordained aristocracy, no social peerage. The first to San Francisco began as equals.

Israelite and Gentile existed in commercial symbiosis, though they rarely mixed socially and intermarried even less often. According to one memoir, "The seclusion of the Gentiles across the street was not distorted into intentional distinction or racial prejudice. No one desired to break through the natural barriers established by differences of race or background."

Whatever the reason for segregation, it was of no moment to Levi Strauss on his late-afternoon promenade; rather, that was a time to review the day's business, to savor his cumulative accomplishments. No Forty-Niner he — that distinction was significant only to obituary writers at the newspaper offices — still, he had come far since his arrival in New York in 1847, a *Yehud* from Buttenheim who spoke no English and had no trade.

San Francisco, too, had changed in these twenty years. The brick sidewalks Levi Strauss sauntered along once had been wooden, the muddy streets planked at $5.00 a foot, nothing so much as kindling for the city's recurring fires. To twenty-four-year-old Levi Strauss, one of 33,000 immigrants to San Francisco that year, the city in 1853 appeared almost as noisy, as roiling a monument to turmoil as New York had six years before. There were twenty-three wharves, thirteen ironworks, four sawmills, five theaters, nine billiard-table manufacturers, 117 dry-goods establishments, twenty-eight breweries, and 399 saloons.

Most of the 78,000 fortune seekers living there crowded into thirty-six blocks close to the waterfront from Clark's Point to the Rincon. A few dairymen and farmers lived farther out near the old Mission, futilely resisting incorporation into the city, shunning the horse-drawn omnibus to the business center on California Street. The wood-frame and tent city had been leveled by fire six times, rebuilt, and leveled again. Each time the number of brick and iron buildings increased, wisdom finally overtaking expedience. Those that survived the ordeal by fire would be shattered by the earthquakes of 1865 and 1868.

It was a turbulent city, waterfront speculators reinvesting hundredfold profits and reaping once again. Residential areas appeared, burned to the ground, and were rebuilt as business blocks, all in the space of weeks.

It was also a violent city: by the summer of 1853, the coroner had dutifully recorded 1200 murders. Another 2400 were rumored; wanderers disappeared as suddenly as they had appeared.

Meanwhile, the sand dunes on the leeward shore of the windy peninsula had been leveled to fill in the bay, whole blocks at a time reclaimed by the "Steam Paddy" that dug out the hills. Where once wharves had squatted on the festering mudflats and beached sailing ships had metamorphosed into noxious boardinghouses, entire city blocks teemed with commerce. Levi Strauss & Co.'s building sat on such filled-in mudflats, a new company on a reclaimed lot in a city of fortune.

Strauss had remained close to the waterfront since his arrival in San Francisco. His first shop in the city had been built on pilings, a haphazard appendage to the Sacramento Street wharf. Where better for a fledgling merchant with little capital and only the small stock he could ship from New York to this gold-infatuated city on the Pacific Ocean? He sold his merchandise to teamsters in work clothes, their grimy pants carelessly stuffed into the tops of muddy boots;

to dapper gamblers and affluent saloonkeepers; to the eager new arrivals, the greenhorns off to the diggings on the next riverboat.

He was left with funds enough to buy more goods at the raucous auctions held when new ships and cargoes arrived. Each vessel, each auctioneer's lot, each speculative bid provided a little more cash in this city which disdained coins smaller than two bits; where the $20 gold piece was the common currency; where merchants habitually told customers, "Ignore the bits," and rounded prices to the nearest quarter. It was a strange, even disquieting, business practice for the youth accustomed to penny and nickel sales.

In a city short of merchandise, in a country where whim and need were dispelled by gold dust, the prices were far higher than Levi Strauss had ever imagined while in New York. A packet of needles he had sold for one cent when tramping through Kentucky just a year before now brought a quarter. A $5.00 blanket went for $40.00 in San Francisco. Tin plates and cups bought for pennies in New York sold for dollars on the way to the gold fields.

The money he took in he paid out at the tumultous auction houses for new supplies until Jonas and Louis in New York could replenish his stores. It would be two weeks, perhaps three, before his letters reached them by the Pacific Steamship Mail Lines, across Panama to the Gulf of Mexico, and from there by packet to New York. Then it might take as long as four months for the goods to arrive by clipper ship around the Horn. If they did arrive. More than one vessel had broached in the torturous seas of the Strait of Magellan. Still, the risks were worth taking: one dollar earned in San Francisco bought two, three, or four dollars in New York goods. As long as Jonas and Louis could provide him with cheap goods made in New York, he could sell dear in San Francisco.

In the meantime, he bought and sold what he could, guarding his money, fretting at the delay, and all the while paying numbing bills for his lodging and meals. One dollar for coffee and doughnuts. Two dollars for dinner, as much as a laborer in New York made in a day. Yet the higher prices meant more odd coins for the adroit businessman to snare.

Levi Strauss was that. He had paid the city business-license fee of $100, $25 quarterly, and opened the shop at the foot of Sacramento Street with his brother-in-law, a one-time peddler from St. Louis, David Stern. David had come to San Francisco late in 1851, the first of the family to discover the riches to be made in California.

By 1856, they had moved to larger quarters a few doors up the street. Fanny and her three children, Jacob, Caroline, and Henry, had joined them. In time, five more children would be born to David and Fanny in their new home, and eighteen-year-old Henry would die there. San Francisco had become home for two former pack peddlers.

Retail sales gave way to the wholesaling of New York goods. Levi Strauss was peddling still, his samples stored in large trunks on the back of the hired wagon, but now only to retail merchants in the oddly named gold towns. Up the Sacramento River by sidewheeler to the new state capital, then following the wagon tracks to the northern mines at Michigan Bluff, where Leland Stanford kept store; to Grass Valley, where Lola Montez, the king's whore, now lived; then south to Placerville, Fiddletown, Murphys, Columbia, and Chinese Camp.

Levi Strauss's merchandise changed with each ship arrival. To the dry goods and men's shirts his brothers sent west, he added the occasional bargains bought at auction on the San Francisco docks — hats one time, yardage the next. It made little difference, so long as he could sell it quickly, take a small profit, and turn his varied stock.

It was a precarious business, one in which the value of a merchant's inventory changed with the arrival of the next ship. Lookouts posted on the top of the tallest hills gave as much as a day's warning before a ship managed to run in through the Golden Gate and dock. Prices dropped 25 percent with word that a vessel had been sighted; unsure of the ship's cargo, merchants slashed the prices on all their goods rather than hold on to high-priced inventories during periods of glut. Only the wealthiest importers and the saloonkeepers could maintain prices, the first because they had the financial reserves to hold out, the others because there never was enough whiskey in water-short San Francisco.

Levi Strauss & Co. had no such financial reserves. Strauss and his brother-in-law frequently slept in their shop on blankets pulled from the stock when they expected the arrival of a ship. While David marked down the goods, Levi was to attend the inevitable auctions of goods shipped by eastern speculators to San Francisco jobbers and auction houses.

Levi preferred that Jonas and Louis ship goods directly to Levi Strauss & Co., but that presented difficulties. Communication between San Francisco and New York was slow, the answering shipment slower still. Even the celebrated Pony Express, which did not begin service until April 1860, took nine days to race the 2300 miles between Sacramento and St. Joseph, Missouri — at a cost of $5.00 for each half-ounce letter. The riders could carry no merchandise; that had to come by ship, either around the Horn or from New York to Chagres in Panama, then across the isthmus to Panama City by wagon and later train, finally by the Pacific Mail Steamship's twice-monthly service between the tropical port and San Francisco.

In addition, money and specie accumulated in San Francisco had to be transported by ship to New York to pay for those goods. The steamship line's day of departure became also the due day for business accounts, a tradition that would survive until the turn of the century.

Not until 1869 and the driving of the Golden Spike in Promontory, Utah, would those problems end. In the meantime, all San Francisco merchants were at the same disadvantage. In such a situation, small though the firm was, Levi Strauss & Co. prospered. On February 1, 1861, when the *California* steamed for Panama on its regular run, it carried shipments of gold from the Rothschild agent in San Francisco totaling $128,000; from Levi Strauss & Co., "clothing jobbers," $59,732.34; from Strauss's competitor, Jesse Seligman, $43,000. (Seligman was to leave the San Francisco dry-goods business to join his brothers in their New York banking house, J. and W. Seligman; he would return some years later to start a bank. Jesse, *né* Isaias, Seligman was one of the first prominent Hebrews in the city, secretary of Howard Volunteer Fire Company Number 3, a signal honor since the volunteer companies, even in fire-beset San Francisco, were elite organizations.)

By the 1860s there were five partners in Levi Strauss & Co.: the brothers Levi, Jonas, and Louis, and their two brothers-in-law, William Sahlein and David Stern. The youngest among them, Levi, was the acknowledged organizer in California, the one with the best head for business. They might have named the company Strauss Brothers, but S. Strauss, no relation as far as they could tell, was already using that name on his Dupont Street dry-goods store. Levi Strauss & Co. it became, and so it remained, long after S. Strauss had given up the ghost.

Levi Strauss & Co. survived, virtually the last of the pioneering dry-goods houses left in the city. There were years of setbacks: 1855, when the local bank of Adams & Co. collapsed on "Black Friday"; 1857, the grim year of the national panic; the war years, during which cotton became scarce and Confederate raiders harassed San Francisco–bound shipping; and 1868, when an earthquake — "in sudden fury like the spring of a tiger upon its intended victim" — had cracked the firm's two-year-old Battery Street building from basement to floriated cornice.

For a Bavarian Jew, even one who was now a citizen of the United States, there were special times of stress. In 1856, the second of the city's Vigilance Committees had sprung up, these good citizens of San Francisco establishing themselves in Fort Gunnybags on Sacramento Street, less than a block from Levi Strauss's business. Behind a five-foot wall of sandbags, the members of the committee had tried and condemned two murderers. In the name of expedient justice, they hanged the two men from the second story of the Truitt Building while the 5000 members of the Vigilance Committee guarded against legal interference. To immigrants like

Levi Strauss, who could recall the treatment of Jews in the Old World, the hanging bodies of the two murderers seemed a threatening harbinger. Few Bavarian Jews supported the vigilantes; most were relieved when they disbanded.

There were disquieting reminders, too, that even though Jews were citizens, they remained "a race apart." In 1858, the State of California adopted a Sunday-closing law, fixing the Sabbath on the first, not the seventh, day of the week. To Levi Strauss, unlike more observant Jews, the law made little difference; his wholesale establishment was open six days a week, from 6:00 A.M. until Philip Fisher closed twelve hours later. The Reform Jews of Temple Emanu-El had little difficulty adjusting their Orthodox upbringing to New World realities.

It was more difficult to accept the slanders of Dr. John T. McLean, the medical-doctor-turned-special-agent of the Treasury Department in charge of collecting customs duties in San Francisco. Questioned about the low rate of collections at the port, McLean told a congressional committee, "A large portion of our under-evaluations are found to be made by that class of people — German and French Jews. I think the Israelites a little more prone to that sort of business than persons who are not of that religious persuasion."

There was no other way for the doctor to explain his lagging collections without blaming himself. The great majority of those importing merchandise to San Francisco were Israelites, and much of what they brought in was dry goods and clothing. The house of Levi Strauss boasted in its catalogues the finest of French and German manufactures, Irish linen, Belgian lace, and Italian shawls.

McLean's tenure did little for the already poor reputation of San Francisco's customs collectors. (The customs house until the Civil War was a haven for second sons of southern politicians, for failed law partners of southern congressmen. The satrapy came to be known along the Embarcadero as "the Virginia Poor House.")

Firing back at McLean — and the very fact that they felt strong enough to answer a government official broadside for broadside is significant — the Israelites of San Francisco snapped: "He [McLean] is a professional man, a doctor of medicine, and by accepting an inferior and not too honorable Government office, he has virtually proclaimed his inability to earn an honorable support by the practice of his profession, but does not hesitate to malign those who do, and who contribute to the public weal instead of slandering others."

An Israelite of San Francisco, Levi Strauss, was secure enough not to be troubled by the Dr. McLeans. He had other, more pressing, matters to consider. The opening of the transcontinental railroad had triggered an even greater flood of immigrants than the city had known during the frenetic days of '49. Daily, land speculators and real estate developers made fortunes.

And then there was the interesting letter from the Reno tailor, mentioning that he had developed a new pair of pantaloons he wanted to patent, one with the seams fastened by copper rivets.

Chapter II

A Credit to His Race

JACOB YOUPHES was eternally restless. Born in 1831 near Riga, the Baltic seaport sometimes Russian, sometimes Polish, sometimes Swedish, and sometimes German — but never Latvian — at twenty-three he had embarked for the New World. A Jew in Riga, German-speaking or not, was always the *untermensch*.

For two years he had sought his fortune, first in New York City, then in Augusta, Maine, but a journeyman tailor made little money. In September 1856, after a month-long sea voyage and Panama crossing, Jacob Youphes, now Jacob W. Davis, arrived in San Francisco.

He worked for six months as a tailor before setting off for the rowdy mining town of Weaverville to open his own shop. He had had only moderate success when rumors of a gold strike on the Fraser River in British Columbia filtered south. Jacob Davis set out for Canada in the summer of 1858.

In the next nine years, Davis's fortunes waxed and waned. He opened a store for outfitting miners; then left that to become a partner in a brewery. He married in 1865, but neither his wife, Annie, nor the birth of his first child could ease Davis's restlessness, the need to be something more than a Jew with a small business.

Two years after his marriage, Davis sold his interest in the brewery and bundled his small family aboard the steamship *Pacific* for San Francisco, once again to start anew. He invested this time in a coal business on Pine Street, only to see it fail disastrously within six months. At a time when the city was wild with rumors of silver pouring from the Comstock into Virginia City, Davis decided to try once more in that boom town.

For all the Comstock silver making others wealthy, in two months Jacob Davis had failed as a tobacconist. His cash gone, he turned to tailoring "in earnest," as he later put it, working by candlelight until midnight and one o'clock. He had debts to pay.

Eleven months more at his old trade was enough. In June 1868, he took his slight savings and growing family to Reno. That railhead on the Central Pacific had just been laid out, and a new town offered possibilities for an ambitious man. There, Davis became a partner again in a brewery; a community populated by as many railroaders and teamsters as Reno would certainly develop a thirst for beer.

The brewery was no more successful than his earlier efforts had been. He fitfully resigned himself to a tailor's shop in Reno.

The workingmen of that town had little use for fine clothing. By the beginning of 1869, Davis was fashioning horse blankets, wagon covers, and tents from an off-white duck cloth his brother-in-law had purchased for him from the San Francisco dry-goods house of Levi Strauss & Co. The duck-cloth goods he sold to the blacksmith, who in turn peddled them to teamsters shipping in and out of town.

The business was steady, if not the financial bonanza he had so long pursued. He could support his family, though there were few spare coins. In October 1870, he ordered a second roll of duck cloth from Levi Strauss & Co., asking for credit; the dry-goods firm, probably with no more than routine consideration, opened a small account for the tailor in Reno.

By the time the woman customer knocked on his door in December 1870, Jacob Davis, thirty-nine years old, was shrouded in his faded dreams. He recognized the woman in his shop as the wife of the huge laborer stricken with dropsy.

The couple lived in a shack across the steel-bright Central Pacific Railroad track behind his shop.

"I want a pair of pants for my husband," she told the tailor. "I can't get a pair large enough to fit him in the stores. I want to send him up to chop some wood, but he has no pants to put on."

"He'll have to come in so I can take his measure," Davis explained.

"He cannot very well come as he has nothing to put on," she snapped. "Besides, he's sick."

Davis shrugged. A sale was a sale. He suggested the woman use string to measure her husband's waist, knotting it to indicate his girth. Observing propriety, Davis advised her to use an old pair of pants to measure the inseam from crotch to cuff.

Her husband needed the strong pants before the first of the year, she continued. A laborer was hard on his clothes; a woodcutter, harder still. Davis nodded; clothes did not wear very well in the labor of the West. Teamsters, surveyors, miners had long complained that their garments came apart, especially where the pockets were sewn to the pants. Davis himself had tried unsuccessfully to develop special stitches to keep the pockets on men's pants from ripping free.

The strongest material he had in the shop was the ten-ounce duck twill. It was hard to work, but he had had some experience with it.

The pants she ordered would cost $3.00 and would not be ready until after the first of the year. As was the custom, she paid in advance, carefully counting out the coins, promising to return with the knotted string.

Davis cut the oversized garment from the tent fabric he had used on the horse blankets. Sitting cross-legged on his bench — the tailor's traditional working posture — he sewed rather than riveted as he did when attaching the front straps and crouper to the horse blankets.

"So when the pants were done," he later recalled, "the rivets were lying on the table. And the thought struck me to fasten the pockets with those rivets."

Davis hammered the rivets into the corners of the pockets, front and rear. If rivets would hold a horse blanket together, rivets would hold a pocket to his pants. "I did not make a big thing of it. I sold those pants and never thought of it for a time." He saw the pants worn just once — as the bulky woodcutter with dropsy set off for the hills.

The following month, the Reno tailor made to order four more pairs of pants of the duck cloth, riveting the pockets and seams. Davis recalled that his customers paid cash but not who they were; like the man with dropsy, the first to wear riveted pants were forgotten.

Selling principally to "travelers" — men he did not know personally, he was at pains to point out — Davis made ten pairs of the riveted pants in February 1871. The following month he sewed a dozen more, to outfit members of a surveying party. The business was unsolicited but steady. His riveted pantaloons were walking advertisements, one teamster noticing them on another, then seeking out Davis.

There was no single style to Davis's pants. He attempted unsuccessfully to order duck cloth in colors other than the off-white. Instead, he added nine-ounce blue denim purchased in bolts from the one dry-goods wholesaler he knew in San Francisco. Some pairs, sold in the cold months of 1871 and 1872, he lined with blanketing for insulation. They were bulky, but warm enough in the Sierra Nevada's bitter winter.

The frustrated tailor from Reno realized he had finally made his strike. He was selling the riveted pants as fast as he could make them, for the first time in his life certain of customers for his wares. He was an entrepreneur now, no longer a mere tailor, having sold more than 200 pairs of the garments in the last eighteen months. The once modest bill at Levi Strauss for yardage and blanketing had climbed to $350, which a year and a half ago would have been a staggering sum.

His success raised a problem for the burgeoning manufacturer. Others might steal his idea, but his wife insisted he spend no more money on patent fees. He had two already, and they had earned him nothing. Worse still, he was spending much of what he made perfecting a steam-powered canal boat and a steam-powered ore crusher. There was just no cash for a third patent.

Even if he had one, he lacked the means to distribute his product widely.

Davis approached the town's druggist, William Frank, a friend he could trust with his private correspondence; the immigrant from Riga had never felt secure about his written English.

On July 2, 1872, the two drafted a letter to the only people Davis knew who might be interested in his riveted pants, the "Gents" of "Mess. Levi Strauss & Co." The very size of his bills suggested he was on to something.

Noting he was remitting a check to balance his account — first things first — Jacob W. Davis added:

I also send you by Express 2 ps. Overall as you will see one Blue and one made of the 10 oz Duck which I have bought in greate many Peces of you, and have made it up in to Pents, such as the sample.

The secratt of them Pents is the Rivits that I put in those Pockets and I found the demand so large that I cannot make them up fast enough. I charge for the Duck $3.00 and the Blue $2.50 a pear. My nabors are getting yealouse of these success and unless I secure it by Patent Papers it will soon become a general thing. Everybody will make them up and thare will be no money in it.

Therefore Gentleman, I wish to make you a Proposition that you should take out the Latters Patent in my name as I am the inventor of it, the expense of it will be about $68, all complit and for these $68 I will give you half the right to sell all such clothing Revited according to the Patent, for all the Pacific States and Teroterious, the balince of the United States and half of the Pacific Coast I resarve for myself. The investment for you is but a trifle compared with the improvement in all Coarse Clothing. I use it in all Blankit Clothing such as Coats, Vests and Pents, and you will find it a very salable article at a much advenst rate ...

These looks like a trifle hardley worth speakeing off but nevertheless I knew you can make a very large amount of money on it. If you make up Pents the way I do you can sell Duck Pents such as the Sample at $30. per doz. and they will readly retail for $3. a pair.

The two sample pairs of pants that Davis forwarded to San Francisco, and the prices Davis charged, convinced the partners. Workingmen's pants sold ordinarily at wholesale for $9.00 and $10.00 per dozen. Davis got $36.00 merely by adding a penny's worth of rivets here and there.

Though the West Coast house had not engaged in manufacturing to this point — Jonas and Louis Strauss contracted in New York's sweatshops for the goods the firm did manufacture — there was no reason workingmen's garments should not be added to the company's line. The $68 patent fee was a trifle, with 50 percent to 75 percent profits in the offing.

To manufacture the pantaloons, the company had a number of options. It could contract the work to other firms already manufacturing men's clothing. Or it could follow the lead of Jonas and Louis in New York, and divide the work among a myriad of small contractors who hired sewing-machine operators to work in their own homes. Or Levi Strauss & Co. might open its own manufacturing facility, that the biggest risk requiring the most capital.

The partners decided promptly. A week after Davis's letter arrived, the patent attorneys contacted by Levi Strauss & Co. forwarded the petition for a patent to the Reno tailor for his signature. By August 9, 1872, he had returned the petition and description of his invention, and the attorneys submitted the application for Jacob W. Davis's "improvement in fastening seams . . . in order to prevent the seam from starting or giving away from the frequent strain or pressure."

It was rejected, examiners in the Washington Patent Office asserting similar rivets had been used to bind seams and tongues in soldiers' boots during the Civil War.

It would take ten months and three amendments totally revising the application before the examiner finally approved

----

Davis's patent for a "fastening for pocket-openings whereby the sewed seams are prevented from ripping or starting from frequent pressure ... by the placing of the hands in the pockets ..." Davis specifically abjured seeking a patent on the use of rivets for all seams in clothing.

The patent was granted to Davis on May 20, 1873, and assigned to himself and Levi Strauss & Co., of San Francisco, California.

Meanwhile, the Reno tailor continued to turn out denim and duck overalls, now labeled "patent applied for," in his small shop. On August 4, 1872, James A. Ferguson, a merchant in Wadsworth, Nevada, became the first storekeeper to buy the garments for resale to his customers. Ferguson paid $12 for four pairs already made, three for customers who had inquired about the riveted garments, and a fourth for himself — without rivets.

On March 30, 1873, the increasingly confident Jacob W. Davis concluded his largest sale. A shopkeeper in Palisade, a Central Pacific water stop 250 miles to the east, ordered "some of your patent riveted pants." Davis sent all he had in stock, twenty pairs of duck, and billed Prichard's of Palisade $60. Prichard was free to charge whatever his teamster and railroad customers were willing to pay.

What Davis could do on a modest scale in the Comstock, Levi Strauss & Co. could do throughout the West. By agreement, on April 26, 1873, the tailor closed his shop hard by the railroad tracks in Reno, gathered Annie and their six children, and moved to San Francisco for the third time. In the city directory for 1874, Davis proudly listed himself not as a tailor but as a manufacturer.

A succession of business conferences with the partners of Levi Strauss & Co. had settled their relationship. As foreman, Jacob would supervise the production of the waist pantaloons, or overalls, as Levis Strauss insisted on calling them. (Cut from white and brown duck twill and from denim, the pants thus could not be "jeans"; jeans were inexpensive pants that Strauss had sold in Kentucky thirty years earlier. Kentucky jeans were fashioned of fabric first woven in Genoa, Italy. Centuries of mispronunciation — the sails on Columbus's ships, some said, were of Genoese cloth — has transformed "Genoese" to "jeans." Denim, similarly, was an ellision of *serge de Nîmes*, cloth of Nîmes, France.)

Davis sold a half-interest in his patent to Levi Strauss & Co. Additionally, he agreed to leave all sales to the dry-goods house while he concentrated on manufacture. With at least a portion of the money received, he bought a comfortable home on Folsom Street, below Market, in the once-prestigious South Park residential area.

The San Francisco partners elected to duplicate the experience of the Strauss brothers in New York: the manufacturing of riveted overalls would be done by seamstresses working in their homes. Essentially, tailor Davis was multiplied a hundredfold. The women would be paid on a piece-rate basis, and the best of them, sewing five pairs of pants a day, might earn as much as $3.00. It was a goodly wage for an industrious woman, as much as her mechanic- or bricklayer-husband earned for a day's labor building the new cable-car lines in the city.

Davis supervised the cutting of the heavy yardage, the bundling of the fifteen or more separate pieces of cloth and the buttons to be sewn into garments, the morning delivery of the bundles to seamstresses' homes around the city, and the evening pickup of the finished pantaloons, still warm from the hot irons.

He made his initial delivery to Battery Street on June 2, 1873. Three days later, the firm recorded its first sale of riveted pants made from ten-ounce white duck. The first denim pants were delivered and sold two weeks later.

Within a month the men realized Davis could not keep up with the demand. Conceivably, Levi might have turned to Jonas and Louis, asking them to produce the finished garments. New York swarmed with desperately poor immigrants willing to work for as little as $6.00 a week in the tenements of the Lower East Side. But whatever Louis and Jonas might save in labor, Levi would pay shipping the riveted clothing to California.

Instead, the company consolidated its cottage industry into a small manufacturing plant. Jacob Davis did it the only way he knew how — as an amalgam of operators, each completing entire garments. Sixty women sat around an overhead shaft in the steam-powered Donahue Building on Fremont Street. Each stitched the denim or duck trousers and jackets, slitting buttonholes, then hammering on the rivets. Paid on a piece-rate basis, they worked against the clock for an average of $3.00 a day; the more garments they finished, the more they earned.

Had Davis any experience as a manufacturer, he might have installed a different system. Eastern clothing houses had learned output in their sweatshops increased, and earnings with it, when a worker completed only certain parts of garments. With specialization came speed, as the relatively fewer tasks became routine operations for the workers.

Instead, Davis set sixty female sewing-machine operators to work in a large loft to meet the demand. They added riveted hunting coats to the line, then blanket-lined pants. By the end of the year, they had sold over 1800 dozen pants and coats for $43,510.

Such success was not to be overlooked by competitors, who quickly moved to imitate the patented pantaloons. On September 1, 1873, San Francisco manufacturer A. B. Elfelt began producing similar riveted clothing. At the same time, a Chinese entrepreneur, Kan Lun, started making riveted pants in a San Jose loft.

In the first of a series of sometimes grinding lawsuits against imitators, patent infringers, and counterfeiters, Levi Strauss & Co. brought legal action in January 1874, against both Elfelt and Kan Lun. Brandishing Davis's patent, Levi Strauss & Co. prevailed.

That year the firm sold 5875 dozen riveted pants, vests, coats, jumpers, and blouses for $148,471. The following year sales rose to $156,000 and, in 1876, to $188,921. Booming sales as far east as Utah and Colorado prompted Jonas and Louis to take on patented riveted clothing as well. Levi dispatched Jacob Davis late in 1876 to open a manufacturing plant at 77–79 Thomas Street in lower Manhattan. (The New York house of J. Strauss, Brother & Co. would sell patented riveted clothing until it was dissolved, after the death of the senior partner in 1885.)

The addition of the profit-rich riveted clothing to the extensive catalogue of Levi Strauss & Co. hardly occupied very much of the partners' time. Levi Strauss himself was increasingly active in business affairs far from the Battery Street building.

The black-clad Strauss was now a formidable figure in the community — despite an affable manner so unlike the severe mein expected of a merchant prince. In one way, he had come to resemble his financial peers: he was achieving a rotundity much favored by the doctors of his day as a sure sign of robust health.

Strauss's commercial prominence inevitably thrust him into civic affairs. When James Lick, a hosteler, donated to the new University of California the observatory bearing his name, Strauss was among the leading citizens who signed the obligatory memorial thanking Lick. The unruly San Francisco *Post*, in a June 1874 editorial, noted that the signatories included former Levi Strauss customer, now Central Pacific Railroad magnate, Leland Stanford; the erstwhile grain king of California, Isaac Friedlander, whose South Carolina–born wife insisted he was a "Hebrew," not a "Jew"; the state's largest individual landowner, Turkish-born James Ben Ali-Haggin; and Levi Strauss — among a sheaf of bankers. The newspaper added slyly: "If these gentlemen have such a profound appreciation of Mr. Lick's action, why don't they show it by going and doing likewise? And in the meantime, the mudsills of the community would entertain somewhat more profound sentiments of grateful appreciation and regard for them if they were to make a point of paying something like a fair share of the taxes."

Amid the success of the firm's business enterprises, on January 2, 1874, David Stern died at the home Strauss and he shared on Powell Street. "The highly respected pioneer merchant," as the newspapers described him in their obitu-

----

aries the following day, was fifty-one years old. David had been the first of the family to travel to California, the path-finder for Levi Strauss & Co. The first of the five partners to die, he was buried by the Eureka Benevolent Society, the Hebrew welfare-and-burial agency for which he had served as secretary when he first arrived in San Francisco.

For Fanny, newly widowed, life would go on much as before. She and her seven children would continue to live with her brother; she would keep his house and maintain a caravansary for the nephews working at Levi Strauss & Co.

For her oldest son, the sober Jacob, the death of gentle David Stern would be more unsettling. As his mother pointed out, there was now no Stern with Levi Strauss & Co. His younger brothers lacked his experience in business and were far too young to assume significant positions in the family firm. It was his duty, his responsibility, to assure his patrimony — for his brothers as well as for himself. Jacob dutifully surrendered his position on Montgomery Street and went to work for his uncles.

First grief, then joy, the proverb states. William Sahlein's wife, Mary, had died seven years earlier, leaving the widower to raise his two sons and his daughter, Rosa. The widow Stern, fifty-one, and the widower Sahlein, fifty-eight, married later that year. Thus the family remained bonded; not only did Fanny and her sons inherit David's fraction of the business, but she would share in Sahlein's as well.

The combined families, thirteen in all, crowded the Powell Street residence. The area had grown more commercial; the property was ideal for a business block. So Sahlein bought a new home at the corner of Post and Leavenworth streets, a quieter neighborhood of substantial houses farther west. At Fanny's insistence, Levi Strauss moved with them.

His routines continued unchanged. He strode about San Francisco, busy with his investments, sometimes on his own behalf, sometimes for the firm that bore his name. He was now a director of the Spring Valley Water Company, once controlled by the bankrupt silver king William Ralston. The firm floundered when Ralston's empire collapsed, but as the principal water source for the city it had to be salvaged. That took time.

As the scattered pieces of property in the city multiplied, Levi Strauss & Co. became a substantial landlord as well as dry-goods wholesaler. Then, in December 1875, Strauss and two friends purchased for $785,000 the combined Mission and Pacific Woolen Mills from the widow of the bankrupt Ralston. That sale, at a knockdown price, symbolized the passage of economic leadership from the financial adventurers of the last twenty-five years to the cunning capitalists of the next twenty-five. The oldest mills on the Pacific Coast, since 1853 they had been the major producers of fabric in the West. Blending wool from California, Oregon, and Australia, the mills had supplied Levi Strauss & Co. with woolen blankets and yard goods. They would become even more profitable as the source for the linings of the patented riveted clothing Levi Strauss was now manufacturing.

That clothing was a considered success, the firm widely advertising, "These goods are specially adapted for the use of FARMERS, MECHANICS, MINERS, and WORKING MEN in general. They are manufactured of the Best Material, and in a Superior Manner. A trial will convince everybody of this fact. USE NO OTHER, AND INQUIRE FOR THESE GOODS ONLY." If the one-time tailor Jacob Davis had any problem, it was finding women willing to work for him. Demand outstripped supply; there were never more than 150 dozen pairs of pants on the shelves at 98 Battery Street, barely a week's supply now.

There was an ample labor pool in the city, but Levi Strauss refused to take advantage of it. Employing Chinese laborers meant that white workers would be deprived of jobs. There was but one Celestial, the cutter, employed by the firm, and he had been hired only after successive white workers abruptly quit. Cutting multiple layers of tough denim and duck with a long knife took uncommon strength; the long hours demanded endurance. The Chinese cutter stayed.

Other manufacturers were less particular about depriving white families of a livelihood. In the smoky warrens of

Chinatown, Levi Strauss's competitors produced their duck and denim work clothes — paying a dollar a day to the queued men who hunched over sewing machines seven days a week.

Where else could they turn if they intended to compete with work clothes manufactured so cheaply in the East, manufacturers protested. They had no patented clothing for which they could charge premium prices and pay good wages. White women turned down seamstress jobs, preferring the better pay of domestics in the ornate houses springing up in the newly developed Western Addition. At least four fifths of the labor in the garment industry was performed by Chinese, one manufacturing survey of the time estimated. "Such an institution as an organized clothing factory, conducted by white labor, can hardly be said to exist on the Pacific Coast."

For years, employers had welcomed Chinese coolies to the Golden Mountains as a supply of cheap labor. Ten thousand Celestials had clawed the Central Pacific east from Sacramento through the Sierras to Promontory, Utah. Thousands more worked as stevedores, laundrymen, houseboys, and miners under debt-bondage. No job was too menial; almost no salary too low. So long as there was a shortage of labor in booming California, the Chinese found work that white laboring men would not or could not perform. So long as they remained in their appointed place, the Chinese enjoyed the toleration of their "betters."

Then, in 1873, the gilded age of industrial marvels imploded, crushed in the collapse of the nation's largest bank, Jay Cooke and Company. Bank runs, tight credit, and strikes followed successive wage cuts; as many as one million men across the country were left unemployed. Golden California was locked in a seemingly unending depression. Unemployed laborers from eastern states who had poured into the state since the opening of the transcontinental railroad four years earlier found themselves unable to earn a living, even in this El Dorado. California was no longer a land where penniless immigrants could find riches or, if not wealth, then at least a place of promise, of respectability. Those who might have farmed twenty years earlier found the best lands sequestered by the railroads. The golden streams had been picked clean of nuggets. The mines now offered deep-shaft work for no more than 30,000 underpaid men, mostly Chinese, where once 100,000 had been employed.

White laborers with no more to sell than their strength roamed the cities, stripped of pride, embittered because their wives alone could find work to support them. Jobs once spurned by these Irish immigrants, who had built the eastern portion of the transcontinental railway, they now grasped — whatever the pay. The contraction became constriction. Chinese laborers cut their wage demands to hold on to what little they had. Formerly enticing townsites laid out by speculators grew weeds, then succumbed to bankruptcies picked clean by scavenging lawyers. Even the prosperous house of Levi Strauss felt the depression; sales once comfortably between $2.5 and $3 million a year fell to $2 million.

The weather only aggravated conditions during the winter of 1876–1877. The worst drought in memory ruined the spring crops. Thousands of head of livestock, their tongues swollen to raw red gags, died of thirst in dusty *arroyos*. The cost of food shot up, other prices following.

Rage focused on the Chinese; victims would feed on other victims. On Sunday, July 23, 1877, the sour resentment erupted. A sympathy meeting called to support eastern railroad strikers exploded on the sand lots across from San Francisco's new city hall. Restless laborers howling "On to Chinatown," the truculent spokesman for the Workingmen's Party, Denis Kearney, lost control of the crowds ostensibly gathered to hear him savage the lords of capital and barons of privilege. Mobs stormed Chinatown, smashing into saloons and looting on their way, sacking shops that caught their fancy. By sheer drunken numbers, they swept aside the constabulary and swarmed up Dupont.

For three days the mob controlled the city. Fires blazed in Chinese laundries torched as their terrified owners fled. Firemen stood helpless, their canvas hoses slashed by the mob.

Chinatown was a smoldering shambles, buildings burned out, lacquer and silk wares spilling into the street to be crushed by the marauders. The riot edged toward the docks, threatening the property of the lords of capital, then receded.

By Wednesday night, fatigue had snuffed out the rage. San Francisco was quiet once more, but it would never be quite the same city. It had been purged by fire of its frontier idealism, the belief that every man might make his fortune with hard work and some luck; fire and the cold bath of Thursday's dawn hardened San Francisco into a city of classes — rich, poor, and poorer. In the guttering fires burned the last organized protest by white laboring men for thirty years.

Levi Strauss, the Sahlein and Stern families had watched the flames in the night sky just blocks from their homes at 621 Leavenworth. As terrifying as the three-day siege had been to the financially secure, the very lords of capitalism the workingmen attacked, for Levi Strauss it was an omen as well.

The firm had pondered expanding production of the patented rivet lines but was uncertain about appropriate hiring practices. The people they sold to, workingmen, had rampaged in the streets. The anger that sacked Chinatown might as easily be directed against Levi Strauss & Co. or the clothes the firm manufactured. If only to preserve its share of the market — perhaps 10 percent of the workingmen's clothes sold — the company would continue to hire "none but white labor." It was only fair that white labor make the garments white workingmen wore. And it was good business.

Electing to employ white women, Levi Strauss was also choosing to pay higher wages, as much as twice that of his competitors. To charge the necessary higher retail prices, Strauss had to offer commensurate quality that would significantly outwear those marketed by his competitors. Levi Strauss & Co. thus imposed a quality and price standard followed for the next hundred years.

Within a year, Levi Strauss & Co. was producing some 100,000 garments, five overalls or jackets per day, per operator. The riveted clothing could be bought in two colors and two fabrics: the off-white, frequently tan, duck, and the indigo-dyed denim. Lacking belt loops, the pants had suspender buttons instead, two in the rear, four in the front. Both denim and duck shrank ostensibly to fit, but an extra inch or two at the waist could be gathered by a cinch strap and buckle sewn onto the back of the trousers.

With expansion of the factory in 1877, Levi Strauss & Co. settled on the design of its patented riveted clothing. A single New England mill, Amoskeag, furnished the fabric, thus assuring Levi Strauss a standard dark blue color. Denim might be had in a variety of colors — all of which faded dramatically — but one mill's indigo blue was significantly different from another's.

In an effort to match the copper color of the unique rivets, Jacob Davis had used orange linen thread for the stitching. To distinguish the pants from those of competitors, the operators sewed in two curving V's, or arcuate rows of stitches, on the back pockets. (The arcuate design may once have been functional, binding the blanket lining to the pocket, but long after the lining had been discontinued, the arcuate design remained. The firm did not register its vestigial stitching as a trademark until 1942, the application stating that the arcuate pattern had been used since 1873. It is seemingly the oldest clothing trademark in continuous use.)

A printed oilcloth guarantee was tacked to the seat of the pants to proclaim this, the company's the "Two Horse Brand." The oilcloth "flasher" sported a steel engraving of two teamsters whipping a pair of dray horses in a vain effort to pull apart the riveted pants. The guarantee promised "a new pair FREE" if the present one of "exclusive XX special top weight all cotton denim" ripped.

In 1886, a second label, of leather, was added to the rear waistband, this too bearing the Two Horse logo. Unlike the oilcloth guarantee, the leather plaque was permanently affixed with orange linen thread.

Some pattern of pocket stitching, the orange thread, the leather patch, the very styling Davis imparted to the pantaloons — a tight-fitting, straight-legged, low-on-the-hips garment that could be tucked into a workman's boots — all became hallmarks of the western work pants. Indeed, the metal buttons, in effect oversized rivets, would also be widely imitated, down to the embossing of the manufacturer's name around the edge of the metal disc.

From year to year, the garments remained unchanged. They were functional, simple, and, above all, durable.

The strength of the garments was based on the fabric itself. Denim was woven from threads spun from long-staple cotton fibers, an inch to an inch and a half long, pulled from the white bolls. The inch-long fibers were twisted tightly in a counterclockwise spiral, binding the ends of the fibers together. Were the spiral of the thread untwisted, the individual fibers at any given point would pull easily from the strand.

The cotton thread was then bathed in the dye made from the indigo plant. The result, theoretically, was a deep blue, though the actual hue and intensity varied considerably from mill to mill, even from crop to crop. The blue yarns became the warp threads of the fabric, the longitudinal strands, forty, fifty, or sixty to the inch.

The fill, or latitudinal threads, were also cotton, somewhat thicker in diameter than the warp yarns, and less tightly spun. They were left undyed, in their natural white or gray-white color. Pulled by a shuttle across the twenty-eight-inch-wide fabric, the fill threads intersected the indigo warp yarns: over one, then under two, over one, then under two. Each successive pass of the shuttle began a step later, the second fill beginning under two, over one; the third fill, under one, over one, under two; the third returning to the over-one, under-two start. The shuttle's invariably repeated sequence imparted a forty-five-degree diagonal appearance or twill to the loomed denim. The over-one, under-two passage of the shuttle left more indigo-dyed cotton exposed on the face, more of the unbleached cotton exposed on the back; the impression was of a dark blue fabric on one side, a light blue on the other.

The hard twist of the blue threads, and the density of threads per square inch — as much as seventy warps and fifty fills per inch — imparted strength to the fabric. That strength was measured in an abstraction, weight per square yard of woven cloth. The more horizontal and vertical threads used, the heavier the material.

Levi Strauss's nine-ounce Double X denim was the heaviest fabric then milled. (When looms were later improved, the weight of the denim would increase to ten ounces per square yard.) The off-white duck cloth was virtually identical, but spun of more costly linen threads. On these two fabrics and their durability the reputation of the Two Horse Brand — and ultimately of the entire corporation — came to rest.

Other manufacturers chose to use a less costly material. That, coupled with the lower wages they paid, produced a 25 percent price differential between Levi Strauss and its competitors. Despite this, sales of the patented riveted clothing steadily increased. By 1881, the firm's invoices and advertisements invariably described the house as "sole proprietors and manufacturers of the celebrated patented riveted duck and denim clothing." Just how many were celebrating the garments beyond the confines of 14–16 Battery Street is problematical, but it is clear that the company was selling the garments to miners, cowboys, teamsters, and lumberjacks. Patented riveted clothes were "excellently adapted to the use of those engaged in manual labor." Sales were confined largely to the Pacific Coast, but Levi Strauss had agents as far as Mexico, the Hawaiian Islands, Tahiti, and New Zealand.

By the early 1880s, the factory had 250 operators. By the end of the decade, Jacob Davis, stomping through the Donahue Building, cursing broken power shafts and belts, supervised 450 factory hands. Another eighty-five worked as stockclerks, salesmen, and bookkeepers at the Battery Street offices and showrooms.

The patented riveted clothing remained a comparatively small, if profitable, part of Levi Strauss & Co.'s sales. In a letter written on July 28, 1881, to the New York office — managed by the sporting Nathan Strauss — the sober Jacob Stern grumbled that sales of clothing had fallen alarmingly.

> It is a pity that after being in the clothing business so long that we should virtually be driven out of it, but there is no use in hiding the fact that such is going to be the case unless a change takes place. We have had so many complaints this season [about quality] that it is discouraging. We had an idea that it was prejudice as we know that all the clothing houses have worked very hard against us, but where there are so many complaints (of which we lately sent you a few which we received in writing), it can't be *all* prejudice.

Clothing manufactured in the East constituted less than 10 percent of the firm's sales. "It was the same with our riveted goods — the sales were steadily decreasing all the time but you will notice that we are selling more than ever now." The duck and denim work clothes were earning more than the shirts, hosiery, and women's undergarments Nathan shipped from New York for resale in San Francisco.

Whatever the problem with Nathan's clothing, the firm was selling more dry goods than ever. Sales in 1880 reached $2.4 million.

That year was almost the last for the first generation of founders. At the beginning of 1881, first Louis Strauss, then William Sahlein died. Fanny was once again a widow. Meanwhile, Jonas, the oldest, had all but retired.

William Sahlein's sons began dropping out of the company. Moses left to open a retail "fancy goods" store, aware that Fanny, his aunt and stepmother, had already nominated the heirs of Levi Strauss. The affairs of the company fell more heavily on the Sterns, especially Jacob, admittedly "the poorest clothing man in the house." Jacob's younger brother Louis had joined the firm as an assistant cashier two years before. Now, with more of the burden falling on Jacob, their mother prevailed on Sigmund to forgo his career as a "capitalist" — so he was listed for two years in the city directory — and assume his rightful place as a buyer for Levi Strauss.

Sigmund was, after all, a favorite nephew of the founder, the most sporting of the four sons Fanny considered the ultimate heirs. It was Sigmund who attended Levi Strauss's parties in the private rooms at the St. Francis Hotel. It was

Sigmund who brought along his younger friends, especially the convivial beet-sugar heirs, John and Adolph Spreckels. (Within ten years, Sigmund would also introduce the young newspaper owner William Randolph Hearst, freshly expelled from Harvard for venting his contempt for his professors with an obscene gesture. Little Willie, who would become a great party-lover under Levi Strauss's tutelage, brought along his acidulous columnist Ambrose Bierce. Bierce provided the wit.)

In Fanny's mind, Sigmund surely had to work at Levi Strauss. He most resembled his Uncle Levi in both business sense and amusements. Jacob was too solemn, Louis too irresponsible, and Abraham, the baby, still too young either for business or the parties.

The marriage of Jacob Stern, her oldest, and Rosa Sahlein, William's daughter, delighted Fanny. The marriage of these first cousins and stepsiblings bonded into a dynasty the financial interests of two of the original partners. Fanny died, a satisfied woman, at age sixty-one, in 1884.

With her death, the oldest of William Sahlein's sons, Henry, left the firm, at thirty-four to strike out in business for himself. The parting was amicable; Strausses and Sterns were delighted with the subsequent storybook courtship and marriage of Henry to Caroline Fisher, the daughter of Levi Strauss's confidential bookkeeper.

In 1886, Levi Strauss closed the books on the old partnership. As part of the settlement, he sold eight pieces of property in downtown San Francisco for $640,000, apportioning that among the heirs east and west.

The firm of Levi Strauss & Co. was now completely in the hands of its namesake and the four Stern brothers. Strauss himself devoted less and less time to the dry-goods house. It was running well enough; clothing sales had improved with the addition in 1885 of a line of work shirts manufactured under Jacob Davis's supervision. Meanwhile, there were other endeavors to occupy his days, some of them far more lucrative than the dry-goods business.

In 1877 he had become a charter member and treasurer of

the San Francisco Board of Trade, organized "to prevent settlements by insolvent debtors without careful investigation; to resist all inequitable and fraudulent settlements; to collect and exchange trade or credit standing information; and to bring about joint action to collect debts..." The Board of Trade would also take an active part in lobbying the United States Congress for a Central American canal. The rotund Strauss served on a special committee that unanimously endorsed a Nicaraguan route as "greatly" preferable to a Panamian crossing. It would be shorter, the committee argued in an 1880 memorial to Congress, and would cost half the price to build.

The lobbying effort was one not only of civic duty, but of enlightened self-interest as well. The transcontinental railroad, by virtue of ruinously high freight rates, which favored east-to-west shipment of merchandise, effectively limited the trading area of San Francisco's merchants. Excessive freight rates prevented goods manufactured in San Francisco from moving much beyond the Sierra Nevadas. A quick sea route between New York and San Francisco would go far to breaking the hegemony of the railroads. (Railroad opposition to such a canal was one reason thirty-four years would pass before the first ship steamed through George Washington Goethals's engineering marvel.)

Strauss had already served as a member of the Honorary Committee of the California Immigrant Union, organized in October 1869 ostensibly to encourage and protect immigration from the Atlantic states and Europe. (In reality, its purpose was to provide a flow of cheap labor for employers confronted with demands for the eight-hour day and higher salaries.) The union had become a booster organization, and Strauss had devoted time to organizing an exhibit of California goods for a Paris exposition in 1878.

By the last decade of the century, Strauss's business interests entwined him with some of the richest men in California. When Los Angeles banker I. W. Hellman reorganized the Nevada Bank, he asked Strauss to become a director. When Hellman went on to found the Union

Trust Company, the first corporate trustee in the state, again he tapped Strauss for a directorship. Additionally, there was the real estate. One contemporary account noted:

> From time to time he invested his surplus funds in city property and became one of the potent factors in building the city. Many of the substantial business blocks on Kearny, Market, Post, Powell, Sansome and other streets [the very core of commercial San Francisco] were built by him. He has bought, built and sold much property, and is still the owner of valuable holdings.

Nor was that the end of his business activities. He was a director of the vast San Fernando Land and Milling Company, of the San Francisco Gas Company, and of the London, Liverpool and Globe Insurance Company, among others.

Though he paid occasional visits to the factory — grown to 500 employees — and still addressed the clerks at the Battery Street offices by their first names, Strauss paid less attention to the firm's day-to-day operations. For the first time, Levi Strauss & Co. was incorporated, Strauss holding 55 percent of the stock, the seven Stern brothers and sisters the balance.

If the firm faced any problem in the last decade of the nineteenth century beyond cyclical business recessions, it was the expiration of the patent allowing exclusive use of the rivet on its garments. Protected so assiduously for the seventeen years of its life, the patent by law passed into the public domain in 1890. Competitors who for years had hungered to imitate the pants stood ready to rush into the marketplace with cheaper versions of the Double X overalls.

To counter this, Levi Strauss & Co. introduced less expensive versions of its own, both in gray and blue nine-ounce denim. The Double X ten-ounce denim, now known around the company by its arbitrary lot number, 501, would remain in the line, inviolate, the quality standard against which all other riveted denim goods were to be measured.

Genoa-born Mary Rossi, 101 years old in 1977, vividly remembered seeing the proprietary Strauss about this time at the brick factory on Fremont Street. "He used to come to the door of the big room where we all worked and look it over. He never came in; he just gave the room a once-over. He always wore dark suits and carried a tall hat in his hand," she said in a voice at once hoarse and faint.

Then a young lady of sixteen, Mrs. Rossi was too shy ever to have talked to the founder. Instead, she busied herself at her sewing machine, stitching the bundles of twenty-four pieces of blue denim into engineers' overalls, or jumpers. "Except for buttons, when I got through, the jumpers were through," she said, her laugh surprisingly firm. Jacob Davis had incorporated that much specialization.

Occasionally, she did speak with the tailor-turned-factory-manager. "He was a nice gentleman," she recalled. "He spent most of his time in the office and didn't bother you," surely the factory worker's highest compliment for a boss.

Mrs. Rossi and the other 500 factory workers punched in each morning, then waited at their machines for the eight o'clock bell to begin work. Mrs. Rossi sewed jumpers, stitching one together in "one half-hour, less." Another bell ended the day at five, eighteen jumpers later.

"It was a good place to work as long as you did your job. I was too bashful to ask questions or socialize with the other ladies. There were all nationalities there — Italian and Spanish and Irish. Most were married."

Mrs. Rossi was satisfied at the Fremont Street factory. "It was clean, a good place to work. The people were nice, but you couldn't talk much to anybody but the person next to you. It was too noisy with all them rows and rows of sewing machines all in one big room, pants on one side, shirts on the other. Besides, you couldn't afford to talk during working hours; you were too busy."

Recurring business recessions, both local and national, and a surplus labor pool drove wages down. "We could earn a dollar-fifty a day when things went right. Sometimes they went wrong," Mrs. Rossi said with a smile. "Belts broke all the time, and machines, too. They had a belt boy and a mechanic to fix them. But when one broke, it was on your time."

Levi Strauss's visits became less and less frequent. He was once again occupied with railroads, this time in a struggle to save the city of San Francisco from the domination established by the Central Pacific tycoons and their new creature, the Southern Pacific Railroad.

Frustrated by discriminatory freight rates, San Francisco saw its trade with the rest of the nation dwindling. Both Portland and Los Angeles threatened to overtake the city by the Golden Gate as the commercial center of the Pacific Coast unless something was done. More infuriating still, the railroad's arbitrary rates made it cheaper for a merchant to ship goods from Chicago to California's interior valley through Los Angeles than for him to ship directly from San Francisco to this traditional market.

The solution was to create a railroad to challenge the Southern Pacific's monopoly — against determined opposition from the railroad and a corrupt state legislature. In 1891, forty San Francisco businessmen, including Levi Strauss, each advanced $1000 to survey a rail line between San Francisco and Salt Lake City. The effort aborted when the group failed to sell the necessary $1 million in stock.

Two years later they tried again. There was more urgency than ever, for the upstart Los Angeles Chamber of Commerce was excitedly talking about building its own railroad northward, thereby solidifying that brash city's claim as the new center of western commerce.

Led by beet-sugar king Claus Spreckels and two of his sons, John and Adolph, and vociferously supported by Willie Hearst's raucous morning *Examiner*, another syndicate organized the San Francisco and San Joaquin Valley Railroad. If they couldn't build a competitive overland route, at least they could open up the interior valley.

Again Levi Strauss was a subscriber, this time for $25,000. The parties of old at the St. Francis were a bond between these would-be railroad barons.

This time they were more successful. Construction began

late in 1895; by May 1898, the rails had snaked 350 miles to the southern end of the fertile San Joaquin Valley. Less than a year later, without the direct consent of his minority stockholders, Spreckels sold the railroad to the Atchison, Topeka and Santa Fe. The AT&SF immediately entered into a freight-pooling and tariff agreement with its putative rival, the Southern Pacific, on the proven business dictum that a shared monopoly was more profitable than free competition. Levi Strauss forsook the railroad business entirely.

He was sixty-six in 1895, an advanced age for a man at the end of the nineteenth century, the last of the Strauss family to have emigrated from Bavaria to this land the Celestials had called the Golden Mountains. He had outlived even some of the second generation.

"I am a bachelor," the now goateed Strauss told a reporter that year, "and I fancy on that account I need to work more, for my entire life is my business. I don't believe that a man who once forms the habit of being busy can retire and be contented . . . My happiness lies in my routine work."

The man whose personal fortune surpassed $6 million added wistfully, "I do not think large fortunes cause happiness to their owners, for immediately those who possess them become slaves to their wealth. They must devote their lives to caring for their possessions. I don't think money brings friends to its owner. In fact, often the result is quite the contrary."

His loneliness reverberated in a quickened interest in the Talmudic admonition of *Gemiluth Chasadim*, doing kindly acts. He became a major contributor to the Pacific Hebrew Orphan Asylum and Home, of which his nephew Jacob Stern was now a trustee. He donated to the Eureka Benevolent Society, David Stern's favored organization. Jacob Reinstein, a close friend in these last years and a regent of the University of California, persuaded him to contribute to the school's scholarship fund. In 1897, Strauss wrote to the regents, offering to match personally the legislature's creation of twenty-eight perpetual scholarships, four from each congressional district in the state.

He had lived to see the turn of the century; that night of December 31, 1899, had been a triumph of hope. Around the world parents had awakened their children to greet the dawn of a new era, to toll off the seconds separating them from a new century, to peer through sleepy eyes into the night sky of promises.

He was seventy-three in 1902, the goatee longer, whiter. This last year he had not been well, though he had felt better after a sojourn at the lavish, sprawling Hotel Del Monte in Monterey — $120 a week for his suite and the privilege of sitting on the verandah with the very elite of America. Three doctors had nothing to offer for a bad heart, and the male nurse Jacob had hired was useless. What could they do for an old man's heart, anyway?

Still, he kept busy. There were affairs to settle, though he had long since told the four Stern brothers that they would inherit his share of the business. Fanny had her way. On Friday, September 19, 1902, he completed a new will; there were grandnieces and -nephews to remember.

He would leave $20,000 to the Pacific Hebrew Orphan Asylum; $10,000 to the Home for Aged Israelites on Silver Avenue; $5000 to the Eureka Benevolent Association; $5000 each to the Roman Catholic and Protestant orphanages. To Philip Fisher, "as a token of my regard for his faithful services as our confidential bookkeeper," he bequeathed $10,000, and to Albert Hirschfeld, the office manager at Battery Street, $5000. To Sahleins and Sachses and Bachmans and Strausses, Hellers and Scholles — the children and grandchildren of his brothers and sisters — he distributed $1.6 million, to be paid in gold coin unless they preferred their bequest in real estate. Gold, the $20 double eagle — in that surely he had become a San Franciscan.

Jacob, Sigmund, Louis, and Abraham would succeed to the firm and inherit the balance of the $6 million estate.

He worked at the Battery Street building the following Monday. Tuesday, not feeling well at all, complaining that he felt cold, he went home early to stay with his nephews' wives, Rosa, Rosalie, and Elise. The doctors announced that he was suffering from congestion of the liver, whatever that was, and sent him to bed. Feeling much better on Friday, Strauss ate with his family, making jokes at the table, enjoying himself before retiring. He slept for an hour and a half, then woke with a moan. The nurse, useless man, asked, "Mr. Strauss, how do you feel?"

"Oh, about as comfortable as I can under the circumstances," the old man muttered. He turned his head away, closed his eyes, and died.

Flags in the wholesale district flew at half-mast the next morning. His obituary appeared in the city's newspapers, the San Francisco *Call* devoting three columns of its front page to the "pioneer merchant and philanthropist" who devoted his life "not only to fostering the highest commercial conditions, but to the moral, social and educational welfare and development of the young men and women of the state."

The funeral at his home on Leavenworth Street on Monday was simple, without flowers or music. The wholesale district downtown was closed, a singular tribute to the affable man who had been so long a competitor. Hours before the midday ceremony, the streets surrounding the Strauss home were crowded with the carriages of the friends who owned those rival firms, and the bankers and businessmen with whom he had shaped a city unique in America.

Murmuring condolences to the four nephews, they filled the crêpe-draped parlor and drawing room, overflowing the porch and the lawn in front of the house. Rabbi Voorsanger of Temple Emanu-El spoke briefly, praising the former peddler for his philanthropy, charging his death a loss to the community "which benefited by his broad ideals and generous deeds."

The casket was carried from the house and placed in a hearse at the head of a long cortège of carriages. Then in a stately saraband of slowly walking horses, Levi Strauss was borne toward the railroad station at Third and Townsend streets, where a special funeral train waited. On this last ride to a new mausoleum in Nabo Sholom, the Home of Peace cemetery in suburban San Mateo county, Levi Strauss was paying his final tithe to the Southern Pacific Railroad.

Three days later, the San Francisco *Bulletin* editorially urged its readers, "We must not forget the men who made this city, [men such as] Levi Strauss, a credit to the race from which he sprung, and the country of which he was an honored citizen."

His name, not his accomplishments, would be remembered.

Chapter III

The Koveralls Complement

THE TREMORS BEGAN in the early dawn of Wednesday, April 18, 1906. The shock waves reverberated from the bedrock of the sandy peninsula, gathering force, then hammering again and again against the sleeping city.

Fourteen-year-old Hortense Thomson sat up in bed, frightened, watching the oil lamp dance on the table in the one-room house she shared with her parents. Her father bolted from his bed, snatched his pants, and pulled them on, hopping from foot to foot in a grotesque pas de deux with the frantic oil lamp. The girl's mother gathered the blanket about herself, cowering in a corner, whimpering, "This is the end of the world." She stayed there, praying, while her husband and daughter ventured outside.

From their hillside street far out in the Portola district, six miles from the city's commercial center, they could see little. The earthquake had struck, then apparently rolled on. As far as Hortense was concerned, there was no reason not to go to work. They needed the eighty-five cents a day she brought home for hammering rivets into Levi Strauss & Co.'s celebrated patented riveted clothing.

"I'm going to work," the young girl informed her mother.

"You're not going anyplace," Mrs. Thomson ordered. Though the earthquake had passed, the religious woman insisted, again and again, "This is the end of the world."

Not for a capricious fourteen-year-old the factory bosses

had stood in a corner as punishment for loosing live mice on a string in the ladies' rest room. It was an adventure. Besides, the earth no longer shook. Her lunch in hand, Hortense Thomson set off for the street-car line.

Along the streets, she saw the damage not apparent from her home. Homes had slipped from their foundations; stores had cracked apart. "I met some girls on Cortland Avenue, and when the street car didn't come, we began walking toward the city. We walked to Twenty-second and Mission, and another big earthquake hit, about eight A.M. We ran all the way home." She laughed, recalling the morning terror seventy-one years before.

Hortense Thomson would not go to work again for five months. She stayed home, playing jacks with girl friends, until Levi Strauss & Co. opened a new factory in San Francisco in September 1906. Her fearful mother firmly forbade Hortense to cross the bay by ferry to Oakland, where the company had set up a temporary factory.

The earthquake's rumble woke Sigmund and Rosalie Stern in their fashionable home near Van Ness Avenue. The Sterns, too, dressed hastily — how unlike the dapper Sigmund to appear publicly without tie and jacket — and gathered in the parlor. The damage to the robust mansion with its bravura turret was apparently slight; plaster had flaked from the walls, but no one was injured. The toppled chimneys were an annoyance, but nothing that could not be repaired.

After breakfast, Sigmund completed dressing and set off for the offices of Levi Strauss & Co. to assess the damage at 14–16 Battery Street. Rosalie ordered the servants to begin picking up the books from the library floor and sweeping the broken crockery into the dustbin.

The Stern's black and brass Pope-Toledo — said to be the first limousine in the city — was of little use to the vice-president of Levi Strauss & Co. Bracketed cornices and brick chimneys had collapsed into the streets. Roads were cracked, pavement lifted in great blocks along macadam faults, street-car tracks skewed in undulating filaments.

By the time Stern made his way to the business district, fires were burning south of Market Street, near the factory on Fremont Street. In the commercial and banking center north of Market, a dozen buildings spewed smoke into the bright morning sky. The Battery Street building they called "the store" was ablaze, ignited by the shattered gaslight chandeliers Levi Strauss had installed a half-century before.

Cursing cracked water mains and hissing gas pipes, firemen fought individual fires, then retreated as whole blocks erupted in black smoke. A city of 400,000 was stricken.

As the fires surged westward from block to block, determined Rosalie Stern began marshaling the family. She summoned her sister Elise, the wife of Abraham Stern — brothers Stern had married sisters Meyer. Elise and Abraham were to bring the valuable paintings from the home of eldest brother, Jacob, off taking the waters in Europe. (Louis Stern and his wife were living in New York, where he represented the company.)

For a day and a night, the combined Stern families, their maids, butlers, and nannys, twenty-eight in all, camped in Sigmund's yard. Repeated aftershocks kept them outdoors, the roof of their house threatening to give way.

Through the night, the fires burned closer to the Stern families. The following day, they bundled into the family cars — a pony cart attached to the rear of the Pope-Toledo — and joined the procession of bedraggled refugees to the parade ground at the Presidio. A day later, they trekked to Golden Gate Park, where they bivouacked again, cooking over open fires, the maids, children, doyennes of culture, butlers, and all coping with vagaries of food supplies and a lack of water. From the park they could hear the faint thuds of dynamite set by army engineers leveling a firebreak at Van Ness Avenue.

Reinforced by that swath of rubble and a shift of the winds, which blew the flames back on already burned-out neighborhoods, fire-fighters were able to contain the inferno on the third day. One third of the city, its commercial and industrial core, smoldered through the following weekend;

damage to property totaled $350 million; 452 were known dead.

Tens of thousands camped for weeks on the sand hills around the city — Hortense Thomson vividly remembers the tents and shacks thrown up on the hillsides, and the long lines at the community well down the street from her once isolated home. Meanwhile, the picknicking Sterns, *en famille*, repaired to their summer home in Atherton, hard by the badly battered Leland Stanford Junior University.

Working out of temporary offices in Abraham's many-splendored home in the city, the Stern brothers moved quickly to restore their shattered business. Patching a wall tumbled into the street, Sigmund and Abraham converted part of their small Oakland factory into a temporary display room for the new goods their brother Louis would ship immediately from New York. By the time Jacob returned home, the Sterns and Simon Davis, tailor Jacob's twenty-nine-year-old son and second-in-command, were supervising construction of a new factory in San Francisco. It was to be the first Levi Strauss & Co. would actually own.

Meanwhile, they planned to build a new "store" on Battery Street, resited from the middle of the block to the corner.

Their first business decision was to revive an old policy: they would extend credit to retail merchants wiped out in the earthquake. Levi Strauss & Co. was serving as a low- or no-interest bank for its hard-pressed customers.*

Their second move was characteristic of the Sterns, if unusual among businessmen of the era. They placed advertisements in the city's newspapers advising the company's 350 employees that their salaries would be continued until further notice and asking them to register their names at the Oakland factory. Some would be put to work there immediately; others, like Hortense Thomson, would not return to their jobs until the new factory opened in September.

---

* The policy of aiding merchants struck by fire or natural disaster continues. It is considered so routine that Daniel Baran, vice-president of the corporation and, in effect, its credit manager, does not keep statistics on the number of times such disaster relief has been extended or the failure-to-pay rate of recipients. The latter is absurdly low, he insists.

That half-block-long Valencia Street plant filled two floors with machinery, offices, and the workers' dining room. It was new and, for a few days, an exciting place for young Hortense, before the routine of the new button machine to which she had been assigned settled over her.

There were other changes as well. Simon Davis replaced his father as factory manager; Jacob still came in each day, but the women rarely saw him. Hortense was a little relieved; Jacob Davis was so stern, so rigid. "He didn't take too much foolishness."

The son, too, was firm, Miss Thomson recalled, but "very nice. We called him Simon. He would once in a while stick me in a corner 'cause I was playing or doing something I shouldn't." She laughed. Having started, when a youngster, sweeping out the offices, Simon had learned factory management at his father's shoulder. His succession was in the natural order of things at Levi Strauss & Co.

The work day began at seven-thirty in the morning, and ended at five-thirty. The girls — they were always girls, no matter their age — were allowed a half-hour for lunch. Miss Thomson would occasionally supplement her bean sandwiches, "and every other kind of sandwich," brought from home with a nickel piece of pie in the lunch room.

Occasionally, the factory would continue operating until ten at night, to meet the backlog of orders. Miss Thomson remembered her mother waiting in the dark for the young girl, who was miffed that she was not permitted to travel alone at night. Six days a week, nine and a half hours a day — when she wasn't standing in a corner — Miss Thomson operated the button machine. "It was piecework. The most I ever made was a dollar-fifty a day doing that. I gave my mother five dollars a week." On Sundays she might go to the beach or to a park with a girl friend; Hortense "just loved the park." It was her only recreation; her mother forbade going to parties or sinful nickelodeons.

The button machine imposed a numbing routine. "You used to have to feed the buttons for the riveted clothes one by one. You had to put the metal buttons in by hand, and you could step on the lever too soon, especially if you were tired. I almost put a button on my finger one time. One girl did — punched a button right in her finger. She just didn't get her finger out."

There were other accidents. "One time a lady's hair caught in a machine. Her scalp was taken off. They didn't have the belts shielded in those days. She didn't die, but she was in the hospital a long time. People sometimes sewed their fingers. When people were hurt on the job, the company didn't pay medical expenses."

Hortense Thomson admired jovial Simon Davis, his hearty affability, his easy camaraderie with the Irish and Italian girls in the noisy factory. Despite Simon's good humor, "they were very strict in those days. You just couldn't do sloppy work. You just did your work right, or if you didn't, you just had to do it over and lose your time."

Centenarian Mary Rossi, the woman who remembered Levi Strauss in frock coat standing in the door of the old factory, liked the new building on Valencia Street. "It was clean," she asserted with a nod, "and a good place to work. The people were nice. We sat next to each other and could talk. You could talk to anybody there, but you really couldn't afford to during working hours.

"I was satisfied where I was. There were no jobs elsewhere anyway." Mrs. Rossi chuckled. Insisting her guests have the chairs, Mrs. Rossi sat on the edge of her bed in the tidy room in the neighborhood retirement home.

"I lived on Valero Street. I could take the street car for five cents, but it's not a long walk when you're young." The money saved on carfare the Rossis could put away for emergencies; there were always those – a broken stove or a sick baby or a confirmation dress.

Mrs. Rossi reflexively rubbed on the great calloused knob that is her right thumb. "I got that," she explained holding up her hand for her visitors to see, "from using the scissors." She was assigned to work at the damage table, her task to find flawed parts of garments, to remove them with the scissors, and to fit patches. She salvaged these "seconds," as they

were called, until her retirement in 1941; she was then earning $20 a week.

The Valencia Street plant was Simon Davis's creation. His
father, a year from retiring, came to the building each day
but did little; at seventy-four, the task of starting over was
too great.

At twenty-nine, Simon Davis had arrived. He was invested
as manager of the factory, but, more important, he had
earned both the trust and gratitude of the Stern brothers. As
if to celebrate, in December of that year, he married twenty-
year-old Ann Paul; the newlyweds lived with Simon's aging
parents across the bay until they could rebuild the family
home in San Francisco.

Simon Davis was on top of the world. The Sterns deferred
to him in matters of production, just as they acknowledged
the business acumen of Philip Fisher, the graying bookkeeper
and, after forty-five years with Levi Strauss, the first employee to become a shareholder. Increasingly, Fisher was relying on his young assistant, Albert Hirschfeld, but the Stern
brothers were satisfied that their company was in good hands.

The Bankers' Panic of 1907, which paralyzed much of the
nation's business for a year, was paradoxically a boost to the
recovery of Levi Strauss & Co. The panic had begun, as most
panics do, vaguely — during a desultory summer on the stock
market. Prices on the New York Stock Exchange had me-
andered up and down for months; speculators lost confidence
and decided to pull out of the market to await better times.
New stock subscriptions went unsold, and the lassitude crept
into the municipal-bond markets.

Lack of interest turned into nervousness. In September,
prices began falling on the market. The major investment
banks headquartered in New York, heavily involved in the
declining market, found themselves short of funds to lend.

On October 22, 1907, the Knickerbocker Trust Company
closed its doors in the face of a Wall Street rumor, quite ac-
curate, that it was overextended. First in New York, then
across the country, other banks took note of Knickerbocker's
fall and began calling in loans, tightening credit, building

their cash reserves. As ever, the self-serving private banks were doing precisely the wrong thing: more liberal credit was necessary to restore public confidence.

Local merchants were forced to turn to their suppliers for extended lines of credit if they were to survive. Levi Strauss & Co., backed by the personal resources of the four Stern brothers, was in a position to be generous when other wholesale houses were not.

Only the imperious J. P. Morgan could reverse the deepening slump. Morgan the Magnificent strong-armed $25 million assessments from the soundest New York banks, coerced another $50 million from the federal treasury, and personally began lending money — steely-eyed Morgan pocketing 20 percent–interest payments — to less affluent banks. By the end of the year, those institutions were able to lend money to stockbrokers again, and timorous confidence returned to the market. That accomplishment momentarily transformed Morgan from grasping capitalist to national hero — at least to the small businessmen and shopkeepers whose enterprises Morgan had indirectly saved.

It would be months before the easing of credit requirements worked its away across the country, months in which Albert Hirschfeld learned the perils of private banking. There was no better time; he emerged from the ordeal the best credit man in the business, according to co-workers.

Riding out the financial aftershocks of both earthquake and Wall Street panic, the company deliberately began shrinking the number of eastern manufacturers it represented. Gone were the Armorside patented corsets, sold with the promise that they would not break down at the sides, as well as the imported laces, ladies' underwear, sewing supplies, and umbrellas. More and more, the firm relied on sales from its own two labels: Two Horse Brand riveted clothing and the men's dresswear manufactured at Louis Stern's order in the East and sold on the Pacific Coast as Sunset clothes.

The task of rebuilding the company all but completed, the Stern brothers' interest gradually turned elsewhere. Millionaires most comfortably, they had no need to work at all;

there were more compelling things to occupy their time. Abe, the youngest, confined his participation in the firm to creeping up the back stairs of the new building in hopes of catching an employee asleep amid the bundles of clothing. Milton Grunbaum, then a stockclerk, later a vice-president, remembered that he buried sleeping co-workers under piles of denim trousers whenever Abe made his periodic forays. Catching no drowsy clerks, Abe lost all interest in Levi Strauss. (He died of food poisoning after dining on lobster at a local hotel in 1912.)

Jacob and Sigmund Stern appeared at the first-floor office with the single large table they shared as a desk, but their involvement in daily operations had waned considerably. Jacob had been with Levi Strauss & Co. since the death of his father, in 1874. As the oldest, perhaps it was natural that he was most dedicated to maintaining the traditions of the firm. He admonished a tardy young clerk, "It is your obligation to be at work at six-thirty or before, and your privilege to be able to work overtime." A yawning Oscar Groebl promised to do better; he did, eventually becoming the firm's New York buyer and retiring a millionaire.

Jacob's attention to the business was diverted by his interest in the family's favorite charities, especially the Jewish orphanage, of which he was now president, and the old age home. There were also the outside business directorates; he had succeeded his Uncle Levi to boards of banks and insurance companies. A growing interest in music complemented an extensive art collection, which the Sterns often lent to local museums. His family was well protected, and he was at an age when he was more eager to give away than to make money. Jacob and Rosa Stern established a capital fund to make permanent the twenty-eight Levi Strauss scholarships annually awarded by the University of California.

Sigmund deferred to his energetic wife, Rosalie, in matters of culture and to his older brother in matters of business. "Jacob rolled the snowballs, and Sigmund threw them," Milton Grunbaum recalled. His fortune no longer tied directly to the company's, Sigmund seemed as interested in the ties he bought from Paris and laid out on the table for admiring clerks to praise than he did in daily sales reports.

The brothers evolved a system of de facto absentee ownership. Simon Davis, in boater, white pants, and striped blazer, hugely enjoyed his new freedom. He met with friends — there were dozens — for long lunches at Schroeder's German restaurant. He spent afternoons at the track during racing season. He showed up at the factory parties — Hortense Thomson recalled many — if only to sample the unending varieties of homemade wines the Italian operators pressed on him. In the evenings he played cards — bridge with the ladies, poker preferably with his cronies. Boisterous Simon Davis brushed aside his wife's fretting about the money he lost, and, no, he wouldn't take her dancing. He attended the annual dances at the factory only because it was expected of him. Simon Davis hated to dance.

If he needed a car, the grateful Stern brothers were quick to buy him one; he invariably chose the best. This time it was a sporty Buick White Streak he had most fancied. If he needed his house painted, he could always have it done when the painters did the Valencia Street factory; any contractor was ready to do small favors like that for a big job. He selected the rag merchant to buy Levi Strauss & Co.'s waste, and he pocketed that little bonus, too.

Simon would have his way. He was strong-willed, a stubborn man who insisted on doing what he thought best. That sort of determination was just what his new project required.

The idea had come to him slowly, from watching his two older children playing. There were no suitable play clothes marketed for active youngsters, he realized.

In 1912, Simon Davis designed such a garment, a one-piece, button-up-the-front overall of blue denim. Auto mechanics today wear garments similar to the seventy-five-cent Koverall — "The Kind of Klose That Keep Kids Kleen." Backed with the traditional Levi Strauss guarantee of "a new pair FREE if they rip," the garments were widely advertised. Simon's three-year-old daughter, Estelle, a large taffeta bow pinned in her hair, a doll dangling from her left hand, became the Koverall girl. For more than a decade, Estelle Davis rivaled the Morton Salt girl, the paintbrush-wielding Dutch Boy, and the sleepy lad yawning "Time to Re-Tire" in national advertising.

The Koverall was Levi Strauss's first product to be sold nationally. Independent sales representatives carried it with the products of other manufacturers in states the firm's own salesmen did not cover. Beyond merely manufacturing the garment, Davis became its merchandiser, its chief advocate, and most enthusiastic salesman; he took to the road himself, selling his prize.

A gold medal for excellence awarded by the San Francisco Mechanics Institute at its annual industrial exhibition reaffirmed Davis's conviction that this garment would free the company from the regional market in which it was confined. What further proof could the Stern brothers need that the Koverall was all he had claimed? Koveralls had won the same medal earlier awarded the patented riveted clothes, an award still advertised by the company.

Variations on the Koverall theme tumbled from the Valencia Street factory — long sleeve, short sleeve, high neck, "Dutch" or square neck, denims, and hickory stripes. The next year, Davis launched Koverall Nighties, "the new hygenic sleeping garment for boys and girls one to eight years old." Five-and-a-half-year-old Jack Davis joined his little sister as one of the garments' models. Front-buttoning, dropseat Koverall Nighties were made in cottons, drills, and flannels, with and without nursery patterns of Indians, ducks, and teddy bears.

Davis's promotional sense was unbounded. At his urging, the company opened a Koverall Playground for neighborhood children next to the factory. He encouraged the Stern brothers to contribute $25,000 to the million-dollar seed fund necessary to build the 1915 Panama-Pacific International Exhibition fairgrounds adjacent to the Presidio. At that celebrated fair, Davis established a twenty-five-operator Koverall factory, producing the children's garments he fervently believed an intrigued parent would purchase. Hardly satisfied, he secured the company's sponsorship of Kids' Day, the first day of school vacation, opening the amusement park at the exhibition and passing out balloons and trinkets. Davis no doubt had as much fun as the careening children at the fair.

The success of Koveralls provoked problems, as the patented riveted pants had earlier. In 1916, Levi Strauss sued J. C. Penney's for infringing on the use of the trademarked name. The suit, too, could be considered a mark of the success of the garments.

If anyone was at all skeptical of Simon Davis, it was a rosy-cheeked youth of twenty more put off by Davis's ebullient personality than his business practices. Milton Grunbaum was eighteen when he started working as a janitor–errand boy at the new Battery Street building in 1909. Wearing long dress pants for the first time — "Oh! Was I proud of that," he later recalled — Grunbaum had been hired by Albert Hirschfeld as a favor to Grunbaum's uncle. The boy was quitting high school to support an older sister and his mother.

Young Grunbaum was ambitious. He doubled as janitor and errand boy for a year, just long enough to suffer the tribal initiations, including the hoary prank of being sent out to find a left-handed monkey wrench. He was promoted to stockclerk, filling customers' orders for a wage of $25 a month. "I liked to get done as fast as I could because I liked to go out and help the other fellows. I wanted to know everything in the business."

Hirschfeld took the ingratiating lad under his wing. The older man "was a wonderful guy, severe, and honest to a degree that you might say he was even harsh. He disciplined me several times because he felt I was a little too ambitious." But the rigid Albert Hirschfeld, now the firm's effective manager, also encouraged the youth to finish his high school education in night classes. Education was the prerequisite of business success.

Scurrying about the building, Grunbaum met Jacob and Sigmund Stern. How well they came to know *him* he learned when he came down with diphtheria.

Grunbaum lay in bed at home for months, in the first

weeks near death. The Sterns sent their family doctor to treat the young man. The doctor's treatments were drastic; they called for alternately sweating Grunbaum and then bathing him in ice-cold water. "But I really think he saved my life."

His recovery was slow, retarded by his anxiety over money; the family was seriously in debt to the grocer and butcher, and Grunbaum could not hope to repay either soon. When at last he felt strong enough, Jacob Stern's wife drove up in her chauffeur-driven touring car to take him for rides about Golden Gate Park.

"When I finally returned to work, I was so weak it was all I could do to get there and sit down in Mr. Hirschfeld's office. Jacob Stern said, 'Come in and see me some time,' which was almost a command.

"Mr. Stern was sitting at the partners' table, clipping coupons with a scissors. It was a job he entrusted to no one. There were piles of stocks and bonds all over the table. 'Come in, Milton, I'm so exhausted from clipping these,' he said with a smile."

Recounting the story more than sixty-five years later, Milton Grunbaum's eyes suddenly teared. "He gave me a check for a thousand dollars. Because I was supporting my family. They gave me a thousand-dollar check! And the doctors didn't have to be paid; the Sterns had met their bills.

"What was I? I was just a boy," Grunbaum recalled, wiping a cheek. "That's the way they were. They were just that kind of people, that's all."

Milton Grunbaum would devotedly repay the Stern family that gift a thousand times over. In the next few years, the young man filled a variety of clerical jobs. He even went on the road, substituting for sick salesmen, but found it difficult. Hard of hearing, he kept asking storeowners, "What did you say?" Both merchant and pinch-hitting salesman were frustrated. Milton Grunbaum decided his talents lay elsewhere.

Still attending night school, Grunbaum moved to the Valencia Street factory. He swept floors, laid out cloth on the cutting tables, learned to operate and repair the sewing machines, studied production and the ordering of piece goods. "The floorladies educated me."

The self-satisfied Simon Davis and the striving Milton Grunbaum took an instant dislike to each other. According to Grunbaum, the favored Davis showed up only when there was no card game. Grunbaum was in a position to know; he spent long hours in the factory, learning the step-by-step operations in manufacturing shirts, pants, and Koveralls. He gave up vacations: "I wanted to learn everything there was to know there."

Grunbaum made his first major contribution to the company in 1915. "I found out that you didn't size children's clothes likes adults'. Children grow at different rates; at certain stages they have big stomachs, for example. I was the first to discover that." He laughed.

"There was an orphanage about two blocks from the Valencia Street plant, and I took candy up there to the sisters and tried the garments on the kids. I had the first Koveralls that fit all ages. We recut our patterns."

Grunbaum's curiosity led him to question the waste fabric the cutters left behind to be sold as scraps to rag merchants. The factory was discarding enough to deprive the company of sizable profits, he told Hirschfeld. Hirschfeld and his new assistant, David Beronio, could only counsel the angry Grunbaum to remain silent, to do the best job possible under the circumstances. The Stern brothers still considered Davis the backbone of the company.

When the manager of the small production line making riding pants left for another job, Milton Grunbaum, twenty-five years old, was ready. Davis protested to the Stern brothers, warning that the production line "will go to hell," but could recommend no one else for the job. At Hirschfeld's urging, the Sterns tapped young Grunbaum.

This first executive appointment was some balm for his anger, that and the Sterns' preferred privilege of buying stock in the company to which he was so committed. Grunbaum bought his first twenty shares at $85 each, paying for them over the next eight years.

The business boom that accompanied the First World War hardly touched the 600 employees of Levi Strauss & Co. The firm had no government contracts; the sales distribution of the patented riveted clothing was much too localized to be affected by the increase in the work force producing war matériel. The children's garments were sold nationally, but the workaday riveted clothing remained confined to its small market of western miners, lumberjacks, and cowboys. Wholesaling of eastern-made goods was a $2-million-a-year enterprise, twice the sales of all the garments manufactured at the Valencia Street plant.

The frustration continued for Milton Grunbaum. He discovered ways to improve the garments, to cut waste, to increase profits, but Simon Davis discouraged him at every turn. Hirschfeld could only nod sympathetically; his hands were tied. Hirschfeld ran the offices and the wholesaling; Davis, the factory. Even though profits were dwindling, the Stern brothers were wary of change so late in the game.

The surviving partners' annual profits of $45,000 at the end of their best sales year, 1918, did not warrant either their continued investment of $1.6 million or the aggravations 600 employees provided as a dividend. None of the four Stern brothers had a son old enough to succeed to the management, nor was there profit enough to hire a competent general manager.

The business was sputtering to a halt. Only family pride kept the Stern brothers from liquidating Levi Strauss & Co.

Chapter IV

The New Company

SIGMUND STERN was heartily delighted. Privately, he might agree with his daughter, Elise; this second grandchild, Peter, was not as ugly and red as the first had been two years earlier. But that was the sort of thing mothers might say fondly and grandparents dared not utter. Grandparents were supposed to believe each newborn in the family was the most beautiful.

Thank heavens they had decided not to name the child John, after Walter's commanding general. That would too soon become Jack Haas — a burden no child should bear, certainly not Sigmund Stern's grandson.

Sigmund's familial pride and suffusing affection embraced his son-in-law, Walter Haas; the new child somehow seemed to assure that Walter would accept the proposition the older man intended to put to him. Sigmund and Jacob Stern had discussed the matter thoroughly; they needed a son-in-law to succeed them if Levi Strauss & Co. was to continue. And Walter was the only one who seemed to be potentially interested or have the proper business background.

Certainly now was the ideal time for Walter to strike out in a new direction. He had just been demobilized from the army after two years' service, his first lieutenant's uniform retired to the closet the night his second son was born. Military service broadened a man's horizons; it would be difficult for the general's aide-de-camp to return to selling groceries in his cousin's wholesale house.

Walter's family was larger now by one-half. While Walter realized he and Elise need never worry about money, the young man was determinedly independent. Though not so independent that Private Walter Haas was not delighted to learn that his influential in-laws had pulled strings to have him transferred from the Quartermaster Corps' Presidio warehouse to Officer Candidate School.

Still, pride would never allow Walter to rely on inherited wealth.

The exchange of compliments, the small talk dispensed with, Sigmund lit a cigar, then made his proposition. "Why go back to the grocery business? Why not come into Levi Strauss & Co.?"

Walter was surprised. Until then he had not considered leaving his job with Haas Brothers. He had even drawn a token salary from the company to supplement his meager army pay; he felt some obligation implicit in that, though neither Haas Brothers nor Walter's father, Abraham, would hold it binding.

Sigmund could be persuasive. "My brother Jacob is retiring in six months after forty-five years with Levi Strauss. Louis is an invalid, and Abe is dead. After me, there's nobody to carry on. I want you to try it for two years. If you don't like it, we'll liquidate it." Diffident, casual, just the right tone for the dapper Sigmund. Walter was not the only one with pride.

Once he thought it over, the offer intrigued Walter. His cousin, Charles Haas, was president of Haas Brothers, and though he and Charlie were great friends, Walter Haas did not want to be the number two man.

Sigmund Stern's offer appealed for other reasons. The grocery business was circumscribed by the perishable nature of the goods; even with the new fleet of trucks, the firm had difficulty doing business in Sacramento, just eighty miles from San Francisco. On the other hand, Levi Strauss salesmen ranged up and down the Pacific Coast, into Arizona and Nevada. Walter was attracted by the broader horizons.

The prospects at Levi Strauss were brighter. Sigmund would replace Jacob as the head of the firm in six months, but Sigmund was, after all, sixty-one. Walter would be starting near the top, the heir apparent, if the firm continued. At Haas Brothers, there was no such immediate opportunity.

Walter discussed the offer with both his cousin Charles and his father, who agreed it was an opportunity Haas Brothers could not match. They brushed aside the modest salary Haas had accepted during his military service, though it was a debt of conscience the young man carried for over fifty years — until "something developed three or four years ago where I was able to do something for their successors which may have liquidated any debt I had. The people I did it for didn't even know I did it, but it was a moral debt [I had to repay]."

In January of 1919, at the age of thirty, the boss's son-in-law went to work for Levi Strauss & Co. Walter's knowledge of the firm was slight. He had sometimes visited his father-in-law at the Battery Street offices and had bought some dry goods to ship to the Orient. There was much to learn.

Milton Grunbaum remembered that "for the first three months, Walter asked questions, sat, and listened. He didn't talk business at all." He was there, however, to take charge, to make changes he believed necessary. The first he based on his own expertise in accounting, learned at the university and since expanded. He revised an antiquated bookkeeping system, installing new procedures over the objections of the clerks, who still sat at high desks adding long columns of figures by hand, quite as Bob Cratchit had for Scrooge and Marley fifty years before. The new adding machines and revised ledgers "caused overwhelming trouble in the business," Walter later recalled. "They thought I was out to destroy it. They had to accept it because, I guess, I was Mr. Stern's son-in-law."

The grudging acceptance was further retarded because the handsome Haas looked far younger than his thirty years. In addition, the young man's actual business experience hardly marked him as a financial genius. He certainly had not demonstrated that he had inherited his father Abraham's extraordinary business *seychl*.

Abraham Haas had immigrated to America from Reckendorf, Bavaria, at the age of sixteen, in 1863. The family had crossed the fetid isthmus by railroad, then sailed by steamship to Portland, Oregon. Raised there, eventually Abraham had opened a grocery store in a small California mining town, accepting scrip from the mines in lieu of cash. As long as the mine prospered, the currency-on-faith was convertible; but when the diggings petered out, the scrip he held became worthless. A wiser Abraham moved on to Los Angeles.

That city in the late 1860s was a scruffy community of 5000, lacking even the pretense of a cultural veneer; local newspapers recorded a murder a day — refusing to tally Indians, Orientals, and blacks in their box score. A decade later, it was more peaceful, the mayhem largely in land promotions. Los Angeles was a self-inflated boom town of 15,000 hucksters, ready to swarm and batten upon the newcomers lured to this perfect kingdom of prosperity by real estate subdividers. Boom turned to bubble turned to boom again during the 1880s, as the competing Southern Pacific and Santa Fe railroads struggled for passenger supremacy. The St. Louis–to–Los Angeles fare fell from $125.00 to $1.00, and literally tens of thousands took advantage of the cheap rates to make their way west.

Speculators abounded; bounders speculated. Between January 1887 and July 1889, more than sixty new communities offering homesites for two million people were laid out in the environs of Los Angeles. Most ended in despair or desertion. Local residents greeted each other with a thigh-slapping "Has your town recovered yet from the boom?"

Eschewing the lure of land promotions, Abraham Haas organized a successful wholesale grocery business, a companion to younger brother William's and cousin Kalhan's, Haas Brothers, in San Francisco. There he met Fanny Koshland while on a business trip, and brought her back to Los Angeles in 1886, the wife of a man of substance.

From wholesaling he branched out into farming and cattle raising. He formed the first flour-milling company in the city, then turned over most of his stock to a brother and organized the city's first cold-storage business.

He ranged farther afield. With three partners he organized the pioneering hydroelectric business in southern California, stringing the first known long-transmission lines thirty miles. He invested in two natural-gas companies to provide gas-lighting and heat to the growing city.

On one of the father's periodic business trips to San Francisco — they lasted long enough for him to move his entire family north — Walter Haas had been born, in 1889. The family returned home to Los Angeles, and the boy attended elementary school there. The city was still small — so tiny that the streets just ten blocks from downtown lacked paving — but a good place for a young man to grow up. Vacant lots became battlefields, playgrounds, and ball fields as needed.

He and his younger sister were heartbroken when, in 1900, Abraham fulfilled a promise made earlier to his mother-in-law and permanently moved his family to San Francisco. As the financial center of the West — the streets were paved sometimes miles from downtown — there were opportunities for a man with such wide-ranging business interests.

Walter skipped a grade, the Los Angeles schools being better than San Francisco's, and proceeded routinely through Lowell High. Latin was a problem — he never did get a passing grade — but he graduated in 1905. If Walter had any special aptitude, it was for mathematics; he considered an engineering career.

The Haas family was in Europe for a year-long visit when the 1906 earthquake struck. They returned to the devastated Bay Area, Walter to enter the University of California. Going to college there seemed the natural thing to do; most of his high school friends were in the freshman class.

Whatever thoughts he had of engineering Walter put aside in favor of a business education. Someone would have to manage the family enterprises his father was creating. The University of California was a warmly remembered experience for the young man. With an allowance of $75 per month from his father, he lived near the campus and commuted home to San Francisco on the weekends. The experience was maturing; he later recalled English and sociology professors among those who had the greatest influence on his later life.

After graduation, Walter decided he needed further business experience and chose to take a job in a New York bank. He was lonely there, and, using the excuse of his parent's twenty-fifth wedding anniversary, he shortly returned to San Francisco. He spent a dissatisfied year working in a cousin's brokerage house but despaired of making any contribution to the economy in that business.

At the beginning of 1912, eighteen restless months out of school, he joined Haas Brothers as a cashier. It was a new beginning for him in business, but one enriched by the presence of his father in the back office of the building. Wealthy Abraham was past sixty, far more involved with banks and utilities than the wholesale grocery business, yet he treated his twenty-three-year-old son as a business equal. Walter would never forget his father's kindness.

In 1913, while on the Powell Street cable car, he met eighteen-year-old Elise, the daughter of Sigmund and Rosalie Stern. The stunning girl had been "strictly brought up," in the phrase of the times, so their courtship was to be closely circumscribed by society's protocols. "It was the first year after my debut," Elise Stern Haas recalled later. "People considered it a very suitable match because we were seated together at almost every party." The romance of the handsome couple infatuated approving hostesses; such pairings still transform viragos into co-conspirators.

Perhaps to test Elise's resolve, the Sterns took their daughter off to Europe; when they returned, the house salesman for Haas Brothers was waiting. "We became engaged on June eleventh, nineteen fourteen, under the big oak tree on my parents' Atherton estate," she recalled. The balance of their courtship was conducted on the San Francisco–Oakland ferry, Elise meeting her intended at noon so that they could ride over and back during the hour Walter could steal from work.

They were married in October 1914, and moved into a small apartment in the city. They were comfortable — with a maid to keep house — but hardly affluent. The birth of their first son, Walter, Jr., in 1916, and the addition of a nurse to care for him crowded the small Powell Street apartment. They rented a larger house.

Life was placid for the young couple. He was a successful businessman with a future in the family business; she, a society matron barely twenty. The entry of the United States into the First World War upset their routines when Walter enlisted. With a wife and a child, he could have been deferred, but Walter felt obligated to serve, to participate in the struggle that would make the world safe for democracy.

As in business, his military career had been spectacularly mundane. This now was the young man who was disregarding decades of practiced procedure in the bookkeeping department of Levi Strauss & Co.

Walter had one ally among the office workers, the quiet assistant Albert Hirschfeld had adopted as his office manager. David A. Beronio had gone to work for Levi Strauss in 1903, first as a salesclerk on the floor, then as an office worker. David Beronio was different from most of the young employees, more intense, more dedicated, unlike even his handsome younger brother, Fred, one of Simon Davis's roistering companions at the factory. David had no interest in such wasteful pursuits; unmarried, he devoted his entire life to Levi Strauss & Co.

Walter Haas agreed with Hirschfeld's estimate of the sober Beronio. In a tactful memo to the Stern brothers, written just six weeks after he joined the firm, Walter noted, "I think that Beronio has a capacity for a large field of usefulness in real sales management." Walter suggested the detail work that filled Beronio's day "be given over to lower priced help." Beronio would become a central figure in the company as Haas reshaped it.

About the store on Battery Street there was a sense of uneasiness. The future of Levi Strauss & Co., and of the jobs of 350 employees, solely depended on Walter Haas and just

how well he did. By the end of 1919, the bookkeepers' fears
were allayed. The new bookkeeping system allowed them,
for the first time in memory, to close the books on the year
without relinquishing their holiday on New Year's Day. The
man who married the boss's daughter might have some ability after all.

It had not been a particularly successful year, in Haas's
opinion. The firm had produced a moderate profit on sales
of $3 million; Hirschfeld calculated the profit amounted to
6 percent on the capital invested in the firm. "If the business
can't do better than that," Haas told Hirschfeld "I would not
be interested."

Still, he realized the company's potential. The fourteen-
man sales force was lackadaisical and needed to be more
closely supervised. There were small economies he could
initiate here and there, and changes in personnel to place
people in the jobs for which they were best suited. That
most concerned him, assessing the personnel at 98 Battery
Street and shifting people around with the fewest hurt feelings. There was no question of firing anyone; Levi Strauss
& Co. did not do that to employees at the store who had
either outlived their usefulness or no longer could manage
the physical demands of the work. At any given time, there
were ten or twelve older men on the payroll, serving out
their years in make-work jobs. When a salesman grew too
old to travel, Milton Grunbaum recalled, "We had him report into Ninety-eight Battery. Their customers were loyal,
though; they wouldn't buy anything from the new line until
they came into the house and got it from Tad Gale or somebody. The house salesmen didn't get commissions, but they
didn't tell the merchants that."

Financially, it was a drain, but "in those days what would
the old workers have done if they hadn't been able to save
anything?" Grunbaum asked rhetorically. The Stern brothers would not turn their backs on employees they considered
loyal friends.

Haas concentrated his efforts on the store; the factory he
put aside for the moment. Simon Davis was in charge there,
and no man was more respected by the Sterns.

Haas's second trial year offered him the sort of challenge he most liked. Through three quarters of the year, the firm had done well. The reforms he launched began to yield results on the monthly balance sheets. In the last three months of 1920, though, the price of cotton began falling in the market. Inventories of cotton fabrics, especially the denim on which the factories relied, purchased when cotton was forty cents a pound, were suddenly worth thirty cents a pound. The company began adjusting the value of its inventory of raw denim and reducing prices of completed goods. The price of the patented riveted waist overalls, which had reached an all-time high wholesale price of $35 per dozen in June 1920, started downward. To have maintained its high prices while other local manufacturers cut theirs would have prevented Levi Strauss from competing. As it was, all the California firms were at a competitive disadvantage in the face of eastern- and southern-made goods. One of the Progressive Era's modest reforms, California's eight-year-old minimum-wage law for women and children, mandated a $16 operator's wage for a forty-eight-hour week. Free of any similar requirement to pay a living wage, southern manufacturers — most of them transplanted New Englanders — were offering ten and fifteen cents an hour. They could ship their bib overalls west and still dramatically undersell the Californians.

By the end of the year, the wholesale price of the waist overalls had plummeted to $23.50 per dozen — and the price of raw cotton kept falling. Levi Strauss's bib overalls sank even lower, from $35 in 1920 to just $18 two years later. "We had a ship bringing us two hundred bales of denim," Haas later recounted, "and I was hoping the ship would go down without loss of life because it was insured at full price."

The ship did not sink, but cotton prices did, to as little as six cents a pound by the middle of 1921. Profits for 1920, which had seemed so promising, were just $263,952, almost one-third less than those of the previous year.

Walter Haas's two trial years were over. Although he did not feel he could return to his family's wholesale grocery business, he had no doubt he could make his way in the world of commerce. The choice of a job did not hinge on money; not now. Abraham had sold out his interests in the Southern California utilities created decades before. The checks, which an awed Walter showed to his father-in-law, totaled more than $2 million.*

Yet to walk away from Levi Strauss & Co. at this point would be to turn his back on a threatened disaster. For Walter Haas, the personal challenge was too great. Besides, he had come to like the wholesale dry-goods business and to appreciate the potential it offered him. The cotton-price disaster was, he hoped, a once-only catastrophe.

With Walter's decision to stay, Jacob Stern retired. He still came into the office to handle his private business affairs, but he much preferred to spend the days riding his well-groomed horses in Golden Gate Park or at his Atherton home. Sigmund stepped up to the presidency, and Walter was elected first vice-president and treasurer. Stern was the nominal head of the firm, but it was Walter to whom the employees came for day-to-day decisions.

To meet the expected losses in 1921, Haas began cutting the budget at 98 Battery Street. That task completed, he weighed reviewing the factory budget for the first time. Hirschfeld had hinted that certain procedures there might bear closer investigation.

A customer's letter from San Diego, complaining that the dollar Koveralls were too expensive, prompted Haas's decision. To answer that letter, Walter began collecting cost figures on all aspects of factory production.

The process was slow. No one had ever done it before, and Simon Davis resented the boss's son-in-law snooping about his, Davis's, factory.

Haas felt the coolness but let it pass. Davis was, after all, a much respected man at Levi Strauss, and Haas in a sense

---

* Haas declined to reveal the exact amounts, adding only that the sale of the Midway and Southern California Gas Company provided the basis for the family fortune. His reticence is a matter of modesty. According to his wife, Elise, "His hobby is business. He has an extraordinary, acute mind for finance, and he cares absolutely nothing about the money he has."

was infringing on Davis's domain. Still, the factory manager had never before costed out his production, and that must be done. Davis did not actually know how much it cost to manufacture and sell the 501s, the Koveralls, the bib overalls, or the shirts, nor could he justify the prices charged.

The figures Haas gathered were surprising. When he added a proportionate share of the overhead to the actual manufacturing costs, it appeared Levi Strauss was selling the Koveralls at virtually no profit.

Stunned, he recomputed the figures; they hardly changed. The profits on the shirts were marginal, largely because they were priced low to withstand eastern competition. The profits on the overalls were handsome — as high as 15 percent — but the returns on their production had masked the lack of profit in Koveralls. Essentially, the product was overadvertised, oversold by its inventor and chief advocate. Sales did not justify the advertising money spent on Koveralls. To keep the production lines at Valencia Street and in Frankfort, Indiana, busy, Davis was opening up new territories, not exploiting already established markets. Levi Strauss representatives swept over cities, then passed on to preach the Koverall gospel to yet unconverted states.

Haas attempted to discuss his figures with Davis. The jaunty factory manager waved them aside, with the airy comment "We're doing well." When Haas proposed raising the Koverall price, to make the garment carry its weight, Davis appealed to Sigmund. "Why is Walter poking his nose into the factory?"

To a sorely troubled Sigmund Stern, Haas explained that their overall and shirt prices had been set by the competition; fortunately, firms such as Eloesser Heynemann or Cohn, Goldwater knew their costs and priced their goods accordingly. Davis and Hirschfeld merely relied on the competition's judgment. But the Koverall had no direct competition, and Davis no ready-made standard against which to set its price.

The rivalry – it had come to that — smoldered through the year, Haas conciliatory, Davis increasingly assertive, Stern all the more undecided. Davis openly complained about Haas's visits to the factory, dismissing them as the meddling of a greengrocer unfamiliar with clothing.

Haas could be just as determined. He understood the principles of accounting, and they were the same for all businesses — overalls, onions, or oilcans.

Walter Haas needed help, someone he could rely on, who would back him up or correct him if he was wrong. Sigmund Stern had earlier suggested Haas get help; one man alone bore too great a burden. Even Levi Strauss himself had had partners. Walter had someone in mind — if he could convince his brother-in-law to return to San Francisco.

Daniel Koshland was not happy in New York. For days at a time he hardly saw the sun. He and his wife, Eleanor, Walter's younger sister, lived in an apartment house on the East Side. Two blocks from his home he took the subway, got off directly underneath the building in which he worked, had lunch there, then took the subway home after the banking house closed. At twenty-eight, he had a none too prominent position in the private investment house of Lazard Frères, and an ulcer.

Three years of New York banking had not been all that Dan Koshland, or his determined mother, Cora, had hoped it would be. Lazard Frères, handling a handful of family accounts, "was nothing but a high-class bucket shop." It did not seem likely that he would emulate family friend Eugene Meyer, the San Francisco boy who had worked at that bank and would become governor of the Federal Reserve Board.

Like the Haases, the Koshlands had been California pioneers, Dan's paternal grandfather joining the Gold Rush to peddle dry goods in Sacramento. Simon Koschland (sic) had moved to San Francisco, opening a wool-and-hide business, marrying, and fathering fifteen children, seven of whom lived to raise families of their own. One was Marcus, a wool dealer like his father. Barney Schweitzer, Levi Strauss's afternoon drinking companion, had selected the young wool merchant as the proper husband for Schweitzer's headstrong daughter Cora.

The Koshlands — Cora insisted on Anglicizing the spelling

and pronunciation of the name — were comfortably fixed. With the election of William McKinley as President and the passage of the Dingley protective tariff in 1897, wool speculators like the Koshlands prospered. By 1900, the Koshlands were wealthy.

Cora "was a good spender. My father used to kick like hell about everything she did, then boast about her when she'd do it," Koshland recalled. The kicking and the boasting increased when Cora began building a family home to match the family fortune. Completed in 1904, the "Petit Trianon," as it was quickly nicknamed, sported marble columns, a fountain in the main hallway, a leather-paneled library, and endless rooms for young Dan and the neighborhood kids to play in.

Daniel lived in the marble halls — still a San Francisco landmark, though no longer set in undeveloped pastures — until he graduated from the University of California, in 1913, with a degree in commerce. The Koshland home was a showplace of San Francisco's Jewish society, shelter for the stream of fund-raising parties to benefit Cora's manifold charities. There, too, she invited forty or fifty fellow patrons of culture to hear concerts by promising local musicians who needed the money a private recital earned. Young Yehudi and Hepzibah Menuhin, Ruggiero Ricci, Ruth Slenczynska, and Isaac Stern gave recitals for Cora's friends and the invited music critics she lobbied on their behalf.

Cora Schweitzer Koshland had planned Daniel's career quite thoroughly. On his graduation, he would embark on an around-the-world trip with members of his family, before leaving them in Europe. "I was to spend six months in Germany, six months in France, and six months in England, working in banks there. And then I was going to be a finished, accomplished banker," a wry Koshland recalled.

World War I upset Cora's plan in the middle of her son's first six-month tour. Koshland left Berlin — very pro-German —on the last special train to take Americans from the country. He remained sympathetic to the kaiser's cause for a year, until the sinking of the *Lusitania*.

Uncertain that he really desired the banking career his

mother had laid out for him, Koshland went to work for New York's Equitable Trust Company. He met Herbert Lehman, and through that banker-turned-social-worker became active in raising funds for Jewish settlement houses in the Lower East Side. He also worked at one of those community centers, leading boys' groups for two years.

With the prospect that the United States would be drawn into the European war, in 1916 Koshland volunteered for officer's training. He was assigned to the Presidio in San Francisco for training as an artillery officer. Unable to ride in true military style the fire horses drafted to train the would-be officers, Koshland was commissioned instead in the Quartermaster Corps.

Eventually, he was sent to Governor's Island, New York. Though he spoke both French and German, Koshland was denied a transfer to the Intelligence Corps because of his German name. He fretted out the entire war in that safe harbor.

While in San Francisco, the sturdy young lieutenant-to-be again met his first cousin Eleanor Haas. She was a seventeen-year-old schoolgirl, and if it was his uniform that first caught her eye, she was to discover more substantial charms in the young man. The two courted secretly because of her youth and consanguinity, fearing the disapproval of her parents. In February 1918, they told their families. Eleanor arranged to be sent off to a finishing school in New York to be close to her affianced; Abraham Haas was not a man to deny his children that which they most wanted. Eleanor and Dan married in September.

His discharge in hand, Daniel Koshland returned to the banking business, "a fair-haired young Lochinvar from the West who was going to become a partner of Lazard Frères and Company." Because of his interest in community work, the aspiring banker accepted a seat on the board of directors of Montefiore Hospital.

He was still buried in the ranks of other candidates for partnership when his brother-in-law's letter arrived, early in 1922. Walter asked Koshland to join him in San Francisco;

he needed help to revive Levi Strauss & Co. It wasn't a big firm; in fact, Walter wrote, it was just muddling along, but it would be a great chance to run their own company in a few years.

It took two months for Eleanor Koshland to convince her husband that he was unhappy at the bank, that her brother's offer was an opportunity not to be missed. On April 1, 1922, Dan Koshland joined his cousin and brother-in-law, Walter Haas, at Levi Strauss & Co.

Sitting at the table the two of them shared as a desk with the Sterns, Walter showed Dan the cost figures he had earlier computed on factory production. They were rough, he admitted, but it appeared the firm was now losing one dollar for every dozen Koveralls it sold. Would Koshland check Haas's estimates?

Koshland spent at least two days a week at the Valencia Street factory, recomputing Walter's figures, further irking Simon Davis with this second barrage of questions. He was also to become acquainted with the women working there. "As a matter of fact," he recounted with some pride years later, "there was a time when I knew practically everybody in the employ of this company by their first name, two hundred and fifty in the factory and eighty or ninety at Battery Street."

Hortense Thomson remembers Koshland in that first year. "He was so nice. He would come into the factory and just stop and talk. We called him Dan, and he was always interested in what we were doing, how we were. Dan, he's my prize." Miss Thomson laughed, insisting on showing her visitors a handsome lap robe Koshland had given her for her eighty-fifth birthday.

Learning what he could about the manufacture of riveted clothing and the Koveralls, Koshland gathered his own cost figures. He spent two months at it, but he reached the same conclusion Walter had. The fast-selling Koveralls were a money-loser.

The new cost analysis angered Davis even more; the factory manager and the first vice-president of Levi Strauss were plotted on a collision course. The confrontation Walter had hoped to avoid occurred in the summer of 1922.

Walter and Elise Haas were staying with her parents at the Sterns' expansive Atherton home when the delegation of Davis's assistant managers visited one night. Taking Sigmund aside, Fred Beronio reported that Davis intended to quit unless Walter stopped pressuring him on the costs of Koveralls. Davis's threat, he assured Stern, was real, and that placed the venerable firm in jeopardy. Everyone was aware of Simon Davis's importance to the company; Stern himself had admitted it many times.

Stern realized that Walter could not back down, not if he was actually to manage the company, now or later. By his ultimatum, Davis was pre-emptively rejecting any compromise, any face-saving agreement. Stern was forced to choose between his still inexperienced son-in-law and his trusted factory manager.

Sigmund was badly shaken as he relayed Davis's threat. Walter offered to resign, sure he could find work elsewhere, but Stern rejected that solution. Koshland's confirmation of the earlier cost estimates had triggered the beginning of doubt.

Stern spent two sleepless nights pondering the dilemma. He visited Davis at his nearby Burlingame home, asking Davis to reconsider his ultimatum. Davis refused. Stern would have to make the most difficult business decision of his life. No matter how he decided, Levi Strauss & Co. could be jeopardized, and seventy years of work building the name into a mark of integrity would be destroyed. For his daughter's sake, he could choose the comparatively inexperienced Walter — and risk the livelihood of more than 300 employees. Elise need never worry about money, but the people who worked in the factory and at 98 Battery had to. If Stern were to support Davis and the man truly not know the costs of production, or how to price his goods, the company would inexorably slide into bankruptcy.

Stern reached his decision. "I've said to this day — though my wife disagrees with me — whether he believed in me or he wanted to keep his daughter happy, I will never know. She claims it was because he believed in me," Haas said later.

The spurned Davis made good his threat, taking with him two of his production managers, including Fred Beronio. The three solicited others to join the walkout and help them form a rival overall firm. The key figure, Fred's brother, David, chose to stay; he was loyal to the company. (In later years, the brothers lived together, though they worked for competitors, each man silent about his employer's business affairs.)

Davis's departure created a vacuum that the boss's son-in-law had to fill — and, it seemed, with no one qualified to fill it.* It was "with some fear and trembling," Walter Haas would later say with a rueful smile, that they turned to thirty-year-old Milton Grunbaum.

Grunbaum understood that he had been selected as the factory manager by default, and sensed that Stern, Haas, and Koshland considered him on probation. "No one realized this was what I had prepared for, that I *knew* I was going to have command some day."

His first day as factory superintendent, the boyish-looking Grunbaum — he would always look boyish, despite the cigars he had taken to smoking with malodorous élan — sum-

---

* Piecing this story together was difficult. Both Haas and Koshland were reluctant to go into details about the departure of Simon Davis, and deliberately declined to comment on allegations of Davis's dishonesty. In hours of interviews, it was the only time either man was even remotely evasive. Koshland demurred, adding, "There are generations still alive," an elliptical reference to Simon's wife and children. (Simon's younger son, Ben, owns a competitive overall factory in San Francisco; Jack, curiously, is an account executive for the advertising agency that has handled the Levi Strauss account for four decades.)

Simon Davis's later career was a sad one. He opened his own overall factory, borrowing extensively to do so, but was unable to achieve financial stability. When that business folded, Davis went to work making overalls for Neustadter Brothers. About 1932, he began a new overall manufactory, the Ben Davis Company, named after his youngest son because the father's credit was so poor. Davis died in 1940, before Ben was able to put the struggling company on its feet. Significantly, Davis's widow, Ann, said wistfully, "Simon threw it all away foolishly. He would have been much better off if he had stayed. He didn't want to get along with Walter. Walter was a lovely gentleman."

moned the floorladies. They were the actual line managers, who had taught him the factory's operation.

"I'm willing to fire anybody who doesn't correct me if they think I'm wrong," he told the women.

They ignored the hollow threat. Besides, they hoped he would succeed in his new job. According to Hortense Thomson, "Milton would come in in the morning, hang up his coat in the office, and the first thing he would do was walk around the factory saying hello to everybody. We all liked him."

Grunbaum's trial period lasted six months, until the year-end inventory. "Mr. Haas felt there must be some error in the inventory we reported, and sent a group to audit. We had produced more than ever expected," Grunbaum remembered. Moreover, he had been able to bring production costs into line with estimates Haas and Koshland believed appropriate. "It was very easy. I knew everybody in the place, knew where the waste was, knew the best workers. Just to begin to correct the situation made a big difference."

Elsewhere in the slowly stirring company Haas and Koshland wrought changes, shuffling personnel, prodding salesmen, tightening financial controls. By 1925, gross sales had topped $4.4 million, though it was the bottom line on the balance sheet, net profit, that most interested Haas. Significantly, the overalls department was the most profitable; less than 10 percent of the company's business that year produced a third of the profits.

The next year, as Milton Grunbaum organized and reorganized the factory on an assembly-line basis, production of overalls fell sharply; still, the profits of that curtailed production, $160,000, accounted for half of all Levi Strauss profits for the year.

Grunbaum was elated. The company was finally headed in the right direction, putting some emphasis on the highly profitable items it produced rather than merely relying on the national brands of clothing wholesaled in the West. Now he decided to imporve the Double X denim pants. It was a good garment, but he could make it even better.

Levi Strauss & Co. had always honored its guarantee —

"A new pair FREE if they rip." Under Davis, the tattered returns had been immediately discarded, sold off for rags as quickly as they came in. Grunbaum began itemizing the reasons for the returns, inspecting the garments with holes, split seams, flapping back pockets.

The most common complaint was of seams splitting, and Grunbaum sought to correct that flaw first. "It was the linen thread," he later explained. "In those days there were no washing machines and dryers. And linen rotted from the moisture, even as it was drying in the sun. I never knew it — no one did — until I began to test it. We thought we had the finest thread money could buy; linen thread is three times stronger than cotton. But it rotted, and the seams gave way."

Grunbaum replaced the linen with a fine-gauge version of the heavy cord used to sew shoes. The incidence of ripped seams fell sharply, and Grunbaum tackled the next problem, defective rivets with sharp edges that eventually nibbled through the cloth. This round robin of correcting the most common defect then moving to the next most prevalent continues fifty years later.

Grunbaum's persistent good humor turned to dismay, then anger in the week before Christmas. Estimating the year-end profits, Haas and Koshland had set down the annual Christmas bonuses for the employees at the Battery Street building and a handful of managers at the Valencia Street factory. Managers were to receive from $100 to $500; the clerks and salesmen, at least a day's wage. As happened every year, the factory workers were overlooked entirely.

Why did the people at Battery Street receive a Christmas bonus when *his* girls did not, Grunbaum demanded of Koshland. Because they didn't wear suits? They were every bit as crucial to the firm as the clerks and salesmen; the balance sheet proved it. The people in the factory worked hard; everyone knew the garment trade was a speed-up business, and Grunbaum admitted he was a hard taskmaster. But the girls had produced for him, despite the unending upheaval caused by his revisions of the production line.

The more he talked, the more irritated he became, his

cheeks redder, his cigar bobbing more emphatically. He insisted on a bonus for the factory workers, a day's wages, just like the stockclerks at Battery Street got.

"I'm getting five hundred dollars and my girls are getting nothing." He stopped suddenly. "I won't accept my bonus unless you give one to all the people at Valencia Street."

Koshland was convinced, and shortly persuaded Haas. Arguments about equitable treatment would always sway the two. Levi Strauss & Co. was to take the "first significant step, revolutionary in the garment industry," in that form of corporate responsibility.

"Very secretly, so it would be a surprise, we got the money out of the bank and moved it to Valencia Street, and we gave everybody in that factory five dollars, a day's wages."

Fifty years later, that day before Christmas was still vivid in Koshland's mind. "It was the most moving day of my life. We gave out five dollars to everybody in the factory — men, women, everybody, two hundred and fifty or three hundred people.

"And it was a scene I will never forget as long as I live. These were mostly Italian women, and they became, well, hysterical. They cried, they laughed, they surrounded me and Milton. It was uncomfortable. They fell on the floor and kissed my fingers. Nobody in their lives had ever given them anything. They'd worked for everything they'd ever had. And all of a sudden, here was somebody, a firm, that gave them five dollars for doing nothing!

"They paraded around the factory, then out onto Valencia Street. It was an indescribable scene, moving, people moved to tears and laughter."

The tears would be bitter soon enough, and the laughter would die entirely.

Chapter V

The Apotheosis

A WORLD OF ZANY NONSENSE — flappers and Prohibition, mahjongg and marathon dancing, flagpole sitting and miniature golf — turned bleak. Thousands of teachers, butchers, and shopkeepers, lured to invest pitiable savings, were betrayed by their perfervid faith in American free enterprise. In a day, Coolidge prosperity was transformed to Hoover depression.

The icon of capitalism, the stock market, lay shattered in the ruins of a bull market that collapsed on Black Thursday, October 24, 1929. No presidential incantation, no Rockefeller blessing, no Morgan prayer asserting that "the fundamental business of the country is sound," could dispel the panic scuttling about Wall Street. Small investors by the thousands were obliterated in those first days. By January, October's paper millionaires had been reduced to bewildered paupers.

Panic gave way to a failure of nerve; that gave way to despair. Stocks steadied momentarily, then began a downward slide that would last for two years.

The fundamental business of the country was decidedly unsound, the President's, the industrialist's, and the banker's assurances notwithstanding. The running of the bulls on Wall Street shredded public confidence. And as confidence evaporated, consumer buying slowed.

Depression. By March 1930, four million people were unemployed. A year later, eight million were looking for work, anything to regain their lost self-respect and income. By the middle of 1932, that figure had swollen to twelve million men and women, one quarter of the labor force.

As many millions more were underemployed, working a few hours or a few days a week, earning barely enough to feed their families. Even those who managed to work five and six days a week had trouble paying for bare necessities.

The Depression hit hardest at the very people Levi Strauss & Co. counted its customers: farmers, miners, lumbermen, and cowboys. Farmers suffered the worst — first from the Depression itself, then from a worsening drought that settled upon the Great Plains. Farm income fell from $12 billion in 1929 to just $5.3 billion in 1932. Beef steers that had fetched $13.42 per hundred pounds in 1929 were selling for $6.70; hog prices sank 70 percent in that same three-year span.

As farm prices fell, farm foreclosures rose, dumping even more unskilled laborers into the employment pool. Jobless thousands crowded into cardboard and tin Hoovervilles on the outskirts of cities, camped under bridges, or rolled in newspapers to sleep in city parks. By 1935, there were 350,000 Okies and Arkies — Woody Guthrie's Dust Bowl refugees — scrounging for work in California alone.

Unable to qualify for relief because they had lived in the state less than a year, the weathered men hired out for less than living wages. Scorned as rednecks, they were despised as cheap labor. A run-down movie house in Bakersfield even posted a sign: "Negroes and Okies upstairs." Still they came — in sagging Model T's crowded with hollow-eyed children, in deadheading boxcars on the Santa Fe, until the highway patrol set up roadblocks along the Arizona border and illegally turned them back.

California needed no more cheap laborers. One out of five state residents already had swallowed what pride remained and sought public relief.

With the rest of the country, Levi Strauss had prospered in the second half of the 1920s, its annual sales more than $4 million. Profits perched well above the 6 percent on capital invested that Walter Haas had deemed inadequate at the beginning of the decade. But the business had subtly changed. As the mail-order houses of Sears, Roebuck and Montgomery Ward opened retail stores, the manufacturers of dry goods represented by Levi Strauss cut their prices to compete. Wholesale bedding, underwear, and shirts produced less and less profit, though the dollar volume remained high. The Double X denim overalls became the company's major moneymaker.

When Jacob Stern died in 1927 and Sigmund the following year, Walter Haas and Daniel Koshland were well in command. Haas was president, a post he would hold until 1955, Koshland treasurer, but neither paid a great deal of attention to titles. Their salaries were the same; at times Koshland personally owned more stock than did Haas. They shared responsibilities according to their interests. Haas concerned himself with finance and merchandising; Koshland, with production and personnel. Albert Hirschfeld was the third of their triumvirate, responsible for credit, increasingly reliant on intense David Beronio.

The years following the crash would test all of them: Haas's fiscal acumen, Koshland's social conscience, and Hirschfeld's credit policies.

Perhaps because they were related, both by blood and marriage, more likely because each respected the other, Haas and Koshland functioned well together. They compromised disagreements and overlooked mistakes. Years later, both would assert there was no second-guessing, no recrimination.

They complemented each other's temperament. By consensus of those who worked with them, Haas was the business innovator, Koshland his sounding board. Koshland also provided a humanistic dimension, demanding of Levi Strauss & Co. the sense of social responsibility learned from his mother; if Koshland was the leader, Haas — who might have taken the businessman's traditional view of such matters, that is, ignored them entirely — quickly followed.

Levi Strauss closed out the year of the crash with sales totaling $4.2 million. The net profit was $296,000 — of which 70 percent was earned by the waist overalls Milton Grunbaum was still attempting to improve. Though a small manufacturer capturing an even smaller percentage of the national market, the company was producing between 10 and 15 percent of all work garments purchased on the Pacific Coast. Through the decade, there were even moments when Haas permitted himself to fantasize annual profits reaching $1 million. The company was in a good position to do it, however parochial. "To be honest," Koshland confessed, "at first we didn't look beyond the cowboy-miner-laborer market in California, Arizona, Nevada, and maybe Colorado and Utah and, in a minor way, Oregon and Washington."

Sales fell by one-sixth in 1930, and, with that drop, the profit of the year before turned into a loss of $88,000. Economizing everywhere, reducing employment through attrition, Levi Strauss & Co. retrenched, waiting for the economy to face about; it had in all the prior panics and depressions.

The next year was even worse. Demand for its overalls slackening, the company for the first time turned to the growing mail-order houses. "We needed to find a product to sell, just to keep the employees working," Grunbaum recalled. The national chain of J. C. Penney offered manufacturing contracts for loose-fitting khaki pants, for an inexpensive boy's waist overall in denim, and for a lightweight duplicate of the children's Koverall. "They said our prices were too high, so we sold knowing it would be at a substantial loss."

Meanwhile, the factory continued to manufacture the 501 Double X denim overall. "We went ahead with production so our people could live. There was no unemployment insurance in those days," Grunbaum continued.

Bundles of the completed garments began stacking up in the factory, filling the lofts at 98 Battery. Levi Strauss dropped the wholesale price from 1930's $19 per dozen to $17, and still the mounds of indigo bundles grew. In the middle of the year, a worried Koshland asked Haas, "Do you know how many overalls are up there?" pointing to the fourth floor of the Battery Street building. "Ten thousand dozen," he answered his own question — a six-month supply.

Grunbaum remained confident, at least outwardly. "The Double X denim was a staple, like sugar in the grocery store. We were fortunate in that we had a unique product even then, with a staple we knew eventually could be marketed. And we had the financial stability that permitted us to do this."

Still, it was close. On purely business grounds, Haas would have been justified in liquidating the company. Levi Strauss was losing money, and the immediate prospects were not good. Cash reserves had long since disappeared; the "financial stability" was the Haas family fortune. Walter's pride, however, would not permit him to close the doors. Levi Strauss had once been profitable, and he would make it so again.

There were no longer sufficient orders to keep the factory operating full time. The company, which had prided itself on offering year-around employment, unlike other firms in the highly seasonal garment trade, sought to stretch out the work. It put its employees on a three-day work week. For men such as Koshland and Grunbaum, there was no alternative. They would juggle production if Haas and Hirschfeld could provide the money. To fire the girls in the factory, to lay off the clerks at Battery Street, was to deprive friends of food and shelter.

Share-the-work plans, unpopular with labor, were the last option. Hortense Thomson, no longer a little girl playing pranks, recalls that she earned $9.00 a week, barely enough to let her contribute a few pennies to the Open Bible Church she attended three times weekly. The factory payroll, which had reached $395,000 in 1929, fell to $275,000 two years later. "It was painful." Koshland winced. "Everybody took a pay cut; everybody shared in it. Christmas that year was the happiest. Everyone had expected the worst to happen, to be let go, and we had managed to get through the year."

Practically, the workers of Levi Strauss & Co. — thousands of other firms elected the same expedient — had assumed the burden of providing relief for their fellow workers.

There was no national welfare system; President Hoover and the national Chamber of Commerce haughtily rebuffed any such proposals as the nonsense of socialistic do-gooders. The economy was to bootstrap its own return to prosperity. The solitary federal agency created in response to the nation's longest economic depression was the banker-run Reconstruction Finance Corporation, which loaned millions of dollars to banking cronies. (The autocratic rationale seemed to be that the wealthy, not needing the money, would lend it out; in fact, the banks held on to the government funds to shore up their own dwindling reserves against the next expected bank run.)

The Depression wore on, 1932 the severest year. Levi Strauss's sales slipped to $2.1 million, half of what they had been in 1929. For the third year in a row, the company lost money. Since the last year of Coolidge prosperity, Levi Strauss had posted losses totaling $426,000.

That cumulative loss was modest, about equal to a single year's profit in the prosperity of the late 1920s, but the cash reserve alone was not great enough to ensure survival. David Beronio, never very voluble, grew more tight-lipped. Bad debts had doubled, then doubled again — to $33,000 in 1931 — as dealer after dealer went bankrupt. It would have been far worse but for his shrewd credit policies; nevertheless, Beronio considered any unpaid bill a personal failure.

The Battery Street store and the factory inundated with denim trousers — and the salesmen wandering in a wilderness of rural poverty — Grunbaum closed down the production lines. If they couldn't make pants, they would refurbish the factory, hastily completed after the earthquake. They laid hardwood floors, solely to keep people busy.

The upward economic swing long predicted would come only with the election of the Hudson River patroon, New York Governor Franklin Roosevelt, to the presidency of the United States. Repudiated in the worst defeat suffered by an incumbent, Herbert Hoover relinquished the White House in March 1933. He was a sadly worn man, bewildered by the failure of the economic system to right itself without governmental aid. Roosevelt had no such illusions; he invoked government participation to save the very capitalistic system business and finance believed him intent on destroying.

The nation's mood was palpable: FDR would get the country going again. He warned, "The only thing we have to fear is fear itself," a well-turned phrase that encapsulated the one truth which the Grand Old Party could not understand. Trust in the new President restored public confidence. Sales of goods beyond the barest essentials began to perk up.

The Depression would not truly end until the Second World War. Indeed, there was a temporary slump in 1938, and Levi Strauss would not surpass 1929's $4 million sales mark until 1941. But the company had survived.

Factory wages increased 50 percent in 1933 as workers returned to full-time employment. The price of the Double X denim waist overalls, reduced to $12.75 per dozen in January 1933, started upward. Six months later, it was $13.75. At the beginning of 1934, it jumped to $16.50. (By the end of the decade, it would rise to $17.00, exactly twice the price per dozen in 1902, the year Levi Strauss died.)

Battery Street's huge inventory of blue denim pants began to evaporate. Their stocks depleted long since, as consumer demand picked up, the dealers began reordering. Levi Strauss's Lot 501 waist overalls *were* like sugar, a staple. As production of overalls in the factory increased, Grunbaum terminated the contracts to manufacture the khaki garments for J. C. Penney. Disingenuously, he told them, "We made a mistake and shouldn't have tried to do business with a firm of your size."

No sooner had the company weathered the Depression than another storm threatened.

With the passage of the National Industrial Recovery Act, its now celebrated Section 7a explicitly assuring labor's right to organize, beleaguered unions stirred.

In San Francisco, an abrasive dockworker from Australia persuaded the newly formed International Longshoremen's and Warehousemen's Union to strike for recognition by waterfront employees. For two months, Harry Bridges's longshoremen tied up the port, until July 5, 1934, when 1500 San Francisco police massed along the Embarcadero to open the way for strikebreakers. In a fury of street battles, two strikers were killed and sixty-four people injured. The governor called up 1700 National Guardsmen with fixed bayonets to accomplish what 1500 police carrying pistols could not.

Other unions rallied to the longshoremen's cause. By July 16, virtually every union in the San Francisco Bay Area had hit the bricks; the general strike lasted four days.

The resulting business paralysis alienated the public, but it also initiated federal arbitration. In subsequent discussions, Bridges secured what he had most wanted, the union hiring hall and, with it, de facto recognition.

Labor was emboldened. In the wake of the strike, union representatives appeared in front of the city's garment factories, passing out leaflets, urging workers to join, arguing that the federal government had guaranteed them the right to organize. One by one, the manufacturers signed contracts, until Levi Strauss was the lone holdout.

Haas and Koshland opposed unionization, as much from the habit of their class as from fear that it would curtail their ability to shift people from task to task. Their opposition was not, however, as militant as the Stern brothers' before them; Jacob and Sigmund had been ardent supporters of the open shop, among the leaders in the largely successful effort to drive unions from the city a dozen years earlier.

Haas recalled, "Our superintendent of shipping came to me and said, 'Our packers and shippers are invited to the union hall. What should we do?'

"And I said, 'Let them go there.' They went, and listened, and they said, 'This is not for us.' "

Haas was not certain why employees at both Battery Street and the factory rejected Bridges's longshoremen's union. "He went after the warehouses, the grocery people, the paper people, everybody. I think the reason our people turned him down was that they were being paid higher wages than he was asking for. And also we had no deductions for sick days. You might call what we were doing paternalistic, but we just thought it was the right way, and our people were well-satisfied."

But there was more to it than that. Bridges's union had been discredited by the general strike; though it won by enforced arbitration recognition from the waterfront employers, it lost prestige elsewhere.

The rebirth of the union movement in the San Francisco area pinched Levi Strauss's efforts to sell the blue denim overalls on which it was increasingly dependent for profits. Unions — especially in the contruction trades — demanded that workers wear only union-made work clothes. As other manufacturers signed contracts and affixed the union label to their garments, Levi Strauss found itself at a competitive disadvantage. The small shops Levi Strauss had so long cultivated, urging in advertisements patronage of neighborhood merchants, could not afford to carry two complete lines of work clothes, one union and one nonunion. In time, Walter Haas recalled, the company could not sell carpenters' or painter's overalls; distribution was reduced to a single store in the strongly unionized city of San Francisco, a saddlery in the suburbs.

The holdout manufacturer hardly resisted the organization of the factory when flurries of leafleters for the United Garment Workers of America appeared in the spring of 1935. "Every time the union came around outside leafleting, the streetsweepers would come inside and complain," Milton Grunbaum said with a chuckle.

The decision to sign with the union, however, was to be the workers', not the company's. The leafleting continued.

"One time it started to rain while they were outside," Grunbaum said. "I really felt sorry for them. I motioned to them and they came running, thinking I was going to say something that would affect the contract, and I said, 'This is foolishness. I don't want you to get soaking wet. Come on inside, and I'll get the boys to get you enough chairs and you can pass your circulars out. This is the only entrance our people use to get in and out.' " The union workers sat on the folding chairs the factory boss provided, dripping water on the new hardwood floors, passing out their broadsides.

The union's organization drive intensified. Walter Haas explained, "They were about to call a strike on my birthday, May eleventh, nineteen thirty-five, to organize the plant. I didn't think my birthday was a good day to have the first strike in the history of Levi Strauss & Company.

"The strike call came after the Wagner Act." Haas shrugged. "It was the law, and a majority of the people in the factory had signed cards for the United Garment Workers. We saw the cards, saw they had a majority, and that was that." Haas's acceptance of the law marked him as a liberal among his business peers.

According to Milton Grunbaum, Haas and Koshland opted for the union because the company "couldn't afford to be picketed. We didn't have the distribution we have now." In Grunbaum's judgment, pickets would have hurt already infinitesimal sales in the San Francisco region.

Hortense Thomson thought the coming of the union "a blessing to us. We did hard work, worked by the minute. It was heavy work, tiring, 'cause you used to have eighteen overalls in a bundle, and it was terrible throwing them up in a truck, way up high, eighteen in a bundle. It was like a slave's job. We worked by the minute to make money." Once unionized, "we gradually got more money, and the dues weren't too much." Miss Thomson attended a few meetings at the union hall on Sixteenth Street, but "wasn't particular about it." She was relieved when Levi Strauss agreed to recognize the United Garment Workers without a strike. She needed her salary.

Having accepted the union, Levi Strauss dealt with it in its idiosyncratic way. Milton Grunbaum was detailed to handle negotiations, a move placing two barriers between the union's business agents and company management. One was Grunbaum himself; the other, his periodic attacks of deafness. To see Grunbaum reach for the battery pack of his hearing aid and shake it was to acknowledge that a wage demand was not getting through to him.

"Even when we were unionized, we had very good relations with the employees. We gave vacations with pay, which was unknown. We'd raise pay when we thought someone deserved it. Pretty soon we found out you can't do that. The union has to have a basis for existence, and it has to fight. So we've learned since then. When we meet with the union, the union wants everything under the sun, and we say we can't give anything, and both sides compromise. It's pro forma," Koshland remarked, smiling.

On one point Grunbaum would not compromise. He refused to sew the union label on Levi Strauss garments. "The union sold those, for one cent each, and I wasn't going to add that to the cost of manufacturing our garments." Union-made Levi's do not carry the union label.

If he was to spend money on the 501, it would be to improve it. Grunbaum devised a way of covering the copper rivets on the rear pockets to satisfy complaints the company was receiving. No longer would the 501 scratch school desks in Arizona, saddles in Colorado, and automobile paint jobs in California. "And besides that," Grunbaum's 1934 patent application conceded, "the rivets are unsightly and do not add but rather detract from the finish and general appearance of the garment."

This alteration was made with no little trepidation. Any change in the Double X denim pants was weighed carefully, usually in afternoon-long meetings involving anyone who had an opinion. Hedging the bet, the firm advertised, "The rivet is still there."

The second change, removing the rivet in the crotch, was mandated by the president himself. There had been some complaints from cowboys about *that* rivet before, but they had been laughed off. However, when Walter Haas, an avid fly fisherman, crouched close to a mountain campfire and the flames heated the rivet in his 501s, it was no longer a laughing matter. The offender was summarily removed.

In time, Grunbaum would change virtually all thirty-five

manufacturing processes for the garment. Only two elements were inviolable: Jacob Davis's sixty-year-old cut and fit of the pants, and the quality of the ten-ounce denim manufactured by Cone Mills to Levi Strauss's specifications. (In 1977, retired twelve years, the still apple-cheeked Grunbaum insisted, "If you take a Five-o-one and just wash and dry it, even before you put it on, you have a beautiful piece of goods. And it's going to get better every time it gets washed because it tightens up.")

By the late 1930s the Double X pants had acquired a mystique of their own. Customers were loyal, sometimes fanatically so. In Montana, ranchers wore Levi Strauss's Lot 501, rather than cheaper overalls, as a badge of success. In the Southwest, Grunbaum boasted, cowboys bought two pairs, one for work and one for dress. "They'd buy them and walk into the river on a hot day and the pants would dry on them, shrinking to fit." If the cowpoke's legs were a pale blue until his next bath, no matter; that was a small price to pay for the proper fit.

The company's one-dollar-per-dozen advertising campaign was reinforced considerably by help from an unexpected quarter, Hollywood. To fill double bills at the Bijou, the studios released herds of Grade-B westerns, and though such stars as Rex Allen and Gene Autry might not wear the faded blue 501s, everyone else on camera did.

Levi Strauss moved to capitalize on the unsolicited endorsement. Its advertising manager, Dick Cronin, affecting western boots and bandanna, began offering prizes to winning rodeo riders. By the end of the decade, the identification of the Double X pants with the western theme was total; working cowboys wore little else. (The power of that motif remains. A generation later, Marlboro cigarettes are tied to a similar theme. Significantly, the models in Marlboro's ads, for authenticity's sake, wear riveted denim pants.)

The effort to link the Double X waist overalls to the opening of the West was deliberate though honest. "When I look back on it," Walter Haas remarked, "it was a combination of luck, opportunity and imagination, and, really, our advertising people. I can't say they put sex into it, but they put a certain imagination into the waist overall. It was different from a workman's garment.

"We were on the western theme continuously in our advertising. Plus wear. Wear; we always stressed wear."

Dick Cronin proudly collected the unsolicited testimonials — even the inadvertent ones. A letter written in 1920 was a favorite of his. For three years, Homer Campbell of Constellation, Arizona, had owned his pair of 501s before he returned them:

> I have worn them every day except Sunday since the early part of 1917. And for some reason which I wish you would explain they have gone to pieces. I have worn nothing but Levi Strauss overalls for the last thirty years and this pair has not given me the service that I have gotten out of some of your overalls in the past. . . . Please consider this and let me know if the fault is mine.

Describing an incident that would be repeated by others in letters years later, Mrs. M. H. English of Otto, Wyoming, wrote:

> Going between here and Basin, we found a man who had run his car off the highway and was stuck. Had no chains or rope . . . but found a pair of old Levi's in the back of the car and tied one leg to our car and one to the front of his. We really had to pull, but the pants held, and out he came.

Milton Grunbaum's shoe thread had proved itself.

The singleminded focus on durability was, by the end of the decade, unusual in American business. Only one other manufacturer had so capitalized on quality in its advertising, and Henry Ford's Model T had become a byword for reliability. In significant ways, the Double X denim paralleled the success of the earlier automobile. Durability bred customer loyalty and, uniquely, an affection for the product that transcended mere serviceability. That, too, formed part of the mystique; in subsequent years, the company would self-mockingly play on that affection for a pair of work pants in its advertising.

Levi Strauss hardly examined its emphasis on quality, according to Walter Haas. "I don't even know that we thought of it. It just came naturally to us. Maybe we believed in Lincoln's theory: you can't fool all the people all the time. Maybe we just thought we had to give honest goods. I think we just accepted this as a matter of course.

"We just believed in furnishing good goods, and believed in the long run quality would tell. In the long run it's just good business. If you depreciate quality, you get found out in the end." *

In the latter half of the decade, Levi Strauss & Co. began expanding. Three men who had started in the shipping room would figure conspicuously: Chris Lucier, Bill Lagoria, and Dick Cronin.

Chris Lucier — he hated his given name, Leo, and used a short form of his middle — had worked for Levi Strauss since 1905, as a fourteen-year-old errand boy, as a wrapper in the shipping department, as the assistant manager of the shirt department, and finally as its manager. Born in San Francisco, the youngest of ten children, Lucier had a keen eye for clothes and an appreciation for the smoothly turned-out Sigmund Stern. Style-conscious himself, he became the company's first true merchandiser, prodding Levi Strauss into producing the decorated western shirt as a complement to the cowboy's Sunday-go-to-meeting pair of Double X denims. The shirts were actually manufactured by local contractors — including a handful of Chinatown entrepreneurs — and sold by Levi Strauss's regular salesmen. He also experimented with leather coats and jackets, a marginally successful enterprise eventually dropped in favor of other lines. (At various times the leather goods included a "Lindbergh" flying jacket and goggled helmet, as well as the full-length overcoats worn by California Highway Patrol officers.)

---

* Haas apologized. "I'm sorry I can't give you answers to these subjective things. We just did them. Maybe we were impelled to do them. Maybe these are some of the reasons we have been successful, because we have curious ideas." Then he laughed.

Lucier was energetic, a man frothing with ideas. Indirectly, he was responsible for the firm's first sally into the East and an advertisement still cherished by the company.

As beef prices had fallen, a scattering of western ranches began taking in summer boarders to stay afloat. Out of the Depression came the dude ranch. The visitors returned in subsequent years to savor the local folkways; but first these mostly wealthy, saddle-sore easterners called on Abercrombie and Fitch, New York specialists in outfitting the outdoorsman, for the proper western clothing real cowboys wore.

Prompted by the demand, Abercrombie and Fitch ordered Double X overalls by mail. Lucier assured the store that it should also order the embroidered shirts his western wear department produced, and to celebrate the 501's debut in New York he placed an advertisement in the newspapers, proclaiming the pants "guaranteed to shrink, guaranteed to fade."

Like Lucier, Bill Lagoria got his first job working in the shipping department on Battery Street. He was eighteen, "too young for the First World War and too old for the Second," when Sigmund Stern hired him in 1917. Lagoria spent thirteen years in the shipping department in a variety of jobs, each with more responsibility than the preceding one. Transferred to the billing department, he once again worked his way through the ranks, eventually heading it. Again he was moved, to become David Beronio's assistant when the venerable Albert Hirschfeld finally retired.

"Beronio was credit manager, sales manager, head of the jeans department, personnel manager, purchasing manager, and insurance manager. I was his assistant in all of these," Lagoria said in an interview. "I was determined to get ahead. I used to come in on Saturdays and Sundays to read his correspondence to see how he handled problems."

Lagoria was just three weeks from his fortieth birthday when Walter Haas informed him that he had been chosen sales manager. Lagoria's appointment marked a new direction for the company. Though the jeans department was just one of many, it was the one in which Lagoria himself was most interested, the one he believed offered the most potential.

The third of the new executives was the advertising manager, Richard Cronin, lately dressed in western garb, probably the one man in the entire company who most clearly understood the value of the connection between Double X pants and the Old West, a link that could be fairly exploited. If he had a human failing, Margaret Vella, then Cronin's twenty-year-old secretary said, "it was because he was so nice, so *nice*. I used to tell him people took advantage of him because he was so nice."

Cronin was a man of grand ideas. Bill Lagoria liked to think of the short Irishman as "the little giant." Out of friendship, Lagoria was willing to overlook Cronin's worst habit, a messy desk. Somewhere beneath the mound of litter before him, Cronin alone could find the precise slip of paper he needed.

Margaret Vella most enjoyed traveling to the rodeos with her boss. For a young lady raised in a strict Catholic home, the trips to faraway Cheyenne, Reno, and Baker, Oregon, were great adventures, made more delightful by the western costume in which Cronin dressed her. Cronin attended rodeos constantly, presiding over well-attended Levi Strauss hospitality rooms.

City-bred Margaret Vella was very careful on those trips. "I started in nineteen thirty-six at the factory, numbering shirts. I was eighteen, and so happy to have a job. When I first started, the boys all paid attention to me, and I wasn't used to that, since I had gone to a girl's school. Then Miss Opal Higgins, in charge of hiring, took me aside and warned me if I didn't do better they would let me go.

"Oh, honestly, that was something *terrible*," she exclaimed. "I think I prayed for two years straight: Please don't let me lose my job. After that warning, I really had my nose to the grindstone." Transferred to Battery Street, the dark-haired woman still attracted male attention, including that of Cronin, who offered her a job as his secretary.

She looked up from her grindstone in 1951 long enough

to spy the tall, graying Bill Lagoria. In keeping with the company's custom, she received a $50 check from Dan Koshland when she married Lagoria.

Lucier, Cronin, Lagoria, and Milton Grunbaum formed a daily luncheon quartet at Henry's Fashion Restaurant "for years, and years, and years," Lagoria recalled. They were all in their forties, close friends, lifelong employees of the same company, and committed to promoting the Double X denim overall. Lucier and Cronin cast out ideas to increase sales; Lagoria and Grunbaum scaled them down to the realm of possibility, then put them into effect.

It was Lucier's idea to add some characteristic to the Double X overall that would distinguish it from the host of other brands on the market. Despite the threat of legal action, competitors had even infringed on the trademarked arcuate design stitched on the rear pockets of the 501. Lucier conceived the addition of a red tab with the word "Levi's" embroidered on it, a trademark to be sewn into the seam of the right rear pocket. On September 1, 1936, Milton Grunbaum began producing Double X pants with the red tab, the first time a clothing manufacturer had externally branded his product.

The folded cotton ribbon, added to the Double X jackets the following July, was to become the most imitated mark the company owned. Four decades later, it is still probably the most infringed-on insignia in the fashion industry.*

The tab, in time, grew into a symbol of prestige, and that,

---

* The ribbon and its placement — as well as the name itself — are protected. To preserve both the concept of the tab and its location, the firm uses a variety of colored ribbons, and 10 percent of all garments have *blank* tabs. Nonetheless, the company's attorneys have handled 200 patent infringements in the past three years alone, including a tab infringement by major competitor Wrangler, won in November 1977. According to Carol Yenne, of the company's legal department, the value of goods sold by companies infringing on Levi Strauss trademarks "easily goes into the millions of dollars." Mrs. Yenne has a closetful of pants and shirts produced under infringement. The number of such cases, and of outright counterfeits of 501s, is increasing as the value of the trademarks is recognized overseas. "Outside of the personnel department," Mrs. Yenne said in April 1977, "I have more files than anyone in the company."

in turn, gave rise to a clutch of teen-agers' tribal rites. In the 1940s, when a fancy for collecting the little red tabs swept Los Angeles, high school students walked around with one hand permanently protecting the right buttock. Periodically, merchants complained that sizable portions of their stock had been stripped of tabs by razor-wielding youngsters under the mistaken impression that 100 or 50 or 200 tabs returned to Levi Strauss could be traded for a free pair of 501s. (That is precisely the last thing the company wants — its identifying trademark stripped from the garment to be transformed into a redemption coupon.)

It was Cronin who suggested that the firm mount an exhibition for the 1939 International Exposition on Treasure Island in San Francisco Bay. Keying the exhibition to the western theme and the rodeos on which he doted, Cronin conceived a mechanical rodeo. Managed by Cronin and Lagoria, the fifteen-foot-square exhibit featured foot-tall figures hand-carved in the likenesses of celebrated figures on the rodeo circuit. In a five-minute show, the announcer made his recorded introductions, a rider hurtled from the chute on a bucking bronco, and a rodeo clown cavorted in sudden jerks and spasms. Employees of the company who saw the mechanical exhibit remember it fondly as a popular attraction at the fair.

According to Lagoria, the fair attracted thousands of visitors. When they returned home, they asked local merchants for the pants promoted by the mechanical rodeo. "We started getting mail inquiries from places in Oklahoma and Iowa and Texas, where we had had only a small mail-order business until then." The awkward mechanical rodeo, which would later tour the country in a large moving truck converted for the occasion, signified the true beginning of Levi Strauss's national sales effort, Lagoria believes.

By the end of the decade, company sales had reached $3.3 million. Profits had not yet recovered to pre-crash levels, in large part because the jobbing was less and less profitable. In 1939, the net profit on sales of the Double X pants and jackets exceeded the company's net profits. Underwear, shirts, bedding, and linens had lost money during the year.

It was about this time — no one can mark the date precisely, for such things happen only gradually — that sales of the Double X pants broke out of the purely western, or workmen's, market. Ostensibly, the fashion started at either the University of California at Berkeley or the University of Oregon; Haas and Koshland believe it was their alma mater's responsibility. Sophomores adopted the pants as their own, prohibiting lowly freshmen from wearing them. Cronin did all he could to capitalize on the fad, offering to dress California's lettermen in the pants if they would only wear them, securing a proclamation from the governor of Oregon reserving the wearing of the Double X denims to sophomores at the state university.

About the same time, merchants began asking company salesmen for "Levi's," the nickname their customers had given the Double X denim, guaranteed-to-fade, guaranteed-to-shrink, Lot 501 waist overalls. Without a thought on its part, Levi Strauss & Company had acquired its most valuable trademark.

The pants had been popularly christened. Already swathed in an ineffable aura of one part quality and one part romance, they now acquired status, as well. Al Sanguinetti, then a skinny high school student growing up in San Francisco's Italian North Beach, remembered, "In nineteen thirty-nine, nineteen forty, I couldn't afford a pair of Levi's. I got a pair of ninety-nine-cent Debb's specials from Debb's Department Store. So I got a little respect for the pants then, 'cause they were two dollars and fifteen cents.

"In school, you had a pair of Levi's, you were King Shit."

Chapter VI

Transition

IT WAS EXPECTED. Whether by himself, his family, or the company, he would never be sure. He had interviewed with other firms during his last year in business school, but it was merely for the experience. Wally Haas was going to work for Levi Strauss & Co.

Brother Peter, two, almost three years his junior, felt differently. Strongly. Enrolled first in the University of California's School of Engineering, switching to economics because his engineering cohorts "could not talk without a slide rule in their hands," Peter felt impelled beyond the company, the family, the protective mantle of "the boss's son."

For a while, Wally had considered medicine as a career. Doctors more than businessmen could help people; certainly a doctor saw the direct results of his work. But by the time he entered the University of California as a freshman, the skinny lad with a prominent Adam's apple and curly hair that defied comb or brush had decided on business, *the* business, Levi Strauss & Co. It was not a particularly exciting firm, he realized; dry-goods wholesaling was not situated at the very frontier of technology or marketing, and, furthermore, Levi Strauss relied on a basically unchanging line of goods, especially its 501 Double X blue denim waist overall. But Levi Strauss was the family business. Someone had to carry on.

The young man was more dutiful than inspired as a student; he studied conscientiously because it was expected of him. He also spent three harrowing years attempting to make the university's tennis team because he expected such perseverance of himself.

After graduating from Berkeley, Wally elected to attend the Harvard Graduate School of Business Administration, then as now the pre-eminent graduate academy for the nation's business leaders. The two years in Cambridge were rewarding. "I went back there immature. I'd been traditionally raised; I'd had a sheltered life. I learned how to attack problems, where to find information, and how to deal with people."

At Berkeley and Harvard, Walter also made lifelong friends, among them Robert McNamara, shortly to become president of the Ford Motor Company, then John F. Kennedy's Secretary of Defense.

"What I really got out of Harvard Business School was my wife," Wally later joked. Evelyn Danzig was attending Wheaton College in Norton, Massachusetts. Near the end of his first year, they had been invited to the same dance in New York, and met on the train to Manhattan. Two girls at the dance interested the twenty-one-year-old Walter Haas, Jr. "I made the terrible mistake of cutting in on the other one first. I was stuck with her an hour. Then I danced with Evelyn, and was cut in on in two minutes. And I decided she was the one I should pay attention to; that was a perfect market test."

While attending Harvard, Walter also took correspondence courses leading to a commission in the Quartermaster Corps. The threat of Hitler's Third Reich darkened Europe, and with it loomed the draft. "We took those courses very spasmodically. We'd let them sit for three months, and then the Maginot Line would be breached, and we'd take three or four in a big hurry."

Walter had some doubts about his military capability. "In one course I got a platoon lost in the woods, and Evie, who was typing the paper for me, got them out."

Haas graduated with a master's degree in business administration in 1939 and returned to San Francisco. There, he began an apprenticeship — "the old-fashioned way" — working in the Levi Strauss factory on Valencia Street, trying to accomplish the tasks Milton Grunbaum set in front of him.

"I even tried to sew a pair of pants, and found out that was one thing Harvard Business School didn't teach you how to do." Nor had the childhood hours perched on the lap of Millie McGuire, the factory's telephone operator, taught him to operate a switchboard.

The first year at the factory would be clearly remembered. "Milton Grunbaum was a great mentor, a great man, with such feeling for people," Haas said softly, shaking his head slowly.

In the factory cafeteria at Valencia Street, Walter learned the most lasting of Grunbaum's lessons. Two former operators, ostensibly retired, were washing the dishes. "My Harvard Business School training told me that was unsanitary and inefficient."

Young Haas asked Grunbaum if he had considered replacing the women with mechanical dishwashers. "I've thought of it, but why don't you look into it?" the cigar-smoking factory manager suggested.

"He was answering my question because he had a perfectly good answer. So I made a typical business school study, and I proved it was more efficient and sanitary. And I gave Mr. Grunbaum all the figures," Haas recalled.

Grunbaum studied the report. "Well, that's all very good. You know, these two ladies are too young to get any garment-union benefits, and too old to work, and each has about thirty years at the factory. What am I going to do with them?"

Haas had learned something else not taught at business school. Almost four decades later, the chairman of the board of the largest clothing manufacturer in the world said with quiet pride, "And it was a good lesson to me."

The instruction was often casual, no more than watching Grunbaum make his first-thing-in-the-morning stroll about the factory, stopping to congratulate Mrs. Ponti, whose oldest son was about to go off to the university; asking Mrs. Finnegan how her husband was mending since his accident on the docks the week before; assuring Mrs. Piccoli that she could use a machine to stitch up her daughter's first-communion dress.

Haas had other teachers as well. Assigned the task of handling a customer complaint, Walter approached it "in best Harvard Business School style. If you have a complaint, that's the time you can make a friend if you handle it right." Haas wrote a conciliatory letter, pointing out that the returned pants had suffered the travails of the damned, over a long period of time, and didn't come within the money-back guarantee.

"A week later I got a letter," he recalled ruefully. "It should have been written on asbestos, it was so hot. She was furious that a big company like us wouldn't stand behind its guarantee, and she called me all kinds of names."

Perplexed, Haas showed the correspondence to David Beronio, asking what he had done wrong. The austere Beronio read the exchange, then peered over his glasses at the uneasy young man. "You signed your name so she could read it."

The apprenticeship of the nominal assistant secretary of Levi Strauss & Co. was interrupted by Pearl Harbor. He spent fifty-two months in uniform, narrowly avoiding bakery school when Colonel Robert Roos, a San Francisco department store executive, recognized Walter's name on a list of officers. Roos tapped the young man for various administrative offices running post exchanges. Haas spent his entire military career within fifty miles of San Francisco; in effect, he was learning merchandising.

Major Walter Haas, Jr., was a seasoned twenty-seven when he returned to Levi Strauss. His father handed him over to sales manager Bill Lagoria with the instruction, "I want you to see he gets a picture of everything." The apprenticeship was almost over.

As the boss's son, of course, Walter, Jr., found that doors were open for him. But rank and opportunity imposed their own burden on the young man. He had to do a better job than anyone else — to prove to himself that his rapid advancement was merited.

As a Haas, he had responsibilities beyond the company as well. Shortly after his discharge, he was asked to solicit for the Community Chest and assigned to canvass a lower-class neighborhood. It was difficult work, he learned. The people who answered the doors when he rang could afford to give so much less than he could. Occasionally, some insulted him. Others were simply suspicious.

The results seemed so niggardly, nickels and dimes fished from purses and pockets barely adding to dollars he could easily donate himself. Troubled, young Haas turned to his uncle, Dan Koshland. "You're always very active in the community. Why do you subject yourself to this? It's a lot of work and I have got a couple of babies at home and I'm doing it on my own time."

"Well, I'll tell you why," the older man answered. "Because you meet the nicest people in the community. They're all doing the same kind of thing." It was another lesson the young man would not forget.

As it had changed Wally Haas, the four years of World War II had also changed the company. Sales of $4.3 million in 1941 had increased to $5.7 million by 1945. The 501 waist overall had been deemed an essential product for the war effort — war-plant workers found it the most serviceable of work clothes — but to secure continuous production of the garment, Levi Strauss had to accept the Office of Price Administration's fixing of the sales price. Costs might rise for denim, for labor, for shipping, for advertising, but Levi Strauss could not adjust its prices correspondingly. By war's end the firm was "trading dollars" on its most celebrated product, Walter, Sr., commented ruefully.

In time, that would appear to be a hidden blessing. When sporadic competitors raised their prices to equal or surpass Levi Strauss, the once premium-priced 501 became a double bargain for consumers. Great numbers who might not have purchased a higher-priced garment now bought the long-wearing work pants.

Demand on the Pacific Coast had also increased with the influx of aircraft and shipyard workers. In effect, large-scale demographic shifts — the westward tilt of population was just beginning — were to benefit the company; the state that had registered 1.25 million on relief just seven years earlier now had a labor shortage. Industrial employers, notably Kaiser shipyards and the expanding aircraft industry in Southern California, recruited all over the country. Lured by high wages, draft exemptions, on-the-job training, workers flocked to the West Coast by the hundreds of thousands. For Levi Strauss & Co., it meant potential customers were leaving the East, *terra incognita* to its salesmen, to come to California, by far the company's most lucrative sales market. Similarly, GIs from other parts of the country found themselves stationed in the West, and discovered the 501 in post exchanges. At the end of the war, they helped create a demand for the waist overall in their eastern home towns.

To meet the increased demand for the celebrated 501s, Milton Grunbaum set up a second factory in the vacant loft of the Greyhound Depot in San Jose, California. Still short of production facilities, Grunbaum located a struggling workpants factory in Wichita Falls, Texas, and arranged for Levi Strauss to buy the plant. By the end of the war, he had opened a fourth factory in a disused automobile showroom in seaside Santa Cruz, California.

Despite Grunbaum's efforts, the company still lacked enough production. Supplies were limited, and Levi Strauss salesmen remained frustrated by the home office's inability to fill commission-rich orders. But even that enforced shortage worked to the firm's advantage; when shipments did arrive, retail stores often advertised their bonanza, luring lines of customers waiting for the doors to open. Americans had learned to queue up for scarce goods. For customer and retailer alike, the scarcity enhanced the 501's social value.

Wartime necessities affected the very garment itself. To conserve scarce materials, the War Production Board directed that unnecessary appendages be stripped from clothes. (Actually, that rule most affected the manufacturers of men's clothing; for "morale purposes" women were to be allowed their frills, flounces, and furbelows.) Cuffs disappeared from all men's pants, and with them went the 501's six suspender buttons, five belt loops, and cinch belt in the back. Since the garment shrank to fit, there was no need for these devices, anyway. What Levi Strauss itself had always been afraid to do — change the garment in any way — was now done for it. Only the belt loops would reappear at the war's end — merely to reassure the more insecure customers.

The board required two additional changes. All-copper rivets were replaced by steel rivets coated with copper, and the unessential use of thread to create the trademarked arcuate stitching on the back pockets were discontinued in favor of paint. The logic of replacing thread with equally scarce paint bewildered the company then, and amuses those who remember the war years now. (The shift from thread to paint apparently hurt sales among Arizona Indians, who refused to accept pants with painted stitching as the authentic article.)

One alteration the firm refused to adopt — the reduction of the weight of the denim. Oscar Groebl, now manager of the New York buying office, pleaded in Washington to be allowed even heavier denim. To reduce the weight of the cloth, ostensibly to save cotton, would reduce the strength of the Double X pants. And they were, after all, being worn by workers in essential industries. Groebl prevailed; the weight of the denim increased to thirteen and one-half ounces.

Amid the expanding production of Levi's — the Double X waist overall's nickname was adopted by the company with a small booklet in mid-1942, "Everybody Knows His First Name" — Levi Strauss & Co. also manufactured dungarees for the navy and fur-lined parkas for Alaska-bound troops.

The war had influenced the company, as it had transformed Walter, Jr. It affected Peter Haas as well.

After his graduation from the University of California, in 1940, Peter was uncertain about his career. At his father's suggestion, Peter talked with a family friend, Leon Livingston, whose advertising agency had handled the Levi Strauss

& Co. account for a number of years. Livingston suggested that Peter work at the agency while making up his mind.

At the beginning of the war, the dark-haired young man was rejected for military service because of poor eyesight. He tried to join the Canadian air force but was again turned down. Thirty-five years later, a joke barely masked his youthful disappointment: "My Seeing Eye dog had flat feet."

A Harvard Business School brochure offered faint hope. Men with degrees from the school could obtain waivers for physical disabilities if the military needed their particular skills. His father and older brother already urging him to go on to business school, Peter enrolled at Harvard. He graduated summa cum laude, a prestigious Baker Scholar, but still a civilian.

Twenty-five-year-old Peter went to work for Hammond Aircraft, a firm in which his father had a financial interest, manufacturing nose assemblies for Douglas Aircraft. The two years at Hammond constituted a time of testing. "I found out maybe I could do something reasonably well, if salary raises are an indication."

At Hammond, Haas met Josephine Baum, the new secretary to the president of the company. Needing a fourth member of his car pool in order to qualify for gas-rationing stamps, Haas invited her to join. A car pool would be more convenient for her than the street car, so, with some skepticism, she accepted. In time, Peter reported with a laugh, he made the car pool even more convenient — by marrying her.

Abruptly deprived of military contracts at the end of the war, Hammond began shutting down. Peter needed a job. (Though the Haas children were independently wealthy the idea of not working never occurred to them.) Jody Baum Haas urged her husband to join the family business.

"Somehow things came together, and it was right to go to work with my father and brother when he got out of service," Haas said later. His abhorrence of taking "the easy way" was gone, yet he remained wary.

His first goal was to be accepted at the Valencia Street factory — he would duplicate the apprenticeship served earlier by his brother — as something other than the boss's son. He found sensitive tutors: Annie Heinzer, who practically managed the factory during Milton Grunbaum's increasing absences; Opal Higgins, the disciplinarian who had terrified the boy-struck Margaret Vella; and a floorlady, Mrs. Garnetta Dunnigan.

Mrs. Dunnigan, "a great lady," particularly impressed Peter. "We had these Christmas parties the day before Christmas. People would officially stop working at twelve. One day Mrs. Dunnigan said to me, 'You know, I think this is really wonderful that the company has a Christmas party. But people lose their paycheck for that afternoon, and I wonder if it's right.' Shortly thereafter we made the afternoon a paid holiday. She was very sensitive to these things and made me sensitive."

Peter was learning, too, those lessons not part of the Harvard Business School curriculum.

Both by his own inclination and the need to fill a gap, Peter gravitated toward production. His father encouraged the choice, for the two sons naturally complemented each other, in much the same fashion as the father and Dan Koshland had earlier divided responsibilities. Walter, the more extroverted of the young men, was interested primarily in merchandising and marketing; Peter, the more introverted, leaned toward production and finance.

With Walter's return from service, the two younger men began to assert an immediate influence on the company, tangential to profit and loss, but critical to their shared concept of corporate responsibilities. Consciously or unconsciously, they were striving for a vaguely realized goal. They would quickly, too quickly, deny they were businessmen of messianic purpose, yet they understood the source of the striving.

"It's in the genes," Walter, Jr., told an interviewer. "It's the way we were brought up, serving in the community, helping when we could. I saw what my parents were doing. I guess we tried to emulate them."

Speaking slowly, carefully, Peter Haas acknowledged, "It

starts way back, maybe with a certain tradition of helping your fellow man, which is a Jewish tradition. I guess the nearest I can think of it is with grandparents on both sides, and then my parents in turn, and coming down to us.

"I've been trying to think how it's passed down. I think part of it is by example, knowing what your grandparents did and seeing what your parents do and how they act and talk, the obligations and responsibilities they feel. It's just something you grow up with, I think.

"I was very jealous of Mount Zion Hospital," Peter said, chuckling, "because it took so much of my mother's time. She was the first woman president, and the second woman president is my sister, Rhoda. In fact, people say it's too bad my sister didn't come into Levi Strauss; we might have been quite successful."

In those first years together, the brothers discussed what they intended to do with their lives. Neither considered public office. Community service was expected; after all, they were the sons of Walter and Elise Haas, the nephews of Daniel and Eleanor Koshland. "We thought we were going to have responsibility for a business. And we said, 'All right, let's make this the best darn corporation in the United States, and maybe we can be an example to someone else,' " Walter, Jr., recalled.

Most businessmen measured success or failure in the simplest terms: profit and loss. Neither son considered that standard sufficient.

As personnel manager, Walter hired the first black, Booker T. Washington, to be employed at the store on Battery Street. Washington was not the first black to work for the company, however; during World War II, the sign propped in the factory window proclaimed "We Hire Freely" as, unbidden, Levi Strauss integrated its work force. (Washington asked to serve as recruiter for other blacks on the grounds that he didn't want the wrong people hired; a bad black worker would jeopardize his own chances for advancement, he argued. He ultimately retired after more than twenty-five years with the company.)

For his part, Peter assisted Milton Grunbaum in organizing a factory in Vallejo, across San Francisco Bay, to manufacture shirts. Deliberately, they hired two blacks among the first fifteen workers employed. The message to the incoming work force was clear: if you went to work for Levi Strauss, you worked with people of all races.

That was true at Valencia Street, as well. The older Irish and Italian women were retiring. They had spent their lives in factories like Levi Strauss, and now their sons and daughters were enrolling in city colleges, pursuing white-collar careers. Increasingly, these women were being replaced by Orientals and blacks taking the first step out of poverty. Smaller numbers of employees at Valencia Street were newly arrived refugees from Europe, especially Jews who either had fled before the war or had survived Hitler's final solution. Julius Phillips was among them. Hired in 1946 to work in the shipping room — he repeatedly declined promotions — forty-four-year-old Phillips was to have an impact on the company far beyond his status as a shipping clerk. A man of uncommon compassion, his advice would be repeatedly sought by other employees — including Walter and Peter Haas.

Even with five factories operating now, Levi Strauss was unable to meet the demand for its waist overalls. The company was forced to institute an allocation program based on past sales, a policy that repaid old loyalties and usually smaller dealers. Despite threats from big customers demanding more than their share, and from department stores that had formerly disdained the guaranteed-to-shrink pants, Levi Strauss hewed rigidly to its allocation scheme. Years later, it was a matter of savored pride for such men as Milton Grunbaum and Bill Lagoria that their allocation program was never compromised. The allocations remained in effect for three years, retarding the company's growth, for they could open new accounts only as production increased.

Grunbaum scouted for additional production facilities. The manager of Levi Strauss's Wichita Falls plant introduced Grunbaum to "Dad" and "Sonny" Stafford of Sedalia, Missouri. Father and son owned their own manufacturing plant, turning out bib overalls for sale in the Midwest and South. Equally important, the Staffords retained a six-man sales force to cover these areas.

The Staffords had unused production capacity; Levi Strauss needed more production. On a handshake, Dad Stafford agreed to transform his unused capacity into Levi Strauss's sixth manufacturing facility. In so doing, however, he was depriving his salesmen of potential income, since he would be unable to expand production of bib overalls if the salesmen could sell more. The solution was obvious: Stafford's sales force began carrying Levi's along with the bib overalls. That tenuous pairing was the beginning of Levi Strauss's effort to grow as a national company.

It was only a matter of time before the firm required more output and proposed to take over all production in Sedalia. Meeting in San Francisco, Dad Stafford asked Walter Haas, Sr., and Dan Koshland, "If you were me, would you turn over your entire business to Levi Strauss and Company without some contract and some prospects for the future?"

Haas was honestly equivocal. "Things vary — such as prices. We've been working together for several years, and this is a decision that you must make on faith in us and how we will do. I cannot tell you what to do."

Ignoring the risk — they would be entirely at the mercy of Levi Strauss — relying on his judgment of Haas, Koshland, and Grunbaum rather than on conventional business wisdom, Stafford threw in with the westerners. Thirty-one years later, Dad succeeded by Sonny, the two companies were still doing business together, Sonny manufacturing only Levi's in his factory, their mutual contract still only a handshake.

Despite the obstacle of a production shortage, in 1948 Walter, Sr., achieved a long-awaited personal goal. For the first time, the company's profits exceeded a million dollars. Almost thirty years before, he had idly fantasized such lavish returns, creeping toward it in the years prior to the Depression, regaining the ground lost after 1933. The firm had come close, recording a net profit of $877,619 on sales of $11.8 million in 1947. This year it had broad-jumped to profits of almost $1.5 million.

The sudden spurt was, in one sense, troubling. The company had planned for it, building production, struggling to keep pace with the demand for Levi's, as the riveted overalls were permanently dubbed now. Yet gross sales between 1947 and 1948 had soared an unnerving 50 percent. Levi Strauss was, after all, a small firm, privately held, its growth financed by Walter, Sr.'s, squirreling away a portion of each year's profits. Was that growth too much? Or too fast? Could they maintain it? Walter, Sr., fretted over that matter for the next twenty years.

Success engendered another problem. The name "Levi's" so firmly fixed in the public mind, people tended to refer to all blue denim pants as Levi's. With a mixture of pride and rue, the company was compelled to an endless effort to prevent its trademarked name from becoming generic for all jeans or dungarees.*

Dan Koshland and Walter, Jr., were soundly optimistic, despite the risks of changing their marketing strategy. Walter kept talking about population growth and pointing to the demand for the waist overall among college men. There was the future, if he was right. If. They had all seen clothing fashions come and go. Would Levi's be one of them?

Grunbaum, Cronin, Lucier, Lagoria, Peter — all sensed the company on the verge of a period of growth. Only David Beronio, now the company's treasurer, was skeptical; but

---

* Trademark or no, a number of protected names have been adopted generically by the public to describe all products of that group: Band-Aid, Dixie Cup, Simoniz, Jell-O, Laundromat, Kleenex, Tampax, Coke, Styrofoam, Deepfreeze, Frigidaire, Dry Ice, Fig Newtons, and, of course, the corporate name that spawned both noun and verb, Xerox. Manufacturers who fail to protect the name — by legal action against infringement and, most often, by delicate reminders to publications that use the name generically — risk losing it. Thermos, nylon, and mimeograph were all left unprotected and now "languish in lower-case ignominy," according to *Time* magazine (July 6, 1962).

David, after forty-four years with Levi Strauss, was too often wedded to the old ways.

Walter Haas, Sr., did not consider himself a conservative. His business peers — including the men who repeatedly voted for him as president of the Chamber of Commerce — believed him rather more liberal than businessmen were wont to be. Progress for Haas certainly was more than increased profits, and he tended to support the more moderate of Republicans, including California's Governor Earl Warren.

Cautionary he was, but Haas could be persuaded to undertake an accelerated growth plan. As Bill Lagoria remembered it, Haas was watching the sales of Levi's "like a hawk." His late-afternoon chats with the sales manager always started with Walter asking, "Well, Bill, what have you got today?"

Four million pairs had sold that year, well over 333,000 dozens, the daily total acknowledged by Haas's ritual response: "Moving right along, aren't they?"

Lagoria's profound respect for Walter — "To my mind, no two men on earth could be better than Senior and Dan Koshland" — would not prevent him from speaking out, urging expansion of production and sales. Haas, in fact, encouraged the exchange, calling it his "Fifth Freedom," after Roosevelt's wartime Four Freedoms. His office door was literally open to any of the 2000 company employees with ideas, grievances, or just wanting a friendly ear. They needed no permission from their immediate superiors.

In a company, in an atmosphere as relaxed as Levi Strauss, where a sewing-machine operator on Valencia Street was only two managers removed from the chief executive — and the president and the operator were on a first-name basis — the Fifth Freedom could and did operate effectively. Haas or Koshland was available. They listened, but made no decision. If they felt a grievance had merit or a suggestion was valid, Haas or Koshland would request that the appropriate manager look into the matter. Of course, the president's request hastened a manager's consideration, or reconsideration in the case of a complaint, but Haas himself issued no orders except through the chain of command. He never jumped managerial echelons to pounce on a subordinate.

Later, he would insist that the Fifth Freedom was his proudest achievement at Levi Strauss. It also provided a valuable information source for him, especially in talking to the *schleppers*, the salesmen in from the field. "I learned more about the business from what they told me. If I was impressed by what they said, I would talk to the sales manager. The salesmen would talk about the lines, say that we needed more depth, we should do this, we should do that, some of which I agreed with and some I disagreed with."

In their late-afternoon conversations, Lagoria continually emphasized the potential of eastern sales. A portion already came from the scattered sales force Dad Stafford had employed; a portion came in "over the transom," by mail from Best and Company in New York, from Carson-Pirie-Scott in Chicago, from St. Louis and Cincinnati. It was Abercrombie and Fitch's "guaranteed to shrink, guaranteed to fade" phenomenon all over again. Former GIs and war-industry workers returning to the East asked for the pants in local stores. It wasn't a lot, but it was growing steadily, Lagoria pointed out. There were even European sales — soldiers stationed in Germany were wearing the 501s off duty. Some gave pairs away to girl friends; others found buyers in Germany's flourishing black market for luxury goods. Post exchanges constantly ordered larger stocks.

Even more telling were the statistics Walter, Jr., had compiled about population trends. The country was entering a baby boom; veterans returned to civilian life were quickly making up for lost time. Historically, too, more children were born during periods of prosperity than during depressions; certainly the country was experiencing the anticipated postwar boom. Births, just over 2.5 million in 1940, had increased in 1945 to 2.8 million, and the total was climbing annually.

To capitalize on that coming youth market — "It was inevitable," Walter, Jr., said in retrospect — meant shifting the sales emphasis from cowboys and farmers to young people. There were not enough advertising dollars for both. That plan, in turn, required a shift in the emphasis on western wear and the western image, with less stress on Levi's-clad cowboys pictured on bucking broncos and more on the Levi's-clad young men and women perched on the corral fence, watching. It played down the West as a workaday reality, recasting the West as a romantic myth. Significantly, this change emphasized Levi's as play clothes rather than work clothes, for young people spent more time at play than at work.

The crucial decisions followed each other, one at a time. Once Haas was convinced they could sustain their growth, he gradually eased the brake. Even then, the large-scale marketing shift urged by Walter, Jr., would have to wait until the shortage of denim eased and the company could abandon allocated distribution. Further, they would need an expanded sales force. In years past, they had sold most of their waist overalls in rural areas, to rural workers; but the bulk of America's young people — their customers in the future — lived in cities, where Levi Strauss accounts were proportionately fewer.

That population factor presented its own problems for Bill Lagoria's expanding sales force. More and more, sales in urban areas were made to large department stores; smaller retail shops, the "Mom-and-Pop" clothing stores that had been the backbone of Levi Strauss's trade, were unable to compete with offer-everything, modern stores. Nowhere was this more true than in their best sales area, Los Angeles, where a new phenomenon was occurring. A phenomenon that only complicated the problem for Levi Strauss salesmen.

Los Angeles County was the nation's first automobile metropolis. It sprawled, over 700 square miles of it, from ocean to mountain to desert. Housing developers hopscotched about, throwing up tracts of green-wood-and-stucco homes, priced to sell on the GI Bill to newly married veterans. (Large numbers of these homes have become decomposing suburban slums in recent years.) The new suburbanites, as mobile as they were in the family car, would not travel to the central city and the department stores there because there was insufficient parking space.

For the department stores, the solution was to create satellites in suburbia, assuring themselves of ample parking by building on open land, then assembling a gaggle of other retail businesses to share the construction expenses.

As the department stores spread, their sales area broadened, strengthening their dominance of the market. Those stores — in Los Angeles and Orange counties, in the mushrooming Bay Area, in Phoenix, Tucson, Dallas — became all the more important to Levi Strauss. But the salesmen met resistance.

The markup on the 501s was but 32 percent, and retailers insisted they needed 40 percent to stay in business. Moreover, department stores expected price cuts because of their volume purchases. Levi Strauss offered only its traditional 5 percent rebate to dealers who bought seventy-five dozen 501s in a six-month period, and 2.5 percent to those purchasing twenty-five to seventy-five dozen. Beyond that discount, the company would not concede additional price breaks. For anyone.

Borrowing a technique developed in Los Angeles by a legendary company salesman, Nat Gredis, Bill Lagoria "used to tell the salesmen that if you can't get the big guy, surround him with all the little merchants you can." However, not all these little merchants were content with the unaccustomed low markup, either. Al Sanguinetti, then filling orders for western wear on the fifth floor at Battery Street, admitted, "We choked the retailer, didn't give him any markup. Retail clerks were instructed, 'Don't sell Levi's. Sell something else. If he insists, go in the back room, behind the curtain, and pull a pair out, but only if he insists.' "

But as customer demand blossomed, and salesclerks made numerous trips to the back room, store owners found it easier to display the Levi's than to stack them behind the curtain. If nothing else, it saved walking. It also alleviated wasted sales effort; Levi's customers tended to be loyal and not easily persuaded to buy another manufacturer's pants.

First the smaller stores, then the department stores succumbed. The chains, however, stocked their Levi's in basement shops; the 501s were, after all, men's work pants or

Levi Strauss, about age forty. The photograph was taken before 1870

Jacob W. Davis, the inventor of riveted clothing, about 1900, no longer a Nevada tailor, but a San Francisco manufacturer

Levi Strauss, about 1890, the successful businessman

Levi Strauss & Co., 14–16 Battery Street, San Francisco, probably about 1870, or shortly after the building was built

Levi Strauss & Co., 14–16 Battery Street, after the earthquake and fire of April 1906

The engraving dates from before 1900 and probably represents an idealized view of Levi Strauss & Co.'s San Francisco factory in the steam-powered Donahue Building

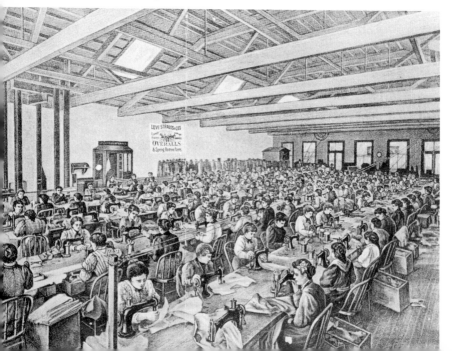

The perils of an old-time drummer. This photo, taken during a snowstorm in Bonanza, Oregon, about 1902, shows legendary Levi Strauss & Co. salesman Joe Frank (third from left, with the shovel) about to set off on a seventy-mile journey to Lakeview, Oregon. It took Frank and the driver, Jim Gormies of Klamath Falls, a week to make the trek. Frank retired, a multimillionaire, in September 1968, at the age of ninety-two, after seventy-two years with the company

A cattle round-up in 1902. The gentlemen are all wearing Double X waist overalls, which came, at the time, with a cinch belt in the rear, to gather the waist, and suspender buttons, to hold them up. Belt loops were not added until 1922

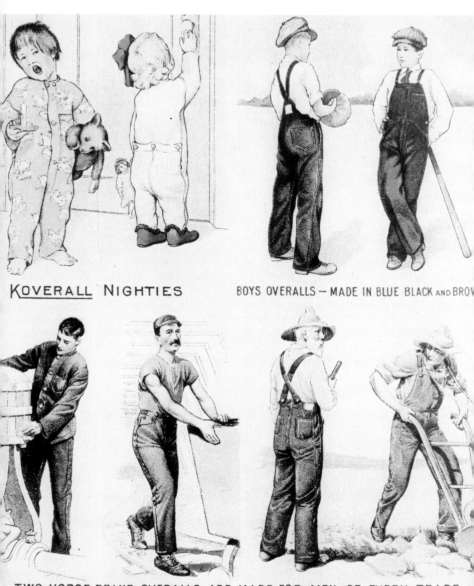

KOVERALL NIGHTIES   BOYS OVERALLS — MADE IN BLUE BLACK AND BROW

TWO HORSE BRAND OVERALLS ARE MADE FOR MEN OF EVERY TRADE

A page from a company catalogue, circa 1915. Koverall nighties sold to merchants for fifty cents, the 501s (lower left) for $13.50 per dozen

An operator in the Koverall factory, about 1919

Daniel Koshland   Walter Haas, Sr.

Peter Haas, Sr. (left), president of Levi Strauss & Co., and Walter Haas, Jr., chairman of the board

children's clothing, and the basement was where the lady of the house shopped for her family. It would take two decades and a revolution in lifestyles for Levi's to find their way upstairs to the "quality" merchandise floors.

The disproportionate contribution of Levi's to company profits was obvious. Walter, Sr., could read the comforting — or troubling — evidence in the firm's financial statements. Levi Strauss was, as it had been for ninety-five years, a dry-goods house, a wholesaler of hosiery and bedding, sweaters and underwear, manufactured by other companies and sold along the Pacific Coast by Levi Strauss salesmen.

The three remaining jobbing departments, occupying the second and third floors of the store on Battery Street, no longer were fundamental to the business. Gradually, their pride of place had been supplanted by work clothes and western wear manufactured by the company itself. Nor were those departments as profitable as they had been formerly. Sales of clothing, bedding, and linen contributed just 19 percent to the company's income, and only a fraction more than 11 percent to the net profits.

Those percentages had been declining over the years, more and more rapidly as salesmen concentrated their efforts on the relatively quick-to-sell 501s. The time of profitable jobbing seemed to have passed. The markup was low, competition from the expanding Sears, Roebuck, J. C. Penney, and Montgomery Ward chains severe. Those companies had eliminated the middleman, or wholesaler, by buying directly from factories — sometimes their own factories — and distributing the merchandise themselves. In that fashion, they managed to cut their prices. So, too, Levi Strauss had avoided a middleman's profit on its denim clothes, for which it was manufacturer and wholesaler both. (Eventually, three small independent distributors in Arizona and Texas that sold Levi's wholesale would be discontinued, the company absorbing the wholesale distribution in those southwestern states as well.)

Wholesaling had another, almost insidious drawback, Walter, Sr., had discovered. The more successful they were, the more likely they were to lose the line. The snake ate its own tail. "We found that in a jobbing department we were at the complete mercy of our suppliers, particularly if we had a branded article. If we developed it well, the manufacturer would set the terms, or he would be prepared to send his own sales force into the field. In other words, when you were jobbing and working with somebody else's goods, you had nothing you could call your own."

It was, in retrospect, a decision as critical to the future of the business as the decision of Walter, Sr., twenty-nine years earlier to join Levi Strauss & Co. The firm terminated jobbing entirely, concentrating on the production of denim garments and western wear, the embroidered shirts and dress pants worn by cowboys.

Levi Strauss was solely a manufacturer for the first time in its history.

The decision once made, then ratified by Dan Koshland, energized the corporation. The jobbing departments would not completely close down until 1954, but from 1948 on, the sales efforts were to be focused on Levi's and western wear.

The transformation demanded changes, many of them, in the way the company did business. As personnel manager, Walter, Jr., argued that Levi Strauss would now be competing with national firms, companies that sought out the best university and business school graduates with new ideas, new strategies, and new research. Levi Strauss should follow that example. If it intended to maintain its present growth rate, it had to attract and develop more managers.

"God bless the Bill Lagorias and Dick Cronins," he said later, but the corporation could no longer afford the leisurely training of all-purpose managers, who started in the stockroom and worked their way up year by year. This traditional practice — "You hired an office boy when the president retired" — was too time-consuming for a rapidly growing company. It needed to bring in men directly as management trainees.

There was grumbling when the first three University of California graduates were hired in 1948. Those who had begun in the stockrooms felt threatened. Al Sanguinetti, nominally a shipping clerk, understood the reason behind the gripes of older employees; he himself had been passed over for the "luxury job" of filling customers' orders on the upper floors of the Battery Street building. The only explanation he received was a limp excuse: "We had a special request from someone." Promotion from within would become a touchstone for the angular Sanguinetti as he levered himself to authority in the corporation.

There were no company management-training programs as such; that refinement would be long in coming. These new graduates merely began as assistants to department heads one or two rungs up the ladder, learned as much as they could, then moved on to other departments. Of the first three, one left after eighteen months to study for the ministry, the second became Levi Strauss's advertising manager, and a third, Mel Bacharach, created a revolution in the garment industry.

Not only did the company need managers; it required greater production capacity and, for that, more money. The firm's recovery from the Depression had been steady, Levi Strauss paying dividends of $6.00 to $9.00 annually. Those payments had been determinedly conservative, sizable portions of the profits plowed back into the company until, by mid-1947, the stock with a nominal value of $100 was actually worth $154 per share. That year, too, the corporation increased its capitalization from the $1.8 million the Sterns had passed on to Walter, Sr., to $3 million. To finance growth, the Haas and Koshland families purchased an additional $450,000 of newly issued stock.

Two years later, Haas, Koshland, and Beronio inaugurated a series of moves that would literally transform a clutch of Levi Strauss employees into millionaires. Fat with retained profits, the firm's capitalization was raised again, from $3 million to $5 million, and the stock split ten for one. The twenty employees who had purchased stock when it was offered found their number of shares increased tenfold. For the moment, it had no meaning, but the day of the windfall was not far off.

Splitting the $100-per-share stock ten for one also meant

splitting the price ten for one. That was essential for a plan which Haas and Koshland had long nurtured: widespread stock ownership among the employees. At a time when the weekly wage at the "store" averaged $50, the workers had difficulty accumulating $100 in savings to purchase available shares. But if the stock cost $10 per share, it was within reach of even the lowest ranks of management.

With the increase in capitalization and the stock split, there were 500,000 shares of Levi Strauss stock, 200,000 of them unissued, to be offered to privileged employees or to the owning families in the future. Those 200,000 shares would be used to finance future expansion.

The firm's centennial approaching, Walter Haas, Sr., and Dan Koshland shaped a plan to involve the corporation more closely with the city in which it lived. With the support of Haas's two sons, they created the Levi Strauss Foundation as a conduit for corporate contributions to a variety of social, educational, and cultural organizations. Fed by annual contributions from the company's net profits — $137,000 the first year — the foundation supplemented the donations the Haases and Koshland made to their favored charities: the symphony, ballet, and opera; Mount Zion Hospital and Homewood Terrace Children's home, the former Jewish orphanage; Mills College, of which Walter, Sr., was a trustee; and, of course, the alma mater of all four, the University of California.

So poised, the company paused for a self-congratulatory moment. In the belief that Levi Strauss himself had come to California during the Gold Rush — the company's early history was lost in the 1906 fire and in the dimming memories of the oldest employees — the firm celebrated its "centennial" in 1950.

It was a small, local fête, a gathering in the cafeteria at Valencia Street to hear greetings from San Francisco Mayor Elmer Robinson. "San Francisco," His Honor asserted, "is as well known for its Levi's as for its cable cars and bridges." Such hyperbole is expected of mayors.

Governor Earl Warren sent a more homey, credible message to his friend and political ally, Walter Haas, Sr. "If it weren't for the durability of Levi's, I'd have been in the poorhouse long ago with *my* five children."

One hundred years. The firm of Levi Strauss & Co. had grown from a small, regional wholesale house into a national manufacturer, from a company that sold whatever goods its founders could scrounge on the docks to a firm that now concentrated its attention on a single, institutionalized product. Once its sales measured in scant thousands of dollars; now it was selling $22 million worth of goods annually. In the last seventy-seven of those 100 years, the company had produced and sold an estimated ninety-five million pairs of the Double X blue denim 501s called Levi's.

They were to match that figure within fifteen years.

Chapter VII

With Utmost Confidence

THE SON OF Antonio and Assunta Sanguinetti had worked since he was eight years old, never very long at any one job, an Italian kid bringing in a few extra dollars, then a young man out for a good time.

During the war, Al had used a forged work permit and a forged boilermakers' union card to obtain summer jobs in the high-paying shipyards. He had bulled cases around the Gallo Wine warehouse during his senior year at Galileo High School. Not until he graduated, in the summer of 1946, did the rail-thin youngster find a place where he enjoyed working, though he took the job only to earn enough for a vacation on the Russian River, north of the city. For an Italian kid, a vacation there was really making it big.

"The objective of working at Levi Strauss and Company was very carefully couched in a career path," he deadpanned, "the career path being I'd start at the Gallo warehouse at Pacific and Battery and walk toward Market, knocking on doors until I got a job."

Five blocks and one lie about his experience as a shipping clerk later, he landed a job. After a year and a half in the shipping department — he never did take that vacation on the Russian River — Alfred V. Sanguinetti snared a coveted spot on the fifth floor. Now he was filling orders for western wear so that someone else downstairs in the shipping department could pack them. It was a good job; the people he worked with, nice. The pay wasn't so hot, but he could get overtime on the weekends. And buy clothes wholesale; the kid from North Beach liked to dress well.

Occasionally, he would be summoned downstairs to post back orders — in which case he had to put on a clean shirt and a pair of slacks. The work there intrigued him. He could spot peaks and valleys in sales, the slow movers and the big hitters. Just by posting back-ordered sizes, he could learn which items were selling in different parts of the country. If ladies' western wear blouses were moving better than men's, he could ponder the swatch cards and try to figure out the reasons.

"So, it became a matter of the guy can add, and the guy can subtract pretty well, and he gets to work on time. He works for the right price — cheap — and keeps his mouth shut and keeps his ears and eyes open." The lanky Sanguinetti was offered a full-time desk job, as a stock-recording clerk. By the time he was drafted, in 1950, he had begun to get a feel for the business.

The Korean War behind him, the twenty-four-year-old veteran returned to his old desk at Levi Strauss & Co. in January 1953. No longer a day-at-a-time youngster, he enrolled in night school on the GI Bill. The twenty bucks a month helped, especially after he married Alma, and the kids "started dropping." A man got serious about things when he had that kind of responsibility. Sanguinetti realized he needed a degree in business if he expected to get ahead — at Levi Strauss or anywhere else.

The company had changed a lot in the two years Sanguinetti was in the service; he could feel it. Their apprenticeships served, the sons of Walter Haas, Sr., had assumed larger roles in the management of the firm. The sons' natural desire to put their own stamp on the business, combined with the company's momentum, created an almost tangible excitement around the Battery Street building.

When the momentum builds, even adversity turns to benefit. In 1952 the company was confronted with a shortage of denim and consequent unused production capacity

----

at its Denison, Texas, plant. To put the idle operators back to work, at the suggestion of Los Angeles salesman Nat Gredis — and with eager merchandiser Chris Lucier pushing hard for the plan — Levi Strauss introduced its first pair of slacks. The Lighter Blues, as they were dubbed, were "kind of abominable," with a rear pocket "that wasn't right," Peter Haas recalled with a grin. However, Gredis and the other salesmen did well with the new garment. Levi Strauss was suddenly in the sportswear business.

After a three-year delay, while Walter, Sr., questioned "whether we wouldn't be fouling our nest" with a product that did not wear as well as the 501, the company introduced boys' double-knee jeans in 1954. This denim was of a lighter weight than the familiar Levi's, reinforced with a patch on the inside of the pant leg at the knee. Kids in Levi Strauss's new jeans no longer displayed scab-covered knees through torn pants; they outgrew the garment before the garment wore out.

The casual line expanded to include twill pants; those, too, sold well. Sales climbed steadily, from $22 million in 1951 to $25 million, then $30.5 million. Profits in 1954 of $1.2 million amounted to 15 percent on the money invested in the firm, two and a half times the percentage a proud Albert Hirschfeld had reported to Walter Haas thirty-five years before.

Walter, Sr., was satisfied by their progress, though hardly content with the status quo. In those thirty-five years, he, Dan Koshland, David Beronio, and a small group of managers had pyramided the value of a share of stock in the company twenty-seven and a half times. The annual dividends had reached $2.00 a share and were rising; in less than five years, an employee who bought a $10.00 share would recoup his investment and still own the share of stock.

They had taken a company dead in the water, revived it, then weathered a grinding depression and a world war. They had expanded it from a small, regional wholesale house into a manufacturer with national distribution. Moreover, they had done it, as the tough-minded Al Sanguinetti liked to boast, with "the first real pair of jeans in the entire world that wasn't prostituted."

Haas's sons could shoulder more of the burden of running the firm. And it was certainly time for Dan to come to the fore as president of the corporation. It was his due, after all these years as vice-president — even if he didn't want the position. Walter Haas remained chairman of the board of directors, but deliberately began the process of turning over the company to his sons. He was sixty-six, and the fishing had been too long neglected.

As chairman of the board, he would be available if he was needed. Dan and a dozen others were there to give advice. It was enough for Walter, Sr., to warn his sons, now vice-presidents, that if they disagreed, he would not act as umpire.

He had consciously planned for this moment; no one was happier when Peter decided to join his brother at Levi Strauss than their father. He had always hoped Peter would, but had said nothing to his younger son. That sort of parental pressure would have surely destroyed the dream.

Walter had seen other men refuse to let go of power, and the effect that had had on their sons, men of middle age either waiting for their fathers to die or hiding in the shadows of self-doubt. As Peter recalled, "There was never any formal decision, a manifesto saying from now on you are responsible for this which you weren't before. I think the role he played in gradually giving Walter and me the reins was one of the greatest things to have happened."

Hortense Thomson also marked a milestone in 1954, her golden anniversary with the company. In that half-century, she had riveted, affixed buttons, or stapled labels on literally millions of pairs of Double X waist overalls. Almost twenty-five years after, she fondly described the party in her honor at the swank Mark Hopkins Hotel. Fifty company executives from around the country — each representing a year she had worked at Levi Strauss — sent telegrams to the woman who had never earned more than $16 a week. Her favorite came from Martin Kulik, sales manager of the Southwest Division: YOU HAVE QUALIFIED FOR PERMANENT EMPLOYMENT BY DILI-

GENT SERVICE THROUGH THE PROBATION PERIOD. NOW LET'S
BUCKLE DOWN AND GO TO WORK.

She worked until she was sixty-five. "They wanted me to
stay two more years so I would be the longest woman employee. But I was just tired." She shrugged. "Retirement
wasn't easy, but I learned to get along." The great, gaping
hole in her day she filled with church work and trips to the
parks she loved. As increasing age made getting about more
difficult, she looked forward to visits from Paula and Lydia
Phillips, sisters of Julius, the kindly stockclerk who had
adopted the Battery Street employees as his own.

"They bring things — steak and eggs, and for my birthday
a basket of fruit. I have to be careful not to tell the others,"
she confided. "I tell them not to do it, because I always feel
that someone needs it. I don't need it. But they don't listen
to you. They're just two nice old ladies." (In addition to her
social security check, the eighty-five-year-old woman received a company pension of $312 per month in 1977. "I was
getting two hundred and six dollars, but they just raised it.")

Miss Thomson is only vaguely aware that the Phillips
sisters, themselves long past retirement age, have been hired
by Levi Strauss to visit some seventy aged company retirees
in the San Francisco area, to bring small gifts of food — too
large a gift would seem like charity to proud people such
as Miss Thomson — and to make certain they are being
cared for.

As Haas's sons took over the management of the company,
and their father's day-to-day involvement in operations
waned, a phenomenon they would all be hard pressed to
explain was about to propel sales beyond their most extrava-
gant fancies.

His name was James Byron Dean. A twenty-three-year-
old actor with a handful of legitimate theater credits, he had
been cast as a restless youth in the 1954 motion picture *East
of Eden*. In his casual slouch, his moodiness, Dean seemed
to embody the yearning and fears of American teen-agers.
In that film, and in the more successful *Rebel Without a
Cause* the following year, the Levi's-clad Dean projected the

turbulence roiling beneath the cashmere-sweater conformity of the nation's youth. Dean seemed to articulate the frustration of youthful dreams by an adult world that measured success in terms of affluence.

Then, with a third film awaiting release, James Dean became a legend.

On September 30, 1955, the young actor died in the wreckage of his speeding Porsche on a California highway. As he might never have done in life, in his reckless death he came to be an enduring symbol.

A host of cowboy heroes twenty years before had helped link the Double X denim pants with the West. So now did films, posters, and publicity stills of the Levi's-clad James Dean inexorably tie the waist overalls to the burgeoning youth population. James Dean's Levi's, T-shirt, boots, and red cloth jacket became a uniform, first among the most rebellious, then for a generation of young men.

A second motion picture in 1954, *The Wild Ones,* added the leather jacket to the costume.* Marlon Brando became the decade's "western" hero, the tender brute of the working class who found freedom straddling a Harley-Davidson motorcycle. Together, Dean and Brando fashioned a new image for the quick-selling 501s, an image that would pain company executives.

The pants acquired — or had grafted to them — an anti-establishment mystique. According to Pat Manning, a market analyst for Levi Strauss International and a woman who has pondered the elaborate social role of these mundane garments, "The anti-establishment image brought the 501 into the market as something more than the work pants Sears sold. It was not a heavy-duty, rebellious thing; it was a kid saying, 'Mom, Dad, I'm tired of you telling me how to dress.' He's not a juvenile delinquent [both Dean and Brando played sympathetic heroes]. He's just a kid who's

---

* The pervasiveness of that uniform is illustrated by the television program "Happy Days." The central character of that comedic re-creation of the 1950s, the Fonz, invariably wears denim pants, a spotless white T-shirt, and a leather jacket.

got a mind of his own and wants to do his own thing." To wear the pants, then, was to proclaim a personal freedom.

Al Sanguinetti, then working in the western wear department by day and attending college at night, remembered, "In the middle nineteen fifties we got this flak, 'If you want to know the good boys from the bad boys, you can tell just by looking at them.' The American Institute of Men's and Boys' Wear, an association of ready-to-wear clothing manufacturers, started going after blue jeans, and schools began to ban them."

Around the country, school dress codes, never very coherent, based on principals' whimsical notions of appropriate dress for the classroom, proscribed Levi's. In urban areas — rural schoolchildren had been wearing denim overalls for decades — for a time, the arbitrary dress codes threatened to curtail sales of the Double X overalls.

The bans would survive longest in the eastern portion of the United States, the area in which Levi Strauss had made the smallest inroads. In the West, the prohibitions collapsed under pressure of economic necessity. Because the pants were so durable, they were the most practical garment for young people, a group notoriously hard on clothing. What did it matter if the school's roughnecks wore them unwashed for weeks at a time? (The contemporary style favored dirty Levi's, pants "you took off at night and stood in the corner," parents complained.) Family pocketbooks eventually prevailed over principals' ideas of propriety.

Levi Strauss confronted other problems as well. Chris Lucier, the intuitive merchandiser who had invented the seat-pocket tab, introduced a ladies' casual line the year he retired. Lucier had sold Lady Levi's during the 1930s and 1940s, discontinued the garment because of denim shortages, and had urged a return to the women's wear business. The new side-zipper pants did poorly; as a sympathetic Al Sanguinetti remembered, "Ladies' casuals fell on its face."

Nor was the 501 doing as well as expected in the eastern part of the country. Easterners disliked the button fly — remedied with a zipper-fly model — and the very shrink-to-fit nature of the Double X denim. Despite the best efforts of company salesmen, retail clerks would not or could not grasp the notion of selling 501s in sizes larger than the customer's measurements. Those who bought their regular size discovered that the pants, after being laundered, were an inch too tight in the waist and two inches too short in the legs. Not until 1960 would the firm be able to market preshrunk denim pants acceptable to company executives.

Though sales in the East lagged, in the more casual western states — where slacks constituted "dress-up" clothing — the 501 barreled along, and the expansion of production and warehouse facilities continued.

Much of the responsibility for that expansion was delegated to a new employee, Paul Glasgow, a thirty-two-year-old industrial engineer who had worked for competitor H. D. Lee. Glasgow had become disenchanted at Lee and had accepted an offer from Levi Strauss "because Milton Grunbaum and Dan Koshland told me they believed in people. I'm a people-believer. That's what turns me on," Glasgow later explained, his speech embroidered with inflections of a Missouri boyhood.

Glasgow took on the role of a troubleshooter, first at the Denison and Wichita Falls plants, then at Blackstone, Virginia. It was at Blackstone that Glasgow would make his proudest contribution to the company.

Levi Strauss's growing number of factories in the states of the old Confederacy — where wage rates chronically lagged behind those of the Northeast and far West — were segregated. Looking back, a self-critical Peter Haas conceded, "We didn't quite have the courage to do it as soon as we would have liked to. We just didn't know if it was right to impose our views on these small southern towns."

Employee turnover at the Blackstone facility was high. Production of denim pants in the white-only plant had fallen badly, to the point where the operation had become marginal. The company needed the plant's production but could not afford the costs. The tough-talking Glasgow was dispatched to right the situation.

Once there, he discovered that blacks had applied for jobs, only to be turned away. Glasgow returned to San Francisco and told the Haas brothers, "I think it's time to integrate that plant." The brothers agreed. They promised to support him "all the way."

Glasgow returned to Virginia to talk to the Chamber of Commerce, churches, businessmen, and politicians. Either Levi Strauss got enough good workers, or the $1.5 million plant would be closed and the town would lose one of its larger employers. "The economic clout, the payroll of several hundred, overcame any objections" those scions of the Old South might have had, Walter, Jr., recalled.

But it was one thing for the white community tacitly to come to grips with reality; it was quite another to cooperate. Glasgow reported to the Haases, "You won't believe. They want a wall between white and black parts."

The brothers refused. Within days, the town fathers proposed that a white line be painted between separate but equal production lines. Glasgow rejected the idea. Not only would there be no line down the middle of the factory; there would be no segregated areas.

Then at least, they suggested, Levi Strauss should maintain separate drinking fountains and rest rooms. Glasgow again refused, confiding to Peter that they had a 50 percent chance of losing the plant.

"What will you do then?" Haas asked.

"We'll move on to the next plant and integrate *it*."

Peter Haas flew to Blackstone and, during a meeting with community leaders, explained that the new policy was a matter of survival. The apparel industry was labor-intensive; Levi Strauss depended on a large pool of workers. It could not afford arbitrarily to discourage people applying for jobs.

The city fathers capitulated. No walls; no line; no separate drinking fountains.

Glasgow conferred with the employees. "We told them we didn't have to do it — equal employment opportunity wasn't the law yet — but we felt a social responsibility, felt it was morally right and we were going to do it."

Glasgow lost only one employee, a woman who admitted she agreed with his policy but was quitting at her husband's insistence.

Initially, blacks and whites avoided each other on the job. In a week they were eating together in the plant cafeteria. Blackstone, Virginia, was quietly integrated.

Glasgow stayed long enough to ensure that Blackstone operated as a integrated facility, and moved on to the next troubled factory, in Warsaw, Virginia. Bluntly, Glasgow summed up the difficulty there: "They didn't know how to run it." He spent three years turning the Warsaw plant from the worst to the best in the company. In the process, he integrated that factory, too.

Elsewhere in the Deep South, the company's plants were quietly desegregated. New facilities would be located only with the initial, explicit understanding that they would also be integrated — from production line to management.

It did not always proceed smoothly. Several small towns declined to have integrated plants, regardless of the economic boost they might provide. In some cases, employees quit and production time was lost, but Levi Strauss became fully integrated.

The moral position, both Walter and Peter Haas maintain, "usually" turns out to be good business. The firm has never suffered a labor dispute because of its integration policy, and no plant has ever been shut down for lack of operators. Walter believes Levi Strauss's policy "actually changed attitudes in a lot of communities," though as recently as 1971 the plant manager in Warsaw was forced to set aside a corner of the company's property for a baseball field so that the integrated Levi Strauss team could play local nines. The city parks were still segregated.

With the steady expansion in the South, for the first time since Walter, Sr., had joined the firm, Levi Strauss was compelled to seek outside sources of finance. Retained earnings, as healthy as they were, were sufficient no longer. A $5 million bank loan represented seed money for the future.

Sales by 1956 had topped $34 million a year. The firm

now employed a staggering 2500 workers in nine facilities, earning $7 million annually. Levi Strauss Double X denims, boys' jeans, twill pants, leisure wear for both men and women were sold in 25,000 stores across the country.

Sales were yet uneven, low on the eastern seaboard, rising steadily as Bill Lagoria moved his finger westward on the map. The larger problem, however, lay in the company's reputation; its goods were still considered bargain-basement merchandise by the large department stores. No matter how well they sold, or perhaps because they did sell so well to value-conscious families, Levi Strauss products had yet to secure the cachet of fashion. Indeed, they remained determinedly antifashion, the 501s and other jeans-cut pants unchanging, impervious to seasonal fancy, resolutely casual attire. By 1959, the company was selling twenty million garments a year, half of them the Double X guaranteed-to-shrink waist overalls, but only in California did department stores dominate in the sale of Levi's.

By the end of the decade, total sales had jumped to $46 million. The firm had ignored the recession of 1958, posting new records each year. Profits had kept pace, totaling $2.5 million in 1959. The firm's net worth, just $6.2 million at the beginning of the 1950s, had leaped to $14.6 million ten years later.

Al Sanguinetti was more or less responsible for the merchandising of western pants. Almost by default, he gradually assumed greater responsibility, traveling with salesmen, consulting with the advertising agency, ordering goods from the scattered contractors who produced the embroidered shirts and pin-striped pants that ostensibly constituted a cowboy's dress clothes.

"By 1958, the company had three years under its belt with men's casual slacks," he noted, adding in a mocking, grave voice, "My God, we're not just manufacturing blue jeans anymore. We're manufacturing peg-bottom pants, lightweight denims, twills. We're selling everything we could make." Even western wear — never a big seller and only marginally profitable — was bringing in as much as $4.5 million a year.

The sons of Walter Haas had proven themselves. It was time, Dan Koshland believed, to step aside. He was sixty-six, had a covey of charitable organizations and philanthropies he wished to attend to, and had accepted the presidency reluctantly in the first place. Koshland asked to be relieved of his position.

The November 1958 board of directors' meeting was an emotional one. Walter, Jr., was elected president; his younger brother, executive vice-president. For their father, it was the capstone of his career. As the matter-of-fact minutes of that meeting noted, "That while it was with regret that the company was acceding to Mr. Koshland's wishes, the chairman had the utmost confidence in the newly elected officers and was proud and grateful that his sons had demonstrated the maturity and judgment which warranted their being entrusted with the top executive positions in the company." Proud, indeed.

There were to be moments in later years when the father, as chairman of the board, was disturbed about various business matters but thought better of speaking out. "It was nothing very serious, but it is not easy when you've spent your whole life at something to relinquish it. I knew it should be done, and if I didn't take an outside job, I wouldn't really let go. With all the best will in the world I wouldn't be able to hold off," the elder Haas explained.

To assure his distraction, Haas accepted the appointment as president of the city's Parks and Recreation Commission. He would devote eight years, almost full time, to that non-paying job — as his mother-in-law, Rosalie Stern, had until her death at the age of eighty-seven, in 1956. In years past, businessman Haas had sometimes questioned his mother-in-law's determination to buy this or that plot for a park, or to add improvements, skeptical about the financial impact on the city. Now, filling the same chair she had occupied, he, too, pushed for more parks and more improvements, his old concern put aside. His task was to encourage the use of parks; it was Mayor George Christopher's to locate the necessary funds.

The formal change in leadership to the new generation

was not only expected but welcomed by company employees. For many, certainly those in the Battery Street building, Levi Strauss counted for more than a biweekly paycheck. It was, in effect, an extended family. The continued presence of the Haas family was pivotal to that feeling.

Jack Lucier, the son of the retired inventor of the firm's most imitated trademark, was a merchandiser at Battery Street, helping to test-market a preshrunk denim that would, they hoped, finally solve the eastern customer's last objection.

Senior, Koshland, Junior, Peter, he reminisced later, long after he had left Levi Strauss to open his own business, "are really moral people. You don't find that too much in companies; you just don't find that. And generous in ways you never heard about.

"I remember a woman who worked there named Reba. She had a cleft palate. They spent a lot of money fixing that up. It was not their responsibility, but the family did it.

"A young fellow, a contemporary of mine, was hurt in the war. He had one eye missing, and had to have an operation, but didn't trust the army doctors. The company paid his salary for three months, the whole time he was recuperating, sent him back east to a specialist, arranged for the doctor to take care of him — and he'd been there only three months."

Frankly admiring, Lucier continued, "They made it a practice to lend money to employees — at a very low interest rate, really just something to keep the borrower's self-respect. When my wife's mother was very, very sick with cancer, my wife borrowed some money from them to cover the doctors' bills. Then she wanted to borrow some more. And Peter came out and told her, 'Yes, you can borrow the money, but you can't borrow any more from us after that. If you need any more money, you come to us and we'll see that you have it, but you can't borrow any more. You're too young to be so much in debt.' "

Lucier shook his head slowly. "And you'd never hear a word about it from them."

On such deeds was loyalty built.

Beyond Koshland's retirement, there were other changes in the executive offices. After thirty-seven years with the company, the imaginative Dick Cronin died. From a $20-a-week clerkship to director of advertising, Cronin had bridged generations and millennia of marketing techniques. In that time, his annual advertising budget had risen from $25,000 to almost $1 million.

The manufacturer of the 1950s was far different from the wholesale house of the 1930s. The settled firm of old, which might be promoted with a mechanical rodeo at a world's fair, had stretched across the continent, marketing a variety of men's and women's pants. Where once it had relied on a handful of unchanging garments, now it was looking to create excitement with its offerings.

For 1959 the company was introducing Walter, Jr.'s, first fashion effort — wash pants with narrow, fourteen-inch cuffs, available in no less than six bravura colors. Three of the six gave the new line its name: "Orange, Lemon and Lime." In addition, there were similarly colored women's pants and Bermuda shorts, all intended to bolster the casual wear line the firm's 110 salesmen were showing.

Orange, Lemon and Lime started with a rush; the firm cut a million yards of fabric in just three weeks to meet the demand. And then sales stopped. Cold. Customers found one bright-colored pair of slacks sufficient unto their wardrobe needs. Still, the abortive line had created excitement, a quality not normally associated with the company's products. Levi Strauss had demonstrated it could have an impact on the apparel business.

By 1960, the company was no longer merely growing; it was skyrocketing. Employees' stock-option and profit-sharing plans had been introduced and expanded. Almost fifty managers held stock in the firm; when any of them quit to take another job, or at their death, the company had first option to buy back those shares. The managers were bound by what has come to be known as "golden handcuffs."

That year, after two years of market-testing, Levi Strauss

was finally ready to introduce preshrunk denim pants. According to Jack Lucier, one of three company executives to guide the test-marketing of the pants, senior managers were overly cautious. "They were extremely afraid of making changes in the garment. The pant was holy. It was churning all this money to them and they really didn't know why, and they were just afraid of making any changes."

Levi Strauss might have adopted the already accepted Sanforizing process of shrinkage control, "with no problem," Lucier added, but elected instead to develop its own method with Cone Mills, the manufacturer of the Double X denim.

Even after the new pants, accorded lot number 505, were successfully test-marketed around the country, Levi Strauss was still hesitant, Lucier remembered. In cut and quality, it was the 501 revisited. But the pants didn't shrink, and the managers were "concerned about disturbing the golden calf." (That golden calf had so far yielded 175 million pairs of the Double X pants.)

The indecision passed. Levi Strauss finally gave its salesmen samples of a pair of waist overalls that met the disdainful eastern market's objections. Their acceptance was encouraging, howevermuch the miner of old might sneer at such niceties as a zipper fly and no-shrink denim.

In the meantime, Walter, Jr., had cast a speculative eye over international markets. As far back as anyone could remember, the company had had overseas sales, but they were scattered, virtually unsolicited. When American mining engineers had been hired to work in South Africa's diamond mines, they sent in mail orders for Levi's. Members of the Sea Bees, the naval construction battalions during World II, had worn the Double X overalls across the South Pacific, incidentally creating a 6000-mile-long sales territory — without a salesman to cover it. In Germany, Levi's had become a fast-selling item on the postwar black market, a staple, along with American cigarettes and nylon stockings. Though all this unsolicited business was not large in dollar volume, it clearly indicated that a foreign demand existed.

Doubts about the strength of that demand in Europe were

dispelled by a slight man, with an unprepossessing air about him, who walked into Levi Strauss's New York office one day. His name was Harry Frankel, he informed Oscar Groebl, manager of the office. He wanted to buy 5000 pairs of Levi's to sell to dealers in France.

Frankel was unknown; that in itself made Groebl skeptical. Groebl's contacts within the apparel industry, his long-standing friendships on Seventh Avenue, in the mills, among the sundry suppliers, were legendary. If Oscar Groebl had not heard of someone, that person was of dubious standing in the trade.

Five thousand pairs of 501s. Even at wholesale prices, that would require a good deal of credit. What about import duties? Shipping costs? Foreign-exchange discounts? Further, Groebl wasn't certain, he told Frankel, that they wanted 501s sold in France; they were, after all, very selective about the stores to which they sold. Advertising and the very image of the overalls themselves were no small consideration. Levi Strauss had long since dispensed with wholesalers, preferring to handle local distribution by itself. There was just no end to the policy questions.

"I'll pay cash," Frankel responded.

"Well" — Groebl brightened — "that puts a new light on it."

Levi Strauss had acquired its first European distributor.

If the company was to expand in foreign markets, Walter believed, Canada was a natural first step. An international border notwithstanding, Canada's western provinces were closer in their casual lifestyle to the western United States than they were to the Maritime provinces. The constant exchange between the two areas would ease the way; for a century, ranchers had grazed their herds on both sides of the border, since cattle did not care whether the grass they munched was Canadian or American. Levi's were already a known commodity in western Canada.

Yet such expansion was not easy. A company-commissioned market study in Canada indicated that a great demand for denim pants existed — but that a single manufacturer, Great Western Garment Company, of Edmonton, Alberta, dominated the market. Breaking in would be difficult, especially for a foreign manufacturer that would have to pay high protective duties if it imported. The opening of a factory in that country to avoid the tariff increased the financial risk.

Instead, Walter dispatched a four-member team, headed by Bill Lagoria, to visit Europe, investigating the potential market in Great Britain and on the Continent. Lagoria's report was glowing; the market was wide open, competition slight, and there was a nascent demand for things American, especially among the youth. The conditions were ready-made for Levi Strauss.

After comparing the two options, Walter and Peter Haas chose Europe and a chain of local distributors. They also decided that those distributors, like Frankel in France, were to be nationals of the country they served, on the simple premise that they knew the local market better than did Levi Strauss. The company would provide a European sales manager, to give advice, to represent European interests in San Francisco; but he would not interject himself in day-to-day operations of the local distributors.

Three months after the Haas brothers made the decision to expand in Europe, Walter received an unexpected caller. Jerry Godsoe was both handsome and personable, a lawyer who had held various governmental positions, Walter learned later. Godsoe introduced himself as president of Great Western Garment Company, of Edmonton, Alberta.

The debonair Godsoe had a problem. Because his wife had inherited Great Western, he and she confronted substantial inheritance taxes and had decided to sell the firm. Would Levi Strauss be interested?

Godsoe was frank. He intended to put the same offer to both H. D. Lee and Blue Bell, Levi Strauss's two major competitors in the ballooning blue jeans market, but preferred to give Levi Strauss the right of refusal. Walter would later attribute that offer to his firm's reputation for integrity. "I knew a lot more about his company than he thought I did, and he knew a lot more about us than I thought he did."

Negotiations for the purchase of the Canadian firm extended over a period of months. In 1961, Levi Strauss bought 75 percent of Great Western Garment for $2.85 million. Godsoe and his wife held the balance, and he would continue as president of the company until his retirement. Ultimately, Godsoe was to select his successor, Levi Strauss was to purchase the balance of the corporation, and Great Western would continue to function virtually as an autonomous corporation, selling under its own label.

Walter and Peter expected the Canadian company to manufacture Levi's in that country, but Great Western had no unused production capacity. The more money it was to put into the company for increased production, the more pants it sold under its own label.

Levi Strauss would not enter the Canadian market under its own brand name for another decade, and, when it did, Great Western continued in its own way, as a competitor. (Practically, the two firms do not compete; they appeal to different economic strata. Great Western makes work garments; Levi Strauss, more fashionable and expensive leisure clothes.)

Such foreign adventures were too remote to concern Al Sanguinetti in 1961. It had taken him seven years, but he was soon to graduate with a bachelor's degree in business from Golden Gate University. The tough-talking kid from North Beach had proved he could do it; now, if his new job didn't kill him first, he was going to continue on for his master's. If that was what it took to compete — the MBAs coming into the company were rising fast — Al Sanguinetti intended to get one, too.

The trouble was his new job. With the retirement of his old boss, Sanguinetti had become merchandise manager of all western wear — pants, shirts, the whole thing. It was a small department with only a few items; it had always been a creature of Dick Cronin's and Chris Lucier's fancy for western flash. But it was Sanguinetti's now, and he realized it was his great opportunity.

In his first three months as merchandising manager, he marked down "all the crap" his predecessor had left behind, "taking a bath" as he cleaned out the dogs. Then, with *his* goods, *his* line, he began to make money. "I didn't have any company assets, no plants. The national production manager had nothing to do with our department. My contractors were making the western wear like I wanted." Sanguinetti was an autonomous anomaly.

His big problem — it would anger him still, fifteen years later — was what his professors at Golden Gate University called "the allocation of scarce resources," in this case, salesmen's time. The company had introduced sand-colored denim pants that year. Within months, customers were asking retail merchants for the new pants as "white Levi's" — customers name a goodly number of Levi Strauss's products. As different-colored versions of the heavyweight twill pants were introduced, including white "white Levi's," salesmen and buyers devoted more of their time to them. Squeezed between the 501s and white Levi's, western wear was orphaned.

"Everybody was waiting for me to croak," Sanguinetti said later. Instead, he harassed the salesmen, badgered Bill Lagoria, fighting for even a small share of the salesmen's time in the stores.

Meanwhile, he scrounged people to staff his department, people he could train to manage things the way he wanted them managed. One of his recruits, plucked from the mailroom, was a restless young black woman.

"I really had no skills," Barbara Clemens-Pitre recalled. "I was twenty-three, divorced, had a four-year-old son, and had spent three years in the mailroom. One day I just told Mr. Sanguinetti — I was really intrigued by him — that I wanted to advance myself.

" 'What would you like to do?' he asked.

" 'I don't know. What have you got?' "

Clemens-Pitre became the western wear department's clerk-typist, then its administrative assistant, then the contract dispatcher. She was learning how to merchandise the gingham plaid shirts with pearl buttons, and the straight-leg pants that fit over cowboy boots. Each job was new to her; each she had to learn while doing it. "I wanted to prove I could do the job, that I could advance. And Sanguinetti was the type of person —" She shrugged.

"He seemed to be interested in me and had confidence in me. I just felt if he was willing to give me an opportunity, I was willing to work."

Recalling how he had been passed over for promotions when outsiders were hired for "the cherry jobs," Sanguinetti was beginning his own campaign of promoting from within.

Beyond giving his support, Clemens-Pitre remembered, Sanguinetti insisted she buy stock, "which I thought was a joke, because when you take your paycheck home every two weeks and find you need an additional hundred dollars, stock is not one of your priorities.

"Two things he told me. Buy stock and save five dollars every payday. No matter what. If you couldn't eat, save five dollars."

By 1962, Sanguinetti's efforts had paid off. "We made so goddam much money that even the old man [Walter Haas, Sr.] got me in the elevator and mentioned it to me. I never forgot that. We sold five and a half percent of the company's [$47 million] gross that year, and got five and a half percent of the net profit. With all our short production runs and high costs per unit."

Al Sanguinetti had made his mark. Now there loomed an even greater claim on the salesmen's time.

Chapter VIII

A Period of Strain

It was a million-dollar crap shoot. Mel Bacharach had worked on it for eighteen months — even longer, if you counted his early experiments curing garments in Vera's oven at home. Finally, Bacharach had found a formula he believed would work.

If he was right, Levi Strauss would have a product that might finally open up those eastern department stores which still scorned Levi's garments as bargain-basement goods. Permanent press could achieve what the 501, Lighter Blues, white Levi's had not. All it required was the right marketing approach, Bacharach argued.

Walter and Peter recognized the big risks, however. Manufacturing permanent press garments required special hot presses to set the pleats, and ovens to cure the resin. It required a new and difficult production step. Workers burned their hands on hot racks, or cooked the garments too long, turning tan pants to faded black, and reds to mottled purples. The production process had to be precise.

Once Paul Glasgow solved the manufacturing problems, they still had to confront the retailers' skepticism. Others had introduced heralded "no-iron" or "easy care" garments in the past, garments that had failed to live up to the advertising claims. There was no reason to believe that a blue jeans house, one not even located on Seventh Avenue, could succeed where the most experienced had failed. Beyond that hurdle lay the consumer, already once, twice, disappointed by airy promises.

It was the brothers' confidence in Bacharach that had taken them this far. One million dollars for the huge ovens and conveyor-belt system that carried garments in and out of the oven, for the hot-head presses to shape the garments before they were cured. That much and more for the piece goods and production costs to manufacture the two styles of slacks they intended to bring out this spring.

Failure, either in producing or merchandising the slacks, would be a severe setback. The money they were risking was considerable, but the loss of prestige would be disastrous. Yet whatever the stakes, who better than Bacharach, their most successful merchandiser, to depend on?

The lanky graduate of the University of California's Graduate School of Business had been hired in 1948 by Walter Haas, Jr., to assist the national sales manager, Bill Lagoria. It wasn't the advertising job Bacharach had applied for through the Student Placement Bureau — that had gone to Bruce Ellerthorpe. The sales job sounded interesting, and he liked the people. Lagoria was as decent, even genteel — that old-fashioned word seemed to apply best — as any man Melvin Bacharach had met. Nor was Lagoria, then diplomatically cutting sales areas to bring in new salesmen and increase their concentration, the only bright spot at Levi Strauss & Co. Even Ellerthorpe, who had beaten out Bacharach for the advertising job, was a good man. It was the firm's loss when Ellerthorpe left, eighteen months later, to study for the ministry.

Over the years Bacharach had come to realize the company's unusual atmosphere stemmed from the offices of Senior and Dan Koshland. They had done the hiring and promoting, staffing the company with like-minded people. Because of those co-workers, the twenty-three-year-old veteran of World War II had "become married" to the firm.

The Korean War interrupted Bacharach's two-year career at Levi Strauss. A member of the Navy Reserve, he was recalled to pilot flare-dropping missions over Frozen Chosen.

Discharged from active duty in 1953 as a lieutenant commander, Bacharach returned to Levi Strauss, first as a salesman in Tulsa, Oklahoma, then for a year as Lagoria's assistant sales manager. But Bacharach had a yen to try merchandising, creating the garments, then managing the inventories. It was a more exciting job and a more demanding one, even in a company such as Levi Strauss, where being first with a fashion was not always necessary or even desirable. He did well at it, gaining the elusive "feel" for the business that makes or breaks merchandisers. He learned how to style a garment that would sell and, most important, how to manage his inventories to increase turnover yet stock enough garments to meet customer orders. Without taking the disastrous markdowns when garments stopped selling. By 1959, Mel Bacharach was the merchandise manager for the firm's sportswear line.

A friend of Bacharach's working for a women's wear manufacturer in San Francisco had been experimenting with a method of permanently fixing pleats in dresses. Henry Weil had hit on a process, secured a patent for it in 1961, and launched Koret of California's production of permanently pleated skirts.

Weil's formula called for coating finished piece goods with a chemical resin and a catalyst. Once the goods had been cut and sewn, creases and pleats were added on a steam press, and the entire garment was baked in an oven. The temperatures of the oven, above 300° Fahrenheit, triggered the catalyst, and that, in turn, transformed the resin into a "cement," bonding the molecules of the cotton together. Creases and pleats previously applied, even the very drape of the garment, were locked into the individual fibers. No matter how often the garment was worn or washed, the fibers retained their "memory" of the cured state and returned to it.

Weil's method had grave drawbacks, however. Aside from the lingering odor of its formaldehyde base — that was bad enough — the resin would cure spontaneously, locking the fibers of the piece goods into a wholly unusable roll of inflexible cloth. Koret was able to use Weil's process only in a limited manner, delivering piece goods to a chemical-treating plant, then bringing them back to the factory on Alabama Street to be cut, sewn, and cured in the proper pleated shape before the spontaneous curing process set in. It was a perpetual race against the clock, with a forty-eight-hour deadline before the piece goods or unfinished garments froze permanently in whatever state they happened to be.

For a small company such as Koret, with but a single manufacturing plant, the daily deliveries of that day's supply of piece goods could be managed. Not so for a larger firm, and certainly not for Levi Strauss, with a dozen facilities scattered about the country, many of them far from chemical-processing plants of any kind.

The following year, a chemist at Sun Chemical, Herman B. Goldstein, devised a new resin, imidazolidone, which eliminated most of the intolerable formaldehyde odor and the forty-eight-hour deadline. Using Goldstein's resin, the piece goods could be treated at the mill during the production process, then shipped across country without spontaneous curing.

Bacharach began his home experiments with Goldstein's resin. There were still problems to be solved — of proper baking temperatures and times, of the design of presses capable of setting the desired pleats and creases. Yet the process worked; it was only a matter of the right technology.

The committed Bacharach secured Levi Strauss & Co.'s support, pushing "a lot of us who were a little conservative or reluctant into backing him and betting on him," Walter, Jr., acknowledged later. He enlisted production engineer Paul Glasgow to help with the design of ovens large enough to handle a production line's output. Together, they devised presses to set the creases.

In the meantime, Bacharach induced George Aufderheide, merchandising vice-president of McCampbell-Graniteville, a Levi Strauss supplier, to install the equipment to add and dry the resin into its piece goods. Aufderheide, too, would have problems.

The effort took a year and one million dollars, but now Levi Strauss was ready.

In January 1963, Graniteville delivered the first of its treated piece goods. Bacharach and Glasgow set to work learning how to mass-produce pants from it, enlarging the ovens and placing them on a conveyor-belt system. Different colors required different curing times and temperatures; too much heat would discolor the cloth, too little would not fully cure the resin.

As sportswear merchandiser, Bacharach designed the first garments Levi Strauss would offer with permanent press, a pair of wash slacks for men to be marketed under the new "Mr. Levi's" label, and a similar pair of slacks for boys. His styling was deliberately conservative.

"In the fashion industries, you don't do the same kind of market-testing you use in instant coffee. You use a constant exposure to people who have a feel for the market, knowing what will happen, following the trends, what stylings, fabrications, colors are being accepted. And you don't try to revolutionize all those things at the same time. You follow the trends," he later explained.

The garments would be made from an all-cotton twill and a sateen,* then very popular, dyed the colors in style at the time. The only difference between Bacharach's slacks and those already on the market was the permanent press feature and the increased price of $1.00 per garment.

By far the bigger gamble was the marketing effort to sell their new "Sta-Prest" process. By producing slacks, not work pants; by delivering on the permanent press quality of the garments where others finally had been forced to adopt "little-or-no-ironing" labels, Levi Strauss was striking out for the high-quality accounts that had eluded them, especially in the eastern portion of the country. To enhance the im-

---

* Sateen is a fabric in which the fill predominates on the face, or exposed side, of the cloth. It is woven with the horizontal fill yarns floating over five, six, seven, or more of the vertical warp yarns before it interlaces a single warp. That pattern is then repeated without variation: five (or six or seven) over, one under; five over, one under. Because the yarns are fine and densely packed, the fabric has a velvetlike sheen and feel.

portance of the new garments, it decided to sell only to the most prestigious stores — a decision, in any event, prompted by the limited production facilities at the new Knoxville curing plant.

Bacharach organized a dozen task forces, each headed by a major executive from San Francisco, to enhance the considered importance of the innovation. They were to visit a half-dozen cities, playing out the same script.

Over a two-and-a-half week period, the teams blitzed through the major cities of the East, calling on the biggest department stores and men's clothiers, inviting their managers, buyers, and corporate officers to a demonstration in a local hotel room. Once they assembled, the Levi Strauss executive present produced a polyethylene bag containing a sopping pair of pants washed in a local self-service laundry. "You know what a pair of pants looks like coming out of a washing machine?" Bacharach laughed, retelling the story.

Into a $99 portable dryer — Levi Strauss bought almost 100 eventually — Bacharach tossed the dripping pants. While they dried, he presented the line of slacks, describing the process, the colors, the fabrics, and anything else he could, to fill the forty-minute period it took to dry the garment.

At the end of the forty minutes, with the élan of a stage magician, he pulled the neatly creased, quite ready-to-wear pants from the dryer. "It was a pretty dramatic way to make a presentation," Bacharach acknowledged with a smile.

As part of the effort to promote Sta-Prest, for the first time in the company's history Levi Strauss offered a cooperative advertising program. The manufacturer and the store would share equally the costs of newspaper ads for the Sta-Prest slacks. In addition, the company arranged for the introductory ads, to run on the same day, in large cities with more than one store. In Chicago, four of the city's largest department stores placed full-page ads in the same editions. "You make an impression on the city," Bacharach added.

The traveling road shows began reporting sales orders, Bacharach remembered. "We said it's a winner. I must have made between thirty and forty presentations in all, with only one turn-down. When we delivered the slacks in February nineteen sixty-four, they sold off the counter with dramatic speed, unbelievable speed."

And then the garments started to come back. Within a week after the first advertisements, customers were returning the slacks with knees worn through, tears along the seams, and material in the seats thinned to indecent proportions.

Suddenly, the stakes had escalated. With Sta-Prest, the company was gambling its carefully nurtured reputation for excellence in quality.

The firm's first move was to guarantee the pants, either by replacement or refund. In some cases, it replaced a store's entire inventory. Still the piles of returned goods mounted, in part because of the large number sold.

Five out of every 100 garments were sent back, a figure that suggested that 35 percent of the customers were buying shabby goods with a Levi Strauss label prominently attached. (The company estimates that for every garment returned for any reason, six others equally defective are not.) If there was any encouraging sign in the flood of returns, it was the high percentage of customers who wanted merely to exchange the torn goods for whole cloth; relatively few were so dissatisfied as to ask for their money back. If nothing else, consumer response proved the firm had the right idea, that America's housewives were happy to forgo ironing their husbands' and sons' pants.

However, Levi Strauss lacked the right fabric for permanent press. All-cotton piece goods were too "tender." The resin locking the molecules of the cotton fiber in place prevented the fabric from distributing stress as untreated cloth did. This brittle quality caused minute fractures in the yarn, leading to tears. Further, in mass production, despite Glasgow's painstaking care, there was no way to maintain precisely the temperatures in the large ovens, as had been done in smaller test lots. Too much heat cured the resin well enough, but it also weakened the fabric itself.

Graniteville's Aufderheide and a nervous Bacharach mounted a hasty corrective effort to strengthen the fabric. A blend of cotton fibers and nylon filaments used in spinning the yarn before it was woven into piece goods offered an immediate answer. Nylon was extremely strong, resisting the abrasion that caused the all-cotton pants to rip. But the nylon had one drawback; it slightly reduced the wash-and-wear characteristics of the finished pants. They would use it, but would keep searching.

Within ten weeks, Levi Strauss was shipping the new version of the Sta-Prest pants to worried retailers. Returns began to fall off as the old inventory disappeared. Still, Aufderheide and Bacharach worked on the problem, under considerable strain until they found another synthetic that would maintain wash-and-wear quality and control abrasion. They finally settled on polyester, in a 65–35 ratio with cotton. Another three months passed before they shipped to retailers the fabric that became the usual blend of natural and synthetic fibers in permanent press clothes.

Largely on the success of Sta-Prest, sales of $77.7 million in 1963 leaped to $106 million the following year. Of even greater importance than the short-term profits, up $2.2 million in the year, they had won entrée to the larger department stores of the East. Salesmen no longer could be dismissed as representatives of the San Francisco overall house.

The firm's exhilaration was muted on May 10, 1964. The awesome David A. Beronio, "D.A.B." of a thousand memos to nervous clerks, after sixty-one years with Levi Strauss & Co., died at the age of seventy-seven. For years, the somber Beronio had been feared; few people in the company realized — as did his replacement, Daniel Baran — how sensitive Beronio could be.

"He was regarded as tough. All credit people are. But he really was a soft touch when it came to people or personal problems. When we had a hurricane in Louisiana or floods in Eureka, California, Beronio contacted the salesmen and found out what damage our accounts suffered. He'd ask the accounts, 'What do you need?' If they had insurance, he'd give them extended credit. If not, he replaced the inventory gratis."

Probably no one else at Levi Strauss knew the stolid Beronio as did Baran. After fifteen years of coaching small-college football, Baran had gravitated into the business world in 1951. Ultimately offered a job as Beronio's second, Baran secured a Dun and Bradstreet report on the then-small San Francisco dry-goods house. There was no sense going to work for a shaky outfit.

Beronio had reluctantly hired Baran, and then only to appease Walter, Sr., and Dan, who sought to convince their corporate secretary-treasurer he was not immortal. For the first year, Baran did little, biding his time; Beronio insisted on deciding all matters, large or small. Finally, Beronio made up his mind. He called in the former football coach and suggested, "Maybe it's time you sat down and we talked over what you're going to do."

Baran had gained Beronio's confidence, no mean feat in itself. Over the next eight years, Beronio gradually turned over credit and finance problems to Baran. By 1960, Baran was running that part of the business, Beronio watching closely.

In that time, Baran had come to admire the crusty Beronio and his sense of integrity. "He died on the tenth of the month, when bills are traditionally due. I always think of him dying on end-of-the-month terms," Baran said.

Only the other members of the company's board of directors had an inkling of the austere Beronio's private life. He had lived for decades with his brother Fred and Fred's family, staying on after 1955 with his now widowed sister-in-law and her two children. They were his major beneficiaries — his Levi Strauss stock alone was worth more than $200,000 — but couldn't receive any funds until the estate cleared probate. To tide over the family that bachelor Beronio had considered his own, the board of directors voted to continue paying Beronio's salary of $2760 per month to the woman whose husband, Fred, had left Levi Strauss & Co. over fifty years before.

On October 1, 1964, the company received another gratuitous boost from its most loyal customers, young students in California. It began at the Sather Gate entrance to the

Haases' alma mater, the Berkeley campus of the University of California. Campus police arrested Jack Weinberg, a former student who was soliciting funds for the Congress of Racial Equality, and hustled him into their squad car. Within moments, students had surrounded the vehicle, refusing to move.

A kinetic philosophy student — who, as spokesman, would come to symbolize for disapproving elders a generation gone mad — leaped on top of the police car and began to rally more students. Mario Savio and the Free Speech Movement would not stop until they had galvanized a nation's college-age population, brought down a brace of university administrators, and forced the retirement of the President of the United States to a ranch in Johnson City, Texas.

The essential demand of the Free Speech Movement, and of the activist groups it spawned, centered on the members' sense of a lack of personal identity. In corporate America, a land whose 200 million citizens were reduced to unemployment statistics or Nielson ratings or numbers in a draft lottery, they demanded to be treated as individuals. They were raucous, but, more galling to their elders, they were right.

The protests spread off campus, melding with the still vigorous civil rights movement. Mass demonstrations against the war in Southeast Asia spilled into the streets. At no time in the nation's history have people so young so influenced public policy.

The unrest in the United States was, in fact, apparent elsewhere, as disapproving, uncomprehending elders would discover when students in Mexico, Holland, Sweden, and France staged similar protests.

The uniform of these earthshakers came to be blue denim, and especially the 100-year-old Double X waist overall. Pat Manning was at that time an eighteen-year-old sorority girl on the turbulent Berkeley campus. The 501 was prevalent on campus, though her sorority barred its members from wearing the pants to classes. "The hippies picked up the Five-o-one in the early nineteen sixties. Hippie girls wore them, somebody else's passed-down, scruffy jeans. Guys from the East Coast wore Five-o-ones, loafers with no socks, oxford-cloth shirts, and Brooks Brothers jackets. And there they were, side by side.

"Then came the college revolution, and the people were all in jeans. The Free Speech Movement was followed by the anti–Vietnam War thing, and the youth feeling that we're important and we're going to do what we want. Jeans were synonymous with all that."

Western work pants had become symbolic of youthful protest. Levi Strauss's sales of blue denim pants flourished. By 1966, the company had surpassed $152 million in annual sales, more than twice the total just three years before. Growth itself became a problem.

"We kept putting plans together and exceeding them. There was no way to plan for the kind of growth we were experiencing," Peter Haas recalled. "Every time we'd make up a plan, it would be obsolete."

Much of the demand was fueled by a wildly creative advertising program deliberately appealing to a younger audience. The newly hired advertising manager, Carroll "Bud" Robinson, tapped "the tremendous creative energy generated in San Francisco at the time — flower power, modern graphics, psychedelic posters, the rock bands. The energies of the nineteen sixties were phenomenal," Joan Saltalamachia, the Jeans Division's advertising manager, recalled a decade later.

With a mandate to cater to the interests of young people, Robinson hired local rock-and-roll bands — including later successes such as Jefferson Airplane and Sopwith Camel — to record radio commercials. He bought air time for these on the most popular of youth-oriented radio stations, beginning in 1965. The company's first television commercials followed the next year.

"Prior to that time, advertising was very straightforward, stressing utilitarian themes," Saltalamachia said. "By the force of his personality, Robinson linked the company to the fun and excitement of the period." A decade later, the venturesome quality and humor were still a hallmark of Levi's advertising, though the target age group had been much expanded.

The company might have grown faster if it had not been stretched thin, both in managers and finances. In 1962, it opened two manufacturing facilities; in 1964, one; in 1965, the year of Milton Grunbaum's retirement, three. During Grunbaum's tenure as production manager, he had launched no less than eighteen factories.

They were not sufficient. In 1966, Levi Strauss purchased the entire Oberman Manufacturing Co., with six facilities and 3000 employees in the South. The Oberman addition boosted output by one-third, enough to keep pace with immediate demand, but far short of the foreseeable orders.

On a more modest scale, the fledgling overseas enterprises were also expanding. In 1964, Levi Strauss & Co. Europe was established with a resident manager. The following year, Mel Bacharach and the new head of Levi Strauss International, Edward Combs, set up a factory for Levi Strauss (Far East) in Hong Kong, accepting a one-quarter partner, the local firm of South Seas Textile Manufacturers.

Walter, Sr., was the one cautionary voice. At times, Peter remembered, the chairman of the board would ask, "How big do you want to grow? Do you have to grow big, to keep running that fast?"

On two or three occasions the sons heeded the father's advice. Perhaps it was the natural conservatism of age, Walter, Sr., later conceded. "It seemed impossible to me that we could sell more and more pants." He chuckled, adding immediately, "Which we have done.

"Also in my time I saw, particularly in nineteen thirty-three, when things were very bad, some pretty big concerns go belly up — and I wanted to be sure we weren't going too fast.

"I had seen people shoot up like rockets, and then fall like rockets. Like Rough Rider, which went belly up a few days ago [May 1977]. We used to look at them and always wonder, 'Why can't we make corduroy pants as well as they do.' "

"I was pretty willing to grow, but not faster than our equity and our financial strength."

With the exception of the $5 million bank loan in 1956, the company had financed its expansion entirely from profits. But to maintain the pace of its growth — it was now effectively doubling sales every five years — required more capital than it could immediately muster.

There were two solutions, one unthinkable. The company could float a stock issue, "go public" in Wall Street terms, and thereby raise more than enough money to finance growth. Sales were booming; the book value of a single share of stock in just six years had rocketed from $3.33 to $39.30; meanwhile $2.00 dividends had arrived promptly. But to go public would offend Walter, Sr.; indeed, embarrass him. Federal law would necessitate disclosure of the family's holdings and some estimate of its wealth. (An estimate only; the Haas family fortune extends far beyond Levi Strauss & Co., into utilities, banks, family foundations, and various stock holdings.) Public disclosure was regarded as a form of ostentatious display by the chairman of the board, and he had avoided such display all his life.

Further, public ownership carried with it responsibilities to the stockholders beyond those the Haases and Koshland bore with their own stockholder-employees — people who understood the business, virtual members of the family, who themselves were responsible for many of the decisions that affected the company's future. No matter how small a percentage of the firm they sold publicly, the sale would infringe on their autonomy.

Deference to Walter, Sr.'s, wishes combined with the directors' own sense of independence ruled out a public stock offering. So the only alternative source of financing was a loan.

In 1966, they negotiated a long-term borrowing of $20 million from Metropolitan Life Insurance Company. Twenty million dollars, a sum greater than their total sales for the year 1949, less than twenty years before.

Finance was not the only strain on the company. By 1966, rapid expansion had breached Levi Strauss's most zealously guarded asset, its quality. Returns were piling up, especially in the multiple lines of casual pants it marketed. A 1 percent rate was acceptable, but the company was getting a 2.2

percent rate of return. Given the one-in-seven return factor, as many as fourteen of every 100 buyers were unhappy with a Levi Strauss product. The firm's major competitor in the expanding casual pants business, El Paso–based Farah, produced a far superior product in both appearance and the quality of the material used. Levi Strauss salesmen were also complaining that shipments to retail stores arrived late and frequently contained the wrong goods. The infection had spread even to that holy of holies, the Double X waist overall; threads were left unclipped, waist and leg measurements were not consistent, belt loops pulled from the waistband.

"It was just a crescendo of complaints about how we were doing in the marketplace," Peter recounted. "Something that we had cherished for so many years, had bragged about, was beginning to go down the drain."

Responsibility for quality control had been vested in the national production manager, first Milton Grunbaum, then Paul Glasgow. But with more than twenty manufacturing plants and distribution facilities to monitor, the San Francisco officers were forced to rely on local managers to maintain the cherished standard.

Imbuing a dedication to excellent quality took time; it could grow only from a plant manager's sense of pride, of belonging to a quality-conscious organization, of responsibility to his co-workers and the customers beyond. In the proliferation of manufacturing facilities to meet demand, the firm had been forced to draft plant managers who simply had not been indoctrinated with that dedication. By the nature of the job, these new managers found themselves caught between a written policy issued in San Francisco ordering high quality, and the incessant clamor of sales managers and merchandisers for immediate production, more production. Considering themselves to be judged by their superiors on the basis of units produced, the factory managers tended to ignore quality control. A pair of pants sent back for repairs meant that an operator lost time; a pair of pants marked as a second — its tab and label ripped off in disgrace — was a permanently lost unit of production.

Walter and Peter themselves shaped a new department to cork the drain. Product Integrity — the name occurred to Walter during a sleepless night spent pondering the problem — was to be completely independent of either production or merchandising. Its manager would have full authority over the acceptance of both raw material — quality had fallen in that area as well — and finished goods.

Finding the right person to manage the new department was critical. They needed someone who had been in the company for years, who understood or, better, believed in the concept of the finest possible quality for its own sake. It would be a demanding job, with a significant amount of travel involved; therefore, the candidate must be relatively young. And he had to be independent and tough-minded.

The criteria preselected the man.

Al Sanguinetti enjoyed his job, running the western wear line — relying on outside contractors for his production, flying off to New York City to buy laces and rhinestones for his gingham and chambray shirts. Since he was showing a good profit, management had let him alone. Sure, he realized the whole western wear line was doomed. In growth it could not keep pace with Lighter Blues and white Levi's and Sta-Prest. Why should the salesmen bother pushing the fancy shirts when they could easily write huge orders for 501s and Sta-Prest merely by walking in the door?

But Al Sanguinetti was stubborn. Previous managers had left to work on other lines. Not him. He turned down two other assignments to stick it out until they actually killed the line.

Walter's argument was straightforward. The company had a problem. Since Al had, in Walter's words, "a reputation of being a heavy with the salesmen," the Haas brothers wanted him to take charge of all quality control.

Sanguinetti was flattered. Quality control — that meant something he knew and cared about, manufacturing the very best product possible. You charged for it, sure, but you stood behind it. In the long run, as Senior had argued all those years, it paid off. Levi Strauss had built its reputation on that guarantee of quality.

"What was I going to do?" Sanguinetti shrugged. He did make one demand — that Product Integrity be responsible for consumer complaints. There would be no better index of how adequate his performance was.

"I had no written job description, no lines of authority, but I was told essentially that I could tell this guy to go fly a kite or that guy to go to hell. And that's all I needed."

Within twenty-four hours, Sanguinetti made his first major decision. Production had long wanted to change the construction of 501s, using wider piece goods for a more economical fabric utilization. But the shift would result in a change in the distinguishing outseam on the *inside* of the pant leg.

Sanguinetti didn't like the change, no matter how much money the company saved by going to wider piece goods. "I said, 'Spike it!' 'Cause I was thinking of the nineteen thirty-seven catalogue, when Roy Rogers used to wear his pants with the leg turned up in a cuff, showing the outseam. 'You took the rivets out. You took the genuine leather patch out. You took out the genuine oilcloth flasher and you put in paper. That's enough! You ain't going to go any fuckin' further!' "

Sanguinetti and the jeans merchandise manager squared off. "So I went to see Number One [Walter Haas, Jr.]. He backed my decision. Actually, I think they rather appreciated me making the decision; I think I got them off the hook."

Sanguinetti's authority was diffuse, his mandate vague. When he learned that Walter had mentioned to various people outside the company that the new manager of Product Integrity had the power to stop shipments or shut down a plant, Sanguinetti confronted Peter. "Is that right? I have the authority to close down a plant?"

"I kind of gulped, but I figured I had to go all the way on this," Peter admitted, "and I said, 'You do, Al, but if you do, let me know right away before the phone starts ringing.' "

It was all the muscle Sanguinetti needed. According to George Layton, now the director of Product Integrity, then quality manager in Texas, "In an hour we had statistical data enough to show that we should shut down the San Angelo, Texas, plant. The quality level was poor; skip-stitching and soiling were the big things. There was oil over everything. Evidently, it had been going on for a long time.

"There was pressure from the national production manager to keep the plant open. They needed the white Levi's production. The union, which had two hundred members in the plant, brought pressure, since its people would be losing money."

San Angelo stayed closed. "The plant was down for ten days. Thirty thousand pairs of pants were involved. Al put people to making repairs on garments and cleaning the plant. Fifty percent of the repairs went back, and he made them do it again. It cost a lot of lost production; the plant had been turning out fifteen to twenty thousand pants a week."

It was not a job for a timorous man. "My first hundred days kinda set the tone." Sanguinetti laughed. "Guy told me, 'I got thirty thousand pairs of boys' Sta-Prest pants and the damn things are discoloring.' I told him to bury 'em." The pants were dealt off as seconds, at a loss of well over $100,000.

He also reached beyond his mandate. No sooner had he barred use of wider piece goods to make 501s than he turned to the arcuate stitching on the back pocket. "For a trademark," he argued, "we're doing a helluva goddam good job of making certain that's the first thing to leave the garment." The sewing was changed from six to twelve stitches per inch.

Establishing piece-goods standards was more difficult. "I said we're going to use my standards because I'm not going to spend the next eleven and a half years getting approval from every damn merchandiser and mill. The customers can't do that, and since I'm their representative, I'm going to do it for them, the best way I know how."

Ten years later, Levi Strauss's fabric standards fill twenty-two pages, stipulating in technical detail everything from breaking strength to colorfastness to formaldehyde content. (At Walter Haas, Jr.'s, insistence, that standard was added;

irritating formaldehyde fumes make for an unpleasant work environment.)

Werner Pels, now in charge of product evaluation, and his laboratory technicians will test between 500 and 600 color and weave combinations produced by thirty-five textile mills this year. For Pels, "Raw material quality is a constant problem. We can count, year after year, upon rejecting five percent of the one hundred million yards of fabric shipped to us.

"Suppliers generally take back substandard goods. The argument is usually not over what we've found, but whether what we found was agreed upon in the beginning as a defect."

The company's very size helps maintain quality. "Our purchasing power makes suppliers see the light faster than they might otherwise," he added dryly. "We get a lot of benefit, without arm-twisting, out of our purchasing power."

Performance standards vary from product to product, depending on end use. Fashion merchandisers, especially in women's wear, repeatedly ask to have fabric standards relaxed on the grounds that a fashion garment does not have a high end use and is not expected to last long. Monitoring the annual one million returned garments, George Layton disagrees. Women's wear returns come in at the same rate and for the same reasons as jeans and boys' wear.

High-fashion houses, the smaller, pace-setting firms, might attempt to get by because style-conscious buyers are more interested in fad than in durability. Not Levi Strauss. For Walter and Peter, the assurance of high quality is more than the continuation of a tradition. It is an affirmation of their youthful desire to make their company the "best darn corporation in America." Both men are keenly aware of consumer dissatisfaction with consumer products, with planned obsolescence, with deteriorating quality; they are, after all, consumers, too.

Beyond that, there was another factor that Walter had especially pondered. Theirs was a large business. Sales in 1968 would approach $200 million, ranking Levi Strauss among the six largest apparel manufacturers in the country, and only one of the other five was solely an apparel house. A corporation of that size, in and of itself, became a societal institution — not only in San Francisco, where Levi Strauss & Co. was a recognized pillar of the community, but beyond, in the twenty-odd towns and cities in which the firm had plants and distribution centers.

Both Walter and Peter believe that corporate America should not restrict its interest to profits alone. Though such an opinion has never had wide currency in the nation's executive suites, on the fifth floor of the Battery Street building the profit-at-all-cost concept was disdained. Profits were important, to be sure; they always would be, for without them the firm could not remain in business. But the maximization of profits at the expense of their 20,000 employees or of cheapening their products or of compromising their own sense of integrity was not to be considered.

The concept of a personal responsibility to the community beyond Levi Strauss had been learned from their parents and Dan Koshland. They had grown up with it, and it had been expected of them. Walter would say later it was in their genes.

It was learned by example, as well, from people like Milton Grunbaum. Younger men such as Mel Bacharach marveled that "the women at the Valencia Street factory really loved that man, working in the drudgery of the apparel industry, and yet they loved him." It was learned from the example of Paul Glasgow, who had managed to save the Blackstone facility without erecting walls, painting lines, or hanging "white-only" signs at the drinking fountains; and of David Beronio, who could find a way to extend credit when a merchant was struck by disaster.

Their personal obligation weighed heavier than it might have on executives of other corporations *because* Levi Strauss was a family-held firm, perhaps one of the half-dozen largest in the nation. But where Levi Strauss & Co. had confined these efforts to employees and customers, Walter and Peter recognized that Levi Strauss in the 1960s could not. This had been a decade of social turmoil. The civil rights movement had flamed into urban riots across the country. However much they might condemn violence, they could not deny the underlying causes: high unemployment rates, discriminatory law enforcement, shoddy education, squalid housing, and barren ghettos. What were their responsibilities, both as citizens and as the president and vice-president of a huge manufacturing firm?

They were about to find out. The White House had asked Walter, Jr., to serve as western regional chairman for the National Alliance of Businessmen.

Chapter IX

Far Too Little Competition

Tom Harris is an affable man with a penchant for jarring combinations of tweed sports jackets and floral-printed ties. The affability may not come easily; the piece of paper taped to his office telephone cautions, "Close cordially. Pay attention!"

Still, Harris exudes the sort of robust good humor expected of a man who has spent most of his adult life soliciting funds for charitable organizations and community services.

For tall, balding Tom Harris, it is a long way from the Hunters Point Boys' Club and hitting up William Zellerbach or Walter, Jr., for donations to take a group of black kids camping. Since 1969, he has helped to shape Levi Strauss's experimental community relations program, much honored but rarely copied around the country.

After a lifetime in youth work, often on precarious budgets, the forty-nine-year-old Harris now heads Levi Strauss & Co.'s Community Affairs Department. His $300,000 annual administrative budget affirms the determination of Walter and Peter Haas to make community affairs as much a corporate function as production and marketing, as great a corporate obligation as profits.

Most corporations maintain similar offices, under one or another title, though few vest in them the authority Harris commands. He reports directly to the president, which accords him the prestige of the northeast-corner office on the twenty-eighth floor of Levi Strauss's headquarters. "It wouldn't be effective otherwise," Walter believes. "It just can't work unless Tom can come in here and tell me what we're doing right and what we're doing wrong."

"People know how to read organization charts, how to interpret them," Harris adds sardonically. In eight years, Harris has learned the Byzantine protocols of corporate politics.

Harris joined Levi Strauss as the company-paid regional executive for President Johnson's National Alliance of Businessmen. The NAB was to be private enterprise's levy in the presidential War on Poverty, a clutch of governmental and private programs intended to alleviate the misery suffered by some thirty million Americans.

Having accepted the regional chairmanship in 1968, Walter also accepted the responsibility for staffing the office. As the first director, he selected newly retired Admiral Herschel Goldberg; a Jew who had risen that high in the navy had to be good. But Goldberg's organizational abilities were needed elsewhere in the company; further, Haas intended to emphasize the firm's community involvement. That goal required a professional.

Tom Harris more than qualified. The years at Hunters Point, San Francisco's stagnant ghetto, had taught him a great deal about community needs in poverty areas. He was a do-gooder with few illusions.

By the end of his first year and NAB's second, Harris had Levi Strauss deeply involved in two complementary efforts to encourage minority businesses.

Both the manufacturing and the retailing programs failed.

"As corporations moved into this area of social concern, they made all kinds of mistakes," Harris criticized. "One of the mistakes was that businessmen took off their business hats and put on community hats."

Nine minority-owned retail clothing stores opened with pledges of a million dollars in credit offered by Levi Strauss, Van Heusen, and other clothing manufacturers. These small stores were offered a year's deferred billing on the first shipment and six months' on subsequent orders.

With the same intensity it poured into a new product

line, Levi Strauss moved into the unfamiliar area of ghetto enterprise. Rufus Butler, a black retailer in Portland, Oregon, told a *Business Week* reporter, "I wrote 'em that I didn't know what extended credit was but that we sure needed it. Next thing, their local Levi Strauss man was here saying if he didn't do business with me, his boss would probably fire him."

"It was done to assist," Harris said later, "but it was the worst possible thing we could have done. We hired an experienced retailer to train people, then put them up in business — without capital. If anyone should know you don't make a retailer in a six-month training course, Levi Strauss should have. But the thought was there.

"We should have known they didn't need extended credit, but did need to be sufficiently capitalized so they could swing in the big world, pay their bills, and hire the lawyers and accountants they needed, rather than wait for charity work."

Nine stores, not all of them in cash-short ghettos, opened. Rufus Butler's survived the longest, five years.

At the same time, the company became interested in the black-owned Ghettos Enterprises, Inc., a self-starting garment manufacturer with no product, no experience, and no contracts. With the assistance of Nat de Palma, then manager of the Valencia Street factory, Ghettos Enterprises set up a production line. Levi Strauss extended a contract for 21,000 reversible vests, paying $1.81 each, or thirty-seven cents more than it was paying a second contractor for the same garment.

Beyond that, the company detailed a full-time employee to aid Ghettos Enterprises in operating the line, lent the hard-pressed company money, and arranged for machinery.

"We were giving them production, we were paying them premiums. It was the worst thing we could do," Harris said, shaking his head. "We were artificially supporting them in a very competitive market, thinking that would assist them. In our naïveté, we financially patronized them."

Beset with difficulties in starting up a production line and meeting quality-control standards, Ghettos Enterprises had a precarious future. To tide the company over, Bud Johns,

Levi Strauss's bearded, Levi's-clad public relations director, suggested another way to support Ghettos.

Levi Strauss had been approached by Now! Designs, a San Francisco firm hoping to use the Levi Strauss trademarks as major design elements on denim-covered clipboards, address books, notebooks, and denim aprons. At Johns's recommendation, Levi Strauss agreed to grant the license — on the condition that the actual production be assigned by Now! Designs to Ghettos. It was the first time, despite dozens of requests from others to license the internationally famed insignia, that the company permitted its trademarks on products it did not actually produce.

From 1969 to 1973, Ghettos sporadically manufactured the Levi's-logo items for Now! Designs — but was never able to establish an economical clothing production line. Ultimately, it sank back into the ghetto.

"A lot of things don't work," Walter acknowledged. "If you lose your faith in human nature, if you lose your sense of humor, you quit."

His brother agreed. "It's easy to back off. But if you think it is right, you are going to keep trying."

Walter's regional chairmanship of the National Alliance of Businessmen ended in March 1970. His sense of community responsibility did not. What Levi Strauss lacked, he believed, was a coherent national program, one in which the company could not only continue to support the good works of old, but could pioneer in new enterprises.

For twenty-one years the Levi Strauss Foundation had contributed to various organizations, $217,000 in 1969 alone. The bulk of the money had been channeled to the family's favored charities, largely in San Francisco. From year to year, profits from the foundation's stock investments were dispatched to the same comparative handful: the University of California, Harvard Business School, Stanford University, Mills College, and the United Negro College Fund (education had always been a preferred recipient); to the Jewish Welfare Federation, the successor to the Eureka Benevolent Association, which David Stern had supported over a hundred years earlier; to the San Francisco Symphony, art museum, and Opera; to the Salvation Army; and to San Francisco Aid to Retarded Children, in which both Peter and his wife, Jody, were active.

The annual foundation disbursement was increasing. The number of recipients was growing, too; requests for contributions multiplied faster than the foundation's ability to screen them.

Levi Strauss & Co. considered itself a leader in community work. If its total cash donation was small compared with such corporate colossuses as United States Steel, General Electric, and Shell Oil, as a percentage of net profits the San Francisco apparel manufacturer was giving more than twice that of most other firms.

The traditional charities were all very well and good, but they were largely San Francisco–based or family favorites. The foundation's contributions were well used, no doubt, but were swallowed up in operating budgets. Levi Strauss might be a leader, but it was hardly innovative.

Walter spurred a dramatic shift in emphasis by appointing a five-member committee to initiate a new corporate effort. Seven years later, the chairman of that committee, now the assistant manager of Levi Strauss International's Canada–Latin America division, quickly plucked the committee report from a shelfful of company documents. "I keep it for sentimental reasons," Edmond Pera said with a grin.

Pera's own involvement was symptomatic of what the Haases hoped to accomplish by investing the company in the community at large. "I really care about this kind of thing," Pera explained, handing over a copy of the revolutionary report, "I don't think I did before I came to Levi's, frankly. It's the philosophy of the Haases. It — it just comes to you," he said slowly, groping for the correct words.

"It's an intangible. It's how they react to people. I've seen them do so damn many good things, just with the little people here.

"My first job at Levi's was setting up entirely new budget systems for the plants, unique in the garment industry. In the process, I got close to Peter. He would always ask, when doing the budgets, 'Is there enough in here for the people?

Do we have enough room for the cafeteria? And what about a park and day care centers,' and the whole works? Their whole philosophy just comes to you."

The committee's major recommendation was to refocus from the San Francisco region to the twenty-odd communities in which Levi Strauss had factories, from the home office to the field. The risks would be greater, the committee acknowledged, but risks were worthwhile. Social problems had not yielded to traditional methods of coping; new ideas might succeed. Five percent of the foundation's grants, the committee advised, should be set aside intentionally "to take on creative, imaginative, high-risk projects."

Pera's committee urged that requests for funding be screened by a panel of employees who would then pass on their recommendations to the foundation board, that is, the Haases. In effect, they would vest real authority in the employees, transforming the Levi Strauss Foundation from a Haas-family concern into an employee-governed agency.

The Pera Committee also suggested that the foundation concentrate its resources, devoting 40 percent of its awards to education — defined far more broadly than the handful of elite institutions previously supported. Another 15 percent would go to health projects; 25 percent to human resources, largely dealing with disadvantaged minorities; 15 percent to environment-related programs; and 5 percent to innovative, experimental projects in a variety of areas.

In 1976, the foundation awarded $225,000 to educational programs, $196,000 to human resources, $94,000 to health programs, and $52,000 to cultural and civic efforts, including such familiar Levi Strauss interests as the San Francisco Opera, Symphony, and Ballet.*

---

* The foundation's interest in these cultural affairs stemmed from Dan Koshland and Elise Haas, Walter, Sr.'s, wife. According to Mrs. Haas, her husband "is allergic to music." His attendance at the opera is limited to opening night, when, according to grandson Douglas Goldman, "he and Marco Hellman of Wells-Fargo would dash out after the start and play cards for the rest of the evening." At the Stern Grove summer music festival in Golden Gate Park — another family charity — Walter listened to an orchestral concert wearing horn-rimmed glasses. Built into the earpiece, a portable radio quietly broadcast a Giants baseball game.

The annual donations do not yet equal the annual contribution received from the company, as the Pera Committee recommended in 1970. The year-end surplus, $1.8 million in 1976 alone, is invested as a hedge against those years when Levi Strauss profits, and contributions to the foundation, may not be great enough to meet needs. By the end of 1976, the foundation's net worth was $4.8 million, and its invested funds were yielding approximately 30 percent of the 1977 budget.

As with most corporations, educational philanthropy dominates. (Scholarships tend to be noncontroversial.) Unlike most corporations, however, Levi Strauss no longer contributes money just to the select few. The 1976 foundation report cited contributions of $24,000 to associations of independent colleges in ten states; $5000 for scholarship assistance to minority students in master of business administration programs at six universities; $7000 for business-study scholarships for disadvantaged high school students in communities where the company has production and distribution centers — some of which is granted to junior colleges; $3500 to provide scholarships for disadvantaged Mexican-American students from areas where the company has facilities; and $25,000 to match employee contributions of up to $100 per person to scholarship funds of their own choice. Twenty-nine children of company employees attended colleges and universities in 1977–1978, aided by Levi Strauss Foundation grants.

The stress on education is also a company tradition — from the first Levi Strauss scholarships at the University of California, made permanent by the founder's nephew, Jacob Stern, in the 1920s. Both Walter, Sr., and Dan Koshland have been instrumental in donating or raising literally millions of dollars for their alma mater, the University of California. (It is said that the one major disappointment in Walter's life was his failure to be appointed a regent of the university; his close friend Earl Warren went to the United States Supreme Court before a vacancy on the Board of Regents occurred, and successive governors of both parties have passed over

Haas. Instead, the senior Haas served twenty years as a generous trustee of Mills College, in Oakland.)

As a family obligation, Haas also administered two trusts created by the widow of Louis Stern, the third of the four nephews to inherit Levi Strauss & Co. Under his financial management, the original Lucie Stern trust of $1.7 million yielded over $9 million, the majority donated to Stanford University, an institution dear to Mrs. Stern.*

Walter, Jr., serves as a trustee of the Ford Foundation and is chairman of its audit committee, overseeing a fund of $3 billion and anual donations of over $200 million a year; he confessed with a laugh that he doesn't understand that amount of money.

Though a graduate of the University of California, Peter accepted a trusteeship of archrival Stanford, but only after reserving the right to root for California's Bears at football games.

The fifth generation continues the tradition. Robert Haas, the son of Walter, Jr., is a trustee of both the University of the Pacific and Mills College.

To correlate with a redirected company foundation, Tom Harris, in charge of the Community Affairs Department, had meantime adopted another concept of corporate participation, the community relations team, developed earlier by Bud Johns and Paul Glasgow.

Each factory and distribution center would organize a volunteer organization of its own employees to provide community service. In a philosophical sense, the size of the team's project was less important than its completion — raising funds to buy equipment for a hospital, painting a senior citizen's home, taking retarded children for an outing, sponsoring a Little League baseball club.

Beyond the creation of Harris's own office, which he structured to support the efforts of these local teams, the com-

---

* At the death of her husband, Mrs. Stern moved to Palo Alto, the site of the university. She entertained students at Sunday dinners and carried on a voluminous correspondence with Stanford men sent overseas during World War II. The school reciprocated the affection of "Aunt Lucie."

pany would institutionalize the concept in two ways. A group that undertook to raise significant amounts of money for a local project could turn to the Levi Strauss Foundation for assistance, and, second, it would be the concern of the local plant manager to see that his facility had a functioning community relations team of rank-and-file workers.

In rhetorical question-and-answer self-dialogue, Harris noted, "Does every plant manager love the community relations responsibility? No. Do most of them support it and think it contributes to their operation? Yes. A lot think it's the greatest thing that ever happened."

It wasn't always so. "You have a plant manager behind in production, getting his ass chewed. The distribution center sent back last week's production, saying they're all bad. OSHA [Occupational Safety and Health Administration] has been around or is coming, and there's a snowstorm and a lot of people are out of work, absenteeism and turnover are up, and Harris walks in talking about community relations teams, bake sales to raise money, rummage sales, and helping community needs.

"And you know the instantaneous reception that received," Harris said gravely, as if the earlier rebuffs smarted still.

"Five years later, I would say the vast number of our managers are involved in, excited about, proud of, what is going on with their community relations team. We have an annual seminar of plant managers and community relations team leaders — often as not they're sewing-machine operators or fork-lift drivers rather than managers — and the whole Levi Strauss board of directors is there, and you listen as employees tell what they've done as a team. You get a manager standing up and saying, 'I've never seen such enthusiasm, fun, esprit de corps'; an employee saying, 'I never thought it was fun working before.' "

In a world where corporate charitable contributions may run to five and six figures, the efforts of the community relations teams pale to near-invisibility. But in a local community, the volunteer efforts of sewing-machine operators and cutters can be enormously influential.

Selected as the outstanding community relations team for 1976, the Clovis, New Mexico, boys' wear manufacturing plant team visited senior citizens; collected clothes and toys for a children's home; gave a Christmas party for adults at a center for the mentally retarded; raised money to purchase corsages on Mother's Day for the women residents of a nursing home; gave the men at the home aftershave lotion on Father's Day; presented the local rehabilitation center with three sewing machines; painted playground equipment; held a bake sale to raise $268 for a muscular dystrophy telethon; awarded a check for $5000 from the Levi Strauss Foundation to a nearby clinic for a prescription drug bank; raised $1200 to buy an incubator for the local hospital; and presented a second foundation check for $1500 to a senior citizens' center for repairs on the bus used to transport the members.

Harris added, "I spend a quarter of my time in capitals of Texas, Arkansas, and Tennessee, where we have the bulk of our facilities, getting to know the state resources available, what government agencies need in proposals.

"We seed programs. We'll give the whole operating budget to get something started, but not to keep it going. It's better to work with the community and show them how to tap resources." After ten years at Hunters Point and coping with short-lived government commitments that died for lack of community resources, this veteran of the War on Poverty has learned the lesson of that well-meaning, abortive effort.

Not everything the foundation funds will succeed.

In the early 1970s, industry discovered the seeming logic of day care centers for the children of employees. Ostensibly, a woman who knew her child was well cared for during the day — especially if the day care center was on the plant grounds — would be more likely to show up for work. If the companies were less than altruistic in their desire to cut down absenteeism, they were willing to provide the best facilities and trained staffs for the children.

Levi Strauss was caught up in the enthusiasm. In Star City, Arkansas, the company built a pilot day care center for $50,000, then spent another $40,000 to staff it. At the end

of the year, twelve children were enrolled. It had been a
dismal failure.

"All over the country, it was the same," Harris said, frown-
ing at the bedraggled fern in his San Francisco office. "It
was our naïveté. The reason it failed? People won't transport kids long distances from home. The centers took care
of kids ages two to five. Who would take care of the older
kids after school, and why do something special just for this
one?

"Parents also haven't read about the values of compre-
hensive day care centers," he added sarcastically, "where the
child will learn manipulative skills, and developmental
skills and come under the professional guidance of a child-
development specialist. All the mother wants is someone to
take care of her kid. We gave the center away to the community, and it filled up."

But this setback would not deter Levi Strauss from attempting to improve day care for children. "In Arkansas
we developed a theory that ninety percent of the kids are
not in day care centers and are being take care of by the lady
down the street. Let's plug the major flaw that now exists,
that most of these ladies are operating in isolation and
probably never read a child-development book, probably
can't afford the highfalutin' educational toys, and let's get
them some training." Harris's Community Affairs Department located a promising model in Portland, Oregon, involving two day care centers as the nuclei of 150 satellite homes
taking in children of working parents.

At the department's prodding, and with a cash contribution from the company foundation, the University of Arkansas created a training program for these housewives-
turned-baby-sitters. A $14,000 grant from the foundation
will establish a similar program in Georgia. An $80,000
Levi Strauss Foundation award to the Texas Department of
Public Welfare will purchase and equip mobile vans to train
home care providers in that state.

Similarly, the failure of the NAB-launched programs of
the early 1970s did not end corporatewide efforts to aid
minority businesses. "It's not a question of whether or not

a business can afford to undertake programs of social reform," Walter Haas, Jr., argued. "We don't think a business
can afford not to."

In September 1972, the company launched an internal
campaign to increase the purchase of goods and services from
minority-owned enterprises. At the time, the company was
buying over $100 million in goods and services; some portion
of this money was deliberately channeled to minority-owned
firms.

Tom Harris recruited the ideal executive to organize the
program, young, committed, and with a unique attribute to
indicate the importance the Haases placed on minority purchasing.

Peter Haas, Jr., had worked two summers at Levi Strauss
while attending Stanford University, the first in advertising,
the second in Harris's fledgling Community Affairs Department. After graduating from Harvard Business School and
spending a year as a full-time volunteer in the office of
United States Senator Alan Cranston, the young man agreed
to manage the minority purchasing program.

It was the first time he had been approached about working in the family firm. "I really didn't discuss it with him,"
his father said later. "He knew he was welcome, and I
didn't want to put the kiss of death on it."

Harris's approach was straightforward. Young Haas was
to work himself out of a job in a year, when the minority
purchasing program would be fully integrated into company
operations, no longer a special function of the Community
Affairs Department.

"Peter, Junior, wasn't sure he wanted to get into business
of any kind. Then he came to Levi for a year to see if he
liked business," Walter, Jr., said. "This was a project we
needed, and one that he seemed ideally suited for and interested in. It was not consciously done to show our interest;
we'd have shown it anyway. I think what it shows is that
he's just like his father, that's all." Young Haas decided he
liked the family enterprise; he is now a middle-level manager in the company's international division.

The program he created transformed Levi Strauss from

a passive purchaser of goods and services from minority-owned firms to an active hunter of such companies. To assure that managers complied — the responsibility was allocated to them — the corporate controller's office prepared monthly reports. Further, managers learned that their evaluations, and consequent bonuses, would in part be based on fulfillment of their quota, just as bonuses were attached to the vigor of a community relations team.

Managers would have to make time-consuming efforts to seek out minority suppliers. They would have to be firm in insisting that construction contractors subcontracted work to minority enterprises, not always easy in the discriminatory building trades.

The program was not intended as a charitable effort; no premiums were paid to minority-owned firms. As Levi Strauss had learned in the Ghettos Enterprises experiment, premiums merely postponed inevitable business failures. Only for sound business reasons, to develop alternative sources of supply or because the work would be of superior quality, did the company accept a minority firm's other than low bid.

Because responsibility is fixed on managers, the program works. Since 1973, when Peter, Jr., relinquished command, minority purchases increased from $1.3 million to $2.8 million. Despite the growth, none of the company's senior managers is satisfied. Minority-owned companies constitute about 3 percent of all manufacturing firms; Levi Strauss is not yet placing 3 percent of its total purchases with black- and brown-owned businesses.

The minority purchasing plan, the community relations teams, the redirection of the Levi Strauss Foundation are fundamental to the sense of corporate responsibility the Haas brothers share. But programs such as these represent only a small part, the public part, of their concern.

"Our first responsibility is to our employees," Walter, Jr., commented, a position articulated through an elaborate benefit program established in the 1950s and since expanded.

Levi Strauss's benefits are competitive with other firms in the garment industry, according to the man responsible for their administration, Ernest Griffes. But animating the farrago of health, retirement, and insurance plans generally considered fringe benefits is a feature virtually unheard-of in such programs — Levi Strauss & Co.'s desire to do what it considers only equitable.

In 1962, with no more reason than that the company's board of directors felt it was owed, the handful of retirees living in San Francisco was granted an 8 percent cost-of-living adjustment. The actual cost to the company that year was a mere $800, but that unanimous action by the board set a precedent. Cost-of-living increases now are routinely awarded to retirees every two or three years, in 1976 a 50 percent increase to field retirees, the following year a similar boost to home office retirees. The annual costs now run in the hundreds of thousands of dollars, according to Griffes.

Quite as expensive, past retirees are raised to the levels of present retirees, again merely on the motion of the board. It costs Levi Strauss $250,000 annually to raise the pensions of the 400 retirees to the level that future retirees will receive under terms of a revised plan. But, as Griffes pointed out, the commitment was not for one year alone, but for all the years those retirees live. Griffes estimates that single gratuitous gesture will cost at least $3.75 million.

Pension programs are hardly uncommon in business and industry in the last half of the twentieth century. But where many companies will deliberately attempt to limit the number of vested retirees, Levi Strauss seemingly seeks to qualify everyone possible.

In 1975, nine years after it acquired the six plants of the Oberman Manufacturing Co., Levi Strauss voluntarily gave the former Oberman employees credit for their years of service to their original employer. Levi Strauss was required to pay into its retirement fund for these surprised people.

The pension plan has been repeatedly amended by the board of directors — as recently as 1976 — to include small groups of people inadvertently omitted by one or another condition of the plan. According to one board member, Paul Glasgow, then a senior vice-president, "They had to go back and fund for them. They didn't have to do it, but it was the *right* thing to do. It was according to the principles laid down by Walter, Senior, and Dan Koshland."

Griffes asserts none of this is demanded by the union contracts. "What the benefit programs are going to be is almost completely determined within the company. If the union negotiates a significant modification of fringe benefits — approximately three quarters of the employees are covered by union contracts — then it is extended to nonunion locations. We try to maintain consistent, similar programs between union and nonunion plants."

Such openhandedness is not without its practical effects. Levi Strauss has had few strikes. The first was the worst, a year-long struggle in Blue Ridge, Georgia, with the International Ladies Garment Workers Union, which sought to renegotiate its contract halfway through the two-year term. At strike's end, Levi Strauss had lost just four days' work, and the union was voted out.

Company industrial relations experts could recall just two other strikes, each of one week's duration at a single plant, and a series of wildcat strikes at a third facility, triggered by conditions left uncorrected after Levi Strauss bought the plant from another manufacturer.

For Roland Selin, head of Industrial Relations, union negotiations are comparatively simple. "Each side takes extreme positions, knowing where they'll end up. Their job is to get all they can get; my job is not to get by with the least I can get by with, because that may hurt us with the costs of turnover and training new people."

Max Cowan, in charge of jeans production and the man who has the most to lose in a strike at a manufacturing facility, may be even more casual about union negotiations. "We have organizing attempts going on right now. We fight these vigorously, but we fight these in a fair way by telling people the truth. We would prefer to deal directly with our people, without the middleman. But in those facilities where we do have a union, we don't have any problem either.

"As long as you're fair, it doesn't make much difference whether you have a labor union or you don't."

To shirtsleeved Paul Glasgow, leaning back in a swivel chair with his arms folded across his chest, labor relations rested on an article of faith. "We're not about to push people around."

In an interview shortly before his 1977 retirement, Glasgow explained, "If we bring in a new piece of automated equipment, nobody must be replaced by this equipment, nobody must suffer a drop in earnings. We'll retrain them on the equipment or on a job of their choice. And to my knowledge we have never displaced anybody yet. God forbid that we ever do."

Glasgow was responsible for the development of a series of automated machines much admired by the labor-intensive garment industry. In some Levi Strauss factories, as much as one quarter of the sewing operations have been automated already, and a seventy-member team is perfecting devices that will handle another quarter.

However, for Levi Strauss to continue to retrain people, rather than lay them off when a function is automated, it must remain a growth company. The moment sales slacken, the pressure to automate and fire workers will begin.

Until that time, automation presents no threat to employees, and Levi Strauss derives the benefits. As Glasgow noted, machines will work until five o'clock on Friday afternoons, and they do not come in hung over on Monday mornings. Production remains more or less constant, and quality is consistent.

Glasgow's concerns at Levi Strauss ranged far beyond the labor-saving devices he introduced into the plants. "We want people to have a more meaningful life. You've got to satisfy basic needs: a roof over your head, some food in your stomach, and a pair of Levi's. But people should get some sort of satisfaction on the job, too.

"What we want to have is more satisfied people and to try and give them a piece of the action and a big piece of the decision-making." Including employees in the decision-making process — beyond the volunteer community relations teams, which Glasgow enthusiastically endorses — has meant experimentation.

In an Albuquerque facility, the plant manager, at Glasgow's urging, organized a small group of eighteen operators to be in business for themselves, making parts for jeans. The company agreed to pay a fixed amount for each unit the group turned out, adding to it regular incentive bonuses for overproduction. The group bought a supervisor's time to deal with cutting-room foremen and mechanics, but did its own hiring and firing. Sometimes.

"Productivity has been all right," Glasgow judged. "Turnover went down half the usual rate; absenteeism went down, except for one person. We told them, 'That's your problem.'

" 'Okay,' they said, and nine of them took her into the cafeteria and talked to her about it, since her absences were lowering their production and pay. The next week was worse.

"So they decided there were too many, and the next time there were three of them. The next week was just as bad.

"So I said, 'Well, what are you going to do with her?'

" 'We're not going to do anything, but *you* got to fire her!'

"They're not used to making decisions like that. But I think people will evolve out of the group who will say, 'I'll handle it,' and I think they will. We want them to work it out for themselves, 'cause if we sit there and guide them, what do we gain?"

Six out of ten workers want merely to learn a routine job and remain at that task, unhindered by such experiments. The Albuquerque effort may not work or may not be exportable to other plants. Past failures of good ideas temper excessive enthusiasm.

A line of twenty-two operators doing more than one operation failed. The variety of jobs shattered monotony, but operators believed that if they concentrated on one task, repeating it reflexively eight hours a day, their productivity and bonuses would increase. The experiment was ended.

An attempt to train women as mechanics — positions for generations considered men's work — put six women in a training class. Two survived; one actually worked as a mechanic.

One female mechanic is hardly a blow for women's rights, but women elsewhere in the corporation are venturing into heretofore sacred precincts. Forty-two of 606 salesmen on the road in 1977 were female, all hired after 1972, when the corporation instituted an affirmative action program for women. One is a plant manager, others are engineers, two are truckdrivers. Glasgow rues still the outcry when the women were trained and hired as truckers. "Goddam wives complaining, 'You going to send my husband on a long haul with that broad?' and me answering, 'You can't take care of him at home, that's your problem.'"

Whatever the risks — some as minimal as an irate wife, some graver — Levi Strauss & Co. is willing to take them. The firm has for some years hired known alcoholics, men with criminal records, drug addicts. "We've lost some," Glasgow conceded. "We never say anything about trying to rehabilitate them, but there are people working here who've made it.

"We've got handicapped people everywhere, blind people in Texas running cafeterias." It is a program Glasgow pushed hard. "It's a gamble when you start with them, and you worry about somebody getting hurt, but we furnish the cafeteria with all the equipment.

"And they do a helluva good job. The profit's theirs, and it goes to the blind. What better could you contribute to?"

For Glasgow there was another pleasure, too. "You ever see the look of satisfaction on the face of someone who's never before had a meaningful job? And you give them one. And you talk to them about it and they light up inside. They now have pride. What's society going to do with them otherwise? You're going to give them a grant every month from the state or the federal government or both."

His enthusiasm overwhelmed the Missouri drawl. "It costs seven thousand dollars a year minimum to keep somebody in San Quentin. You get that guy out here on the street, and he's making fourteen thousand as a mechanic, paying taxes; and isn't that better than having a drain of seven thousand over there? Okay, then you can take that seven thousand and do something for the landscape, or more parks, or more art. Isn't that better?"

But a training program for prisoners at the state prison died aborning, probably Glasgow's biggest disappointment in twenty-five years with the "people-believers" of Levi Strauss. Despite five years of his efforts — offering to place twenty-five ex-convicts as trained mechanics around the country, securing pledges of equipment and manuals from the sewing-machine manufacturers, getting commitments from would-be employers (including competitors Blue Bell and Swank) — the State of California refused to cooperate. Glasgow demanded the men work five days a week on the grounds "you got to show them there's a better world than behind those damn bars." The state balked.

However altruistic minority purchasing programs, equal employment efforts, or community action teams, the executives of Levi Strauss insist they are good business.

"If you can add some fun to sitting there all day making a belt loop, if you can raise money by throwing water-filled sponges at your supervisors, that just has to have an impact in that plant on morale. My God, if you have good morale, you're going to cut down absenteeism, turnover. You're going to get more pants out," Tom Harris argued.

How many more pairs of pants, Harris could not say. "I wish I could measure it."

According to Paul Glasgow, "I want people not only to make more money and have a better standard of living. I think people should be rewarded, told they're needed and wanted, and that they contribute. That's important to all of us. If they get self-satisfaction on their job and get paid reasonably well — we have to remain competitive — the more they stay with us, the more we can do for them. Hell, yes, these efforts are good business. They cut down turnover. They keep production on an even keel so we can ship [to] customers. We're selfish, too."

Anything that trims turnover by even a fraction benefits

the company. Levi Strauss employed 16,000 operators in 1977. Turnover averaged 75 percent annually, though most of those who quit did so in the first month, were replaced, then replaced again. Ten percent efficiency common the first two weeks, it cost the firm in training time and wages $2500 for each new hiree, or about $3 million per year. (This does not include related personnel, advertising, and clerical costs.)

Similarly, absenteeism is costly. A company study found that in one plant, for one month in 1974, if each employee had worked at 100 percent efficiency, putting in forty-hour weeks, the company would have reduced the sewing costs of a pair of pants from $1.21 to fifty cents — or $65,320 for the twenty-three working days of that month.*

Like his father and uncle before him, Walter Haas, Jr., is convinced that there is a real business advantage to corporate altruism. "Attracting people is *the* one. Fifteen or twenty years ago when we used to recruit at Harvard and Stanford Business schools, particularly Harvard, we could get three or four people to interview. Today, if we go back we couldn't send enough interviewers. We can compete with IBM or Procter and Gamble and all the others for the

---

* Hundred percent rates and bonuses for overproduction are fixed by the company but are routinely surpassed by operators. Just paying attention to the operators increases production substantially, Glasgow noted, confirming the so-called Hawthorne Effect. "I thought nobody ever tells these people what a good job they're doing. So I started going by and saying, 'Mary Ellen, I just took a look at your record, and you haven't missed in two days, and you're a hundred and six percent operator, and you're a fantastic person.' Christ, the next week she gave me a hundred and twenty-six percent!" Glasgow may well be the only garment-industry production expert willing to admit, "Sweatshops have bugged me since I entered the industry." And that attitude may explain why, on Glasgow's sentimental journey, prior to retirement, to Warsaw, Virginia, where he had managed for five years, Elizabeth S. Arrington wrote to the local newspaper: "Joy and excitement ran high in August as the word got around that Mr. Paul Glasgow was on his way to Warsaw to visit the Levi plant. All the workers that had worked with Mr. Glasgow fifteen years ago just couldn't wait to see him again ... He finally arrived, just a little stouter but the same wonderful person he has always been ... The only sad thing about the whole evening was when Mr. Glasgow announced he was retiring, but we know he has done his share for Levi Strauss so he deserves to retire."

top graduate school students, because they want to identify with a company that has this philosophy. And that assures our success twenty years from now."

The manifold efforts in the broad and often amorphous area of social responsibility have brought Levi Strauss considerable national attention. Walter, Jr., especially has spoken widely about it, accepted awards for the company's endeavors, and seen little come of the example. He no longer gives such speeches. Accepting its award in 1968 as "business statesman of the year," Walter told the Harvard Business School Association of Northern California that he had won it "if not by default then at least in the face of far too little competition.

"I think that instead of being the good example we should merely be one of an overwhelming majority doing what should and must be done."

Chapter X

The Reorganization

CHILLED BY the cold November wind, they crowded into the Wells-Fargo building, surprised by the size of the turnout. No wonder they had to hold the meeting here, whatever it was about; there was no room big enough at Battery Street for all of Levi Strauss & Co.'s stockholders.

Walter, Jr., worked his way to the front of the room, stopping to chat momentarily. He seemed excited, yet there was a quality of sadness in his manner, thought Barbara Clemens-Pitre, now a stockholder for four years.

"Knowing how much speculation there would be about a meeting of this type, we did not give much advance notice," Walter read from the paper in his hand. The scattered conversations stopped, the whispers sighing to silence. "Our announcement is so important that we wanted to tell as many of you as possible in person, hence this informal meeting."

Here and there a few people guessed the purpose of their summons and sat forward, listening closely.

"The news is something about which all of you have been wondering about for some time." Walter paused and swallowed.

"Levi Strauss and Company is going public."

After 117 years, the family-owned company would sell its stock on the open market. The Haases had resisted the move for years, partly in deference to Walter, Sr.'s, adamant opposition; the patrician was still a man to be respected. But even his financial wizardry could postpone the inevitable no longer.

"Until March of nineteen sixty-six," Walter continued, "Levi Strauss and Company had been able to finance its growth through the use of short-term bank borrowings and retained earnings. Then it became necessary to augment these sources, so we obtained a twenty-million-dollar, long-term loan from Metropolitan Life Insurance Company. . ."

In the four years since, the directors had committed most of the $20 million to new factories, Sta-Prest curing plants, and distribution centers, yet demand for the expanding Levi Strauss lines continued to outstrip production. Finances and personnel were stretched thin. Young men with but months in the company were managing entire Levi's operations overseas, filling production and merchandising positions at home that previously had demanded a decade's effort to learn.

Levi Strauss had been swept up in an unimaginable jeans boom; the western work garment had become an international symbol of leisure, and, ironically, a status symbol. Jeans no longer could be banned in public schools when movie stars wore them to $50-a-meal restaurants, when wash-soft denim had become a ubiquitous uniform for young men and women under twenty-five, when well-patched American jeans commanding two and three times their price as new goods sold out in Montmartre boutiques and Carnaby Street shops.

"Since then, our company continued to expand very rapidly and it was very obvious to all that additional outside financing would have to be obtained," Walter continued, his voice strained.

Beyond the Haases, probably no one better realized how quickly the company had grown in recent years than Mel Bacharach, now Levi Strauss's vice-president for marketing. In 1960, his first year as a stockholder, the company had sales of $50.9 million and profits of $2.2 million. This year, sales would be just short of $350 million, a sevenfold increase, and profits had skyrocketed to more than $80 million. The firm was virtually recession-proof, thanks to the 501 and the corduroy jeans introduced in 1962; the recession of 1967 had barely slowed its growth.

In 1968, the company had reorganized along new marketing lines, Bacharach breaking out the first separate department, the handful of ladies' garments. At the introduction of Levis for Gals, one wag had noted, "It took Levi Strauss almost a hundred and twenty years to find out girls were different from boys."

That small department had gotten off to a healthy start, putting the company visibly into the $3-billion-a-year women's wear business. Potentially, women's wear could be larger than jeans, Bacharach realized.

As Walter Haas spoke, Barbara Clemens-Pitre looked around the room. The confusion she felt, she noticed on the faces of others. She didn't know whether to clap or cry.

Maybe both. She had bought small lots of stock each year, as Al Sanguinetti had advised her to, paying for them bit by bit. Until now, she had never thought of the shares as money. They were her investment to pay for her eleven-year-old son's college education. She bought them and forgot about them.

It struck her suddenly. Once the company's stock went on the open market, her shares would increase in value. Around the room, others had realized the same thing.

"You could hear their brains clicking. They knew they were suddenly much wealthier. But they also knew something just had to change; that family-type feeling we had just had to change." The thirty-year-old black woman had a glimmer of memory: Walter, Jr., in his shirtsleeves, walking around the office, visitors supposing him just another clerk. She wondered if she would ever see him like that again.

Later, when she reconsidered, it occurred to her that listing the company on the New York Stock Exchange would have another drawback. The Haases would be diverted from problems they had inside the company, especially with the Gals department.

The immediate response from retailers to the Gals models

was overwhelming, as if the market had been waiting for the company to acknowledge that it needed a fuller line of women's garments. Levi Strauss had orders to fill six months' production. The firm was filling a gap; retailers did not like women shopping in men's departments — such crossovers inhibited men — yet where else could the growing number of women who routinely wore jeans shop for them?

Gals had not lived up to the first year's promise. The department had to fight for production time, especially in the jeans factories, which were working overtime to meet demand for the 501 and corduroy pants. The mills could not produce enough denim to meet the runaway demand — a problem that would plague the company for the next seven years — and the small Gals department often felt overlooked in the allocations.

It was frustrating, especially when she remembered Sanguinetti's tightly run western wear operation. Sanguinetti was on top of everything; when he said something was going to happen, it happened. How different from Gals.

Clemens-Pitre had not been sure she wanted to transfer to the new department, but Mel Bacharach had convinced her. She would be one of the best trained, a veteran of the now disbanded western wear department, surely capable of handling two models of slacks in ten fabrics produced almost as an afterthought in a men's sportswear factory. It was a line no one else had wanted, a stepchild, but then Clemens-Pitre sometimes believed the entire Gals department a stepchild.

Especially now, when it needed direction from a manager with experience in the women's market. The honeymoon was over; the department had learned that women's wear was much more fashion-conscious than the men's. Gals boasted no 501-type garments produced season after season after season, no highly profitable staples on which it could rely year after year. It had started with a straight-leg, recut version of men's jeans at just the right time, when straight-leg jeans were stylish. But this year the market had shifted from straight legs to flares.

For all the little triumphs, like getting into Bigi, the prestigious teen department of New York's Bergdorf-Goodman, it was taking so long to catch up with the market, Clemens-Pitre fretted. Gals had introduced its own flare-legged pants, but they had been styled badly. That finally corrected, she was still trying to overcome the competitors' lead.

With all the effort that going public would require, and the attention focused on that for the foreseeable future, would anybody have time for the problems of a stepchild? It was just, oh, so *damned* frustrating. Clemens-Pitre blinked back the tears of anger. Or was it sadness that had made her cry? She could hardly follow as Walter continued to read the prepared statement.

". . . Additional outside financing would have to be obtained. We postponed this inevitable development for as long as possible . . ."

Partly the delay had again been in deference to the wishes of Walter, Sr. But much of the reason for his opposition had vanished the previous year, when, to comply with federal law, the company revealed its sales and earnings for the first time.

The statute required that even privately held corporations disclose sales and earnings if they had assets of more than $1 million and more than 500 shareholders. Levi Strauss might have avoided making the announcement, which publicly placed the firm among the six largest apparel companies in the nation, but to do so would have meant severely limiting the number of employees permitted to buy stock. It already had 480 home office employee-stockholders, and the Haas brothers strongly believed in broad employee ownership.

Staying below the 500–shareholder level would mean depriving loyal workers of a share of profits, after more than six decades of employee stock ownership. Reluctantly, braced with the conviction that it was the correct thing to do, the directors had released the firm's earnings.

That public announcement had ended one problem for a handful of company executives. For generations, the annual reports had been closely guarded family secrets. To meet the law's requirement that each shareholder see an annual report, every year David Beronio had typed one copy and personally carried it around the room, showing it to each stockholder attending the annual meeting. The junior executives and minority shareholders got only a brief glance at the balance sheet before it disappeared into Beronio's locked drawer.

As the board expanded and the fiscal problems multiplied, so had the copies of the report. But each had been numbered, and was collected at the end of the annual meeting. A group of younger stockholders, dividing the task among themselves, each committed a portion of the report to memory, then reconstructed the entire document after the meeting.

They all had repeatedly pondered the year-end balance sheets and understood why Walter was saying, "Additional outside equity financing can no longer be postponed."

Standing in the back of the auditorium, Bud Johns paid less attention to Walter's statement than to the reaction of people in the room. He had known the purpose of the meeting, had helped draft the prepared statement, and was curious now about the impact it would have on the old-timers.

The day Levi Strauss stock was offered for public sale its value would rise dramatically. Brokers had already told the Haases that the stock should be put on the market at a price somewhere around twenty times the annual earnings. Shares bought years ago for $1.00 and $2.00 would suddenly be worth between $40 and $45.

Johns counted twenty-nine people in that room, beyond the Haas family, who stood to become instant millionaires. Dozens more would find themselves rather wealthy. Johns watched as the shipping clerk's frown turned to a hesitant smile. A concentration camp survivor who had taken a job in the shipping department two weeks after arriving in the United States, the clerk had never earned more than $200 a week. Yet he had saved, and over the years since 1955 had invested $21,300 in company stock. When Levi Strauss went public, his investment would be worth $394,800.

Slowly reading the statement in his hands, Walter was now explaining that the expected $45 million stock offering in the spring of 1971 would be one of the five largest issues marketed in the last fifteen years.

As a member of the board of directors, Harry Cohn had been aware of the purpose of the meeting but was excited anew by the prospect. For years he had been one of a group of younger managers urging the company to expand faster. Nearly everything the company produced sold well; the Levi Strauss name was like money in the bank. Cohn himself had proved it five years before when, as merchandise manager for casual pants, he had introduced a half-jeans–half-slack combination made in hopsacking. Now the department used between 200,000 and 250,000 yards of fabric, producing 100,000 to 125,000 pairs of Nuvos a week. That one model accounted for as much as $30 million a year in sales and was almost a staple.

With $45 million in new capital from the sale of stock, there was no telling how big the firm would grow, how many more lines like Nuvos it could merchandise. And as general merchandise manager, responsible for everything but Levi's for Gals, Harry Cohn was the man to head the expansion.

There was nothing Cohn liked more than merchandising, designing men's and boys' slacks and pants, picking fabrics and details, setting up production schedules, and getting salesmen behind the line. He had been working toward this for twenty-one years — longer, if he counted his three years as a part-time wrapper in the shipping room while attending high school.

Cohn had learned it all, like everyone else at Levi Strauss, starting from the bottom. A German immigrant, Cohn had come to the United States with his parents in 1940. Fellow immigrant Julius Phillips had gotten him his first part-time job, at seventy cents an hour.

When Cohn graduated from high school, sales manager Bill Lagoria offered him a full-time position, with a five-cent-an-hour raise. The youngster debated between Levi Strauss and college, and decided to try working for a year. If nothing else, the money would come in handy when he did go to school.

Cohn never left. (Years later, his personal fortune greater than $2 million, he would still wonder if he had done the right thing. He had taken night school courses, enough to qualify for a degree, but not the ones necessary to satisfy graduation requirements, he quickly explained.)

The lure of becoming a salesman was too great for the eighteen-year-old youth. "Salesmen were making a lot of money, money that was unreal to me at the time. I had those kinds of ambitions, and I wanted to do it early, when I could enjoy it," Cohn acknowledged later. Salesmen, too, were drafted from the shipping room, and Cohn waited his turn.

Instead, he was offered a job as an assistant clerk in the small western wear department. (Al Sanguinetti would join him a few months later; for the next twenty-two years they would follow parallel careers, the rivalry between the two men friendly, intense, and never far from mind.)

In 1956, Cohn was promoted to assistant manager of the western wear line, responsible for men's pants and shirts. Three years later, Mel Bacharach, about to launch Levi Strauss's casuals line, wooed Cohn away as his assistant merchandising manager. Cohn would second Bacharach for six years, through white Levi's, through Orange, Lemon and Lime, through Sta-Prest, to become the firm's casual slacks expert.

Now he was the general merchandise manager and a member of the board of directors. "When a whole group of us became directors in nineteen sixty-eight — I mean — " Cohn fumbled. How could he describe the pride? He sighed. "That was a day. That was *really* an accomplishment, when all of us moved up together." There would be subsequent promotions, but nothing could quite equal that day.

Walter neared the end of his statement to the 200 stockholders in the Wells-Fargo auditorium. "At the same time, we expect to split our stock so that each of you will receive two shares for each one you now hold."

For the first time it struck Cohn: he could quit work right now at forty-one and live comfortably. The notion evaporated just as suddenly. What the hell would he do with himself if he did retire?

Walter paused, swallowed, then began again. "That about sums up everything I can say, and I hope answers most of the questions you may have. Even though our operations from now on may be more visible to public scrutiny, I assure you that we expect to conduct business as we have in the past, recognizing our responsibilities to our shareholders, to our employees, to our customers — " He faltered. His eyes were wet, his voice too choked to finish the statement: " — to our community, and to our nation, a socially aware and responsible corporation."

Levi Strauss had reached the end of an era.

In April 1971, the company made its first stock offering to the public, the 1,396,000 shares representing 13 percent of the stock. Despite the public scrutiny inherent in accepting thousands of investors as junior partners, the Haas family intended to run Levi Strauss as it had since 1919. One of the three paragraphs describing the firm in the stock prospectus noted:

> The Company's social responsibilities have for many years been a matter of strong conviction on the part of its management. Well before legal requirements were imposed, the Company was an "equal opportunity employer." In 1969, the Company received one of *Business Week* magazine's first two "Business Citizenship" awards in the field of human resources.

The corporation's underwriters believed this to be the first such statement in a stock prospectus.

The offering sold out within a single day, at $47 per share. Levi Strauss made its New York Stock Exchange debut on March 4, 1971, priced at $64, Wall Street investors ignoring their fear of the cyclic apparel industry in their rush to buy.

As a condition of the offering, the Haases insisted that 126,000 commission-free shares be reserved for Levi Strauss employees, to be sold under a formula devised to spread ownership of the company beyond the 500 employees who already held shares.

Though there was a minimum of ten shares — which would cost the employee $446.50 — 1495 bought between ten and 270 shares, the maximum allowable. The average was ninety shares per employee; a number of the workers discovered that their local banks would lend them the money to buy the stock, with the shares themselves as collateral.

By the end of the day, almost 2000 employees owned a piece of the company for which they worked. At year's end, 20 percent of the firm's stock was in the hands of employees at all levels, from operator to board member.

Through the public offering, Levi Strauss had acquired the necessary capital to finance its expected growth. Even with that additional money, it was doubtful the company could keep pace with demand.

Blue denim sales had soared, not only in the United States, but internationally. The once humble workingman's garment had become a standard of high fashion. Fifty-dollar pairs of tight-fitting, flare-legged jeans imported from Europe — they were dry-cleaned to circumvent the shrinkage problem — filled fashionable shops. The jeans market subdivided, then subdivided again, as manufacturers rushed to fill perceived needs: European-cut jeans for midwestern housewives, buttocks-tight jeans for girls sixteen and under, others sized for girls twelve and under, faded jeans patched together from reclaimed denim imported from the Far East, jeans for older men of more ample girth, jeans that barely covered the pubic area, and bib overalls, which covered almost everything. Manufacturers — fifty of them in California alone — tumbled into the market bewildering arrays of blue denim pants, baubled, bangled, and beaded.

Still the international demand grew. In Amsterdam, Levi Strauss's local distributor sold incoming shipments of denim pants to clamoring dealers literally from the backs of delivery trucks. In Paris, two young women offered, at $5 per pair, to wear newly purchased blue denim pants into their bathtub, shrinking them to fit, as cowboys had done for decades. European manufacturers bought fifty million square yards of American denim; Japanese clothing houses, another thirty million.

Denim was ubiquitous. A symbol of the California lifestyle, where for a decade jeans had been acceptable wear in virtually any social situation, it was to be found everywhere. Explanations for the phenomenon ranged widely. Utilitarians pointed to ease of care and to comfort, letting it go at that. Social scientists argued for the once lowly blue denim pants a reverse snob appeal, labeled it a manifestation of a galloping youth culture, or viewed it as a harbinger of spreading emphasis on leisure and the affluence to maintain such affectations.* (The 501 was blackmarketed among Soviet teen-agers, largely children of well-placed bureaucrats, for as much as 100 rubles, or $120; used, it commanded forty rubles, or about six times the American retail price for a new pair. It became commonplace for touring Soviet dignitaries and athletes to stock up on 501s when visiting the United States.)

The manic boom propelled Levi Strauss & Co., manufacturers of the best-known blue denim pants, faster than any other firm. By 1972, the company employed 22,000 workers in fifty facilities around the world. Its salesmen sold to 15,000 accounts in the United States alone, among them 125 LOSs, Levi's Only Stores.

The LOS was another manifestation of the jeans innundation. Levi Strauss would be a major beneficiary, though it was neither the innovator nor an investor in the new marketing concept.

Daniel Baran, Levi Strauss's credit manager, recalled a meeting in his cramped office in the Battery Street building on July 19, 1969. It is not a date Baran is likely to forget.

---

* For example, in his best-selling *The Greening of America*, Charles A. Reich argued, "Jeans make one conscious of the body, not as something separate from the face, but as part of the whole individual." Jeans then "were a declaration of sensuality, not sensuality-for-display as in Madison Avenue style [that is, advertising, mass marketing], but sensuality as part of the natural in man."

"Three weeks earlier, Mel Bacharach had told me about this great idea a guy had for stores which would sell only Levi's products." Baran had agreed to talk to the man.

Donald Fisher was a wealthy, forty-one-year-old, some-time real estate investor and Sacramento, California, hotel owner. Fisher's idea was simple enough: he would sell Levi's as fast-food franchises sold hamburgers or fried chicken. He would have a standardized inventory, a relatively narrow selection with fast turnover, low overhead, and would depend on the Levi's reputation to bring in customers.

"Fisher had set up a corporation with a nebulous ten-thousand-dollar financing. I couldn't see the ten thousand dollars, but because of his great idea, I said, 'Okay, I'll give you ten thousand dollars in merchandise,'" Baran recalled. With guidance from Levi Strauss, Fisher settled on a location in San Francisco, close to a city college and a state university.

Seven years later, the first Gap store had grown to a national chain of 304 shops buying more than $50 million worth of Levi Strauss merchandise. In seven years, Baran added, Fisher had never been late paying a bill.

Fisher's success spawned dozens of imitators, some selling only Levi's, others more catholic in their buying. By 1976, 1200 of these chain-owned "pants-only" stores spread across the country, though most of them carried inventories that included shirts, blouses, and sweaters, too.

Industry and Wall Street observers alike insisted repeatedly that there had to be an end to the madness. The craze for denim, a child of fashion, would expire as suddenly as it began, they argued, forgetting that, however fashionable jeans might be at the moment, once discovered as a utilitarian garment acceptable in almost any social situation, the pants would continue as a part of every man's wardrobe.

Denim shortages reached an estimated 100 million square yards annually, enough to produce another fifty million pairs of pants. Unable to meet customer demand, Levi Strauss returned to allocating its production for the first time since the Korean War. Among divisions of the company, managers fought for a share of the denim. Five years later, the bitterness lingered, the lost opportunities rankling still.

Though at capacity production, 400 million yards of denim a year, the mills declined to add production. A denim mill cost at least $25 million to build, a huge investment to repay if the boom withered. Nor could mills producing other fabrics be converted. The thicker yarns of cotton fibers woven into denim required heavier looms, and contamination from indigo dye barred use of the mill for other yardage once denim had been introduced.

The pell-mell growth brought on other problems for Levi Strauss, Harry Cohn remembered. "Our organization got very heavy because all merchandising, with the exception of Gals, was coming through me. All production was coming through Paul Glasgow. All sales were going to one sales manager. Three or four merchandising departments were reporting to me, all with different requirements. The business got huge, so the control wasn't there anymore." Cohn wrinkled his nose in distaste.

The Haas brothers recognized the necessity for reorganization, and appointed a committee of fifteen executives to recommend a new alignment. Cohn, a member of that committee, recalled the long meetings. "We could continue on a functional basis, or divisionalize, become a General Motors. If we divisionalized, the question was: How? By age group? By product group? By geographic group? By production group, or merchandising group?"

The committee recommended a structuring along existing merchandising lines, breaking the company into four domestic divisions and an autonomous international organization selling everything. In the United States, there would be a Jeans Division, the largest; Levi's for Gals, already set up, requiring only its own production and sales force; a Boyswear Division; and a men's Sportswear Division.

Each of the four would be supported by its own production facilities and its own sales force. Though not intended, the divisions would compete against each other, quite as

General Motors' five marques — Chevrolet, Pontiac, Olds-mobile, Buick, and Cadillac — compete for the automobile customer.

Jeans would manufacture some fashion-oriented garments, snaring dollars from the Sportswear Division. The larger sizes in Boyswear would overlap the smaller in Jeans. As long as unisex fashions held sway, Levi's for Gals would have to fend off all three other divisions.

Walter Haas offered Harry Cohn his pick of either the Jeans or the Sportswear divisions. The choice was easy. There would be little designing, little merchandising in Jeans, Cohn believed; the 501 reigned there.

"Because my heart was in Sportswear, and because it was the greatest challenge," he later said, "I told them, 'You need the best man for the toughest job. So I want Sportswear.'"

Cohn paused. "I've regretted it many times. But not really." His laugh sounded a little thin.

"I didn't realize how tough it was going to be when you pulled it out of the mainstream. So I developed a separate sales force. I took the merchandising people intact, took the factories that were making sportswear, hired a production manager with a different type mentality, because this was no longer a mass-produced, one-type, Five-o-one business. It was a variety of pants, shirts, jackets, with several style changes every year."

Al Sanguinetti had been waiting. For four years he had run the Product Integrity Department, tough, demanding, uncompromising, and restless. He snapped up the Jeans Division offer.

Jeans was the flagship, representing $180 million of the company's $432 million in 1971 sales. It would be responsible for the 501, the foundation of Levi Strauss, the one instantly identifiable corporate product, "the only jean that Levi Strauss himself made," as Sanguinetti said later.

The garment was sold on two bases: its romantic link to the West and its reputation for durability. Sanguinetti understood both elements. The romance he had grown up with in the western wear department. The quality he himself had defended for four years.

Sanguinetti had a freebooter's zest for seizing the opportunity. He had one now — the international denim craze and virtual freedom. A newly appointed executive vice-president, the man to whom Sanguinetti was responsible, "was the best thing that ever happened to me. Ed Combs was a lone wolf who left a lone wolf alone. He said, 'Bring me a fifty-two-million-dollar bottom line.' I did, and they let me run the division the way I thought best."

In six years Sanguinetti would drive Jeans Division sales from $180 million to over $700 million. He reintroduced the discontinued western shirt; it should never have been scuttled in the first place, he maintained. He tentatively organized a fashion jeans line, then watched it develop into a unit the size of the entire Gals and Sportswear divisions. He flogged corduroy sales until that line rivaled denim. Were his division's sales tabulated separately, Sanguinetti would rank among the presidents of the 290 largest corporations in the nation.

At the same time, Sanguinetti was repaying a moral debt, transforming his division into a training ground for corporate executives. "I stole one guy — a personnel man, and made him my planning and finance man. Two years later, I made him production manager for jeans. Two years after that they took him to run the Boyswear Division."

At forty-five, Thomas Borrelli made a midcourse correction in his career. A former seminarian, then a graduate psychologist, Borrelli was working for Lockheed Missiles and Spacecraft, laying out controls and displays for space vehicles. Frustrated by "the Cold War environment," blocked from promotion because he was not an engineer, Borrelli quietly went job hunting.

From a friend he learned that Levi Strauss was seeking a national training director. Despite his wife's misgivings, Borrelli was confident he could survive. One more abrupt change in career merely presented a new challenge.

After eighteen months' shaping programs to train Levi's operators, Borrelli was named corporate personnel director. Two years later, Sanguinetti lured him away; the offer of a line rather than a staff job was too great to miss.

In May 1974, after just eight years with the firm, Tom Borrelli became president of the Boyswear Division and a corporate vice-president. He was the only division manager who hadn't learned the business from the marketing-merchandising side. (Borrelli also bears the burden of being the only division manager whose slender-hipped daughter prefers to wear a rival manufacturer's jeans because the fit is more stylish.)

Secretly pleased, Sanguinetti growled that the company had bled him of trained managers. "I took a guy into western wear thirteen years ago, a mayonnaise salesman. I hired him for five hundred and twenty a month, broke him in on cutting ranch pants for ladies out of Chinatown. Now he's running the Womenswear Division."

Not mayonnaise, Jim McDermott demurred. Jell-O. A University of Illinois graduate, McDermott discovered San Francisco while in the service, and had finally landed a job selling for General Foods. "They screwed around with the bonus arrangement, and I got pissed off and applied to an employment agency.

"I was sent out to interview for one of the first management trainee classes, and somebody on the committee blackballed me. But Sanguinetti had another opening in western wear, so he hired me. Probably because I was cheap." At the time, Sanguinetti's small group was responsible for boys' double-knee jeans, and McDermott was detailed there. Within four years of their introduction — McDermott credits Sanguinetti — Levi Strauss's double-knee jeans had driven Farah, the largest rival manufacturer of branded boys' wear, from the market, leaving Levi Strauss unchallenged.

Now forty, a thirteen-year veteran of the four-season guessing game called merchandising, McDermott has been charged with redirecting the drifting Womenswear Division.

Borrelli and McDermott are Sanguinetti's most successful protégés, but there are others. The company's most militant advocate of promoting from within, Sanguinetti has Levi Strauss's largest division in which to locate talent. "Before somebody's nephew comes in, we're going to exhaust all means to get the blacks, the browns, the women, then the other employees of this company to advance their careers and make more money." In Sanguinetti's domain, it is an edict. A large poster on the walls recruits sales trainees, pointing out that twenty-five of the division's 400–strong sales force once worked in low-paying clerical and stock jobs. Eight of the twenty-five are from ethnic minorities; three are women.*

Not all of Sanguinetti's personnel moves are roundly applauded, he admitted. He "took crap" for a month after the promotion of one young woman to manage the entire fashion jeans department. It was booking $140 million a year in business, too much responsibility for a twenty-eight-year-old; others in the company wanted the job, people with more experience. Still, for Sanguinetti, who said nothing to the woman about the furor her appointment unleashed, the decision was simple. "What I looked at were the people doing the training and selection. Tom Kasten, who got the good marks from McDermott, says she can fill the job."

Just five years out of college, Susan Fantus became one of the most powerful women in American business.

---

* "Because somebody gave me an opportunity and you don't forget stuff like that," Sanguinetti's passion has extended beyond promotion. In 1971, Levi Strauss & Co. established a small factory for the Jeans Division in Eutaw, Alabama, county seat of one of the four poorest counties in the nation. The reasoning was that a Levi Strauss payroll in that community of 10,000 would be the best method of alleviating the numbing poverty. "We invested a lot of corporate resources," Sanguinetti remembered. "These were people who needed help, people who needed opportunity, people who needed incentive. We knew we would take a bath." The company tried a succession of plant managers, devoted thousands of hours of management time and more thousands of dollars. "We used to talk for hours about why we couldn't get a bar-tack operator to go a hundred and twenty percent, like we do other bar-tack operators." Absenteeism was high; production levels and quality, low. Years later, the firm's inability to overcome the culture of poverty — employees would work only long enough to meet immediate financial needs — still pained Sanguinetti.

Chapter XI

Waiting for the Numbers

IT WAS STILL SOME MINUTES before eight in the morning. For a half-hour, Susan Fantus had been studying computer printouts, shaping her department's budget for the coming year. A strand of hair had slipped from the tight coil on the back of her head; occasionally she brushed it off her cheek, annoyed, but unwilling to take the time to rewind it into that schoolteacher's no-nonsense hairdo. The subdued skirt and plaid blouse only enhanced the impression of a lady not accustomed to dallying in front of a mirror before work.

The Locatelli concerto hummed softly in her corner office. That Fantus has a corner office, with a westerly view of San Francisco's orange-red sunsets, is a measure of her status. There are few perks at Levi Strauss & Co. — no executive dining rooms, no carefully graded thicknesses of rug pile, no chauffeur-driven limousines. The corner office remains the only prize.

To hold on to her corner office, Fantus sees successions of those glorious sunsets. Merchandisers routinely work ten- and twelve-hour days, one reason there is heavy attrition among their ranks.

Susan Fantus learned to handle the pressure of bringing out twenty to thirty different models a year in a variety of colors and fabrics, to make the quick decisions ending production of the slow-sellers rather than allowing the inventory to build inexorably at the rate of ten, twenty, or thirty thousand garments a week. She learned to administer a departmental operating budget of $500,000 and to supervise four junior merchandisers and their secretaries. She learned, too, how to deal with mill representatives, with the division's 400 salesmen, with plant managers — mostly men older than she.

Fantus succeeded without role models. "The women in the New York garment industry are stylists, with no cost or profit responsibility. I am responsible for profitability of my line," she stressed, absently toying with the pencil in her hand.

Promotion came rapidly, too rapidly, carped critics elsewhere in the company. "I really was not ready for the fashion jeans job when I got it a year ago. There were a lot of people around the company more qualified, except that I was probably more qualified in that I had the support of Tom [Kasten, vice-president of marketing for the Jeans Division] and Pete [Jacobi, general merchandise manager of the division]. They believed in me."

Women's liberation has not been a factor in her meteoric climb. "I can attribute a lot of my success to being in the right place at the right time," she noted.

Holding a degree in psychology from the University of California at Berkeley, Susan Fantus was twenty-three when she went to work as a clerk-typist at Levi Strauss. "Liberal arts degrees were a dime a dozen." After six months, she applied for a production scheduler's position, and was hired by Tom Kasten, himself just twenty-nine and responsible for the small Gentlemen's Jeans line of clothing for men between the ages of twenty-five and thirty-five.

It was a big jump for her, from a grade five to a grade thirteen. Most promotions range among three salary grades, but Kasten was fast-rising himself and not one to be intimidated by protocol.

There was some resistance, Fantus realized, among plant managers. Her job was to make sure fabric moved from the mills to the plants on time, "helping make the whole thing function. The plant managers were all men, tough, out of Texas and little counties of Georgia, with three hundred operators and production schedules to meet. I was responsible for keeping those operators working.

"As a woman, that was one of the toughest battles I won. And one of the more important. Those people really support me and respect me," she said quietly. The struggle there was to prove herself to those plant managers who depended on her to keep their lines supplied with materials. Any newcomer would be suspect; that she was a woman only heightened the suspicion.

Dealing with people outside the company, she encountered "the little-girl reception, a lot of basic, general sexism," more overt and easier to cope with.

"The first problem I had was not being taken seriously. I think I'm over that for the most part, but going back a couple of years, when I was a merchandising assistant, I was 'a cute little something,' that kind of thing. Now I'm the manager, and the one thing I love and find fascinating is that there's a certain amount of respect for the title and position that I hold and the responsibility I have. As a result, a lot of the sexist crap is cut out, 'cause they can't afford it."

Fantus laughed, an outrageous guffaw from such a slight woman.

"Some of those mill people would kiss me on the hand or on the cheek. And that was tough to deal with — at first. Depending on the person, it was really a matter of saying, 'I really would appreciate it if you would just not do that.' But so many times, with the older men, it was a matter of totally 'grossing' the guy out, so I'd throw in a 'fuck you,' and cure the problem."

Susan Fantus is perfectly capable of strong language. Like other women promoted to managerial ranks at Levi Strauss — there were 166 among the 792 executives throughout the corporation in 1977 — there is a quality of strength about her.* There is also a fillip of independence. Unlike men,

---

* Despite their number, none of the women as yet is a corporate officer. The highest-ranking woman is Karin Håkanson, director of product development, who reports directly to the corporation's chief operating officer, Robert Grohman. Finnish-born and educated, Håkanson is regarded as one of, if not *the* foremost textile engineer in the country. Her professional opinions carry great weight within the industry.

most women in America are not taught to be competitive team players. They are freer to make their own way in the business world. A Susan Fantus can decline afterwork cocktails — she doesn't drink — or ignore the weekend football scores, and still prosper. Men are held more rigidly to prescribed roles.

That year as a production scheduler was the first of her apprenticeship as a merchandiser. As described by Pete Jacobi, Fantus's immediate superior, "Merchandising is where you decide what to make, how many to make, and in what colors and fabrics. You purchase the fabric for as low a price as possible. You take the idea through prototype, sales samples, then coordinate with production for a place to make it on a timely basis, to make sure it is ready for delivery from the distribution centers." Jacobi leaned forward, a forefinger jabbing his desk. "The company lives or dies with its merchandisers in the final analysis."

Normally, the job demands a long apprenticeship. Al Sanguinetti spent thirteen years in a variety of positions before assuming charge of western wear. Harry Cohn — rated by some as the best merchandiser in the company — worked eleven years before he was awarded a line of casual slacks.

Many are called; fewer survive. "The dropout rate among merchandisers," Jim McDermott explained, "is not because they're fired for failure of a line they produce, but the pressure, and our saying, 'If you're not going to make it, get out.'

"Even in the training period, everyone has to carry their own weight. It's pretty easy to see which ones have the mental agility and can handle the strain. You have to have a pretty strong ego, too, because everyone is always bombarding you and no one's happy for more than one day."

According to McDermott, one of Levi Strauss's more successful merchandisers before he became an executive, it requires some seven years "before a merchandiser is really competent."

Still marveling at his own rapid rise, Pete Jacobi agreed. "On paper, there's no way in the world that the Jeans Division, the largest division of any apparel manufacturer in the world, should have a guy with four years' total merchandising experience being general merchandise manager."

He shook his head slowly. "I'll do it. I'll do my damnedest, get ulcers, or have a heart attack, or be successful, or any combination of all of them to do the job, but the fact is, we shouldn't have been in a position as a company that we had to call upon somebody like me."

But Levi Strauss in the 1970s was a vastly changed business from the dry-goods house of the 1940s. Sales increases and international expansion strained the company's ability to train executives. As Sanguinetti's senior managers were plucked for assignments in other divisions, the way opened for younger people, like Max Cowan, to move up rapidly.

In a more settled corporation, the dapper Texan would have spent most of his career climbing the corporate ladder before assuming responsibility for the production of clothing worth over $700 million annually. But when predecessor Tom Borrelli was named president of the Boyswear Division, the twenty-nine-year-old Cowan, just eight years out of North Texas State University, moved into the job of the Jeans Division's national production manager.

The manufacture of a pair of pants — the division runs between fifty and fifty-five construction types at any given time — is a well-established routine, little changed since the rationalization introduced a half-century ago by Milton Grunbaum. Automation is in its infancy; out of thirty-five actual cutting, stitching, and assembly operations necessary to produce a pair of 501s, only six have been fully mechanized. Levi Strauss introduces the automated equipment only when local managers request it, where dislocation can be controlled. None of Cowan's twenty-six plants has all six of the automated devices yet.

From the first sewing operation, serging the edge of the fly to prevent its fraying when the garment is washed, to the last, attaching belt loops, production proceeds from one end of the 130–operator line to the other.

Each of those lines is devoted to a single product, manufactured day after day, 10,000 per week. From the 9500 operators, mostly women, in twenty-six plants flow some seventy-five million Jeans Division garments annually.

And each of those production lines is a ganglion of human problems. "You know who would make a good line manager?" Paul Glasgow asked, his brows beetling skeptically. "That's probably a Mexican-American woman who lives in Albuquerque. She's got six kids, and her husband is sick half the time. She's got to make a living to feed those kids, and everything else."

Responsible for the line of 130 operators, that Mexican-American woman is a first-level manager. She earns between $14,000 and $15,000 a year, and for her the next step up the ladder is assistant plant manager, with a starting salary of $18,000.

The way is open. "A lot of our plant managers started as material handlers and came up through the ranks. We have several women coming along now," Cowan says in his north Texas drawl. Four of his twenty-six plant managers are Chicano, two of them Mexican citizens who cross the border each day to run Levi Strauss's Laredo, Texas, plants.

"The key man is the plant manager. The overwhelming characteristic they must have is the ability to handle people. If they can't do that, if they can't identify with their line managers and operators, black or Chicano, they don't make plant manager." The drawl toughened; Cowan had iterated the first rule of management.

Their problems are human, not technical. Turnover is an ever-present reality, its rate varying from job to job within the plants, and from area to area in the country. In those cities and towns where there is little job competition, turnover is lower. In those places where per capita income is high, turnover is high. In those towns where an operator's status is high — because of relatively good wages and/or a tight job market — turnover is low. An insensitive plant manager will complicate his usual problems.

Nonetheless, he must maintain production while holding garment defects to a minimum. Whatever the efforts to reduce human error, 8 percent of the garments that reach final inspection will be sent back because of defects. Ninety-eight percent of these, many of them machine-caused, can be repaired. The total seconds rate in all Jeans Division facilities is less than 1.5 percent; most industries, Cowan noted, expect 2.5 percent.

Operators, line managers, plant managers, and Cowan are all crucial to Susan Fantus's success as a merchandiser, more so now than at any time in the company's history.

Late in 1974, the fashion jeans market shifted radically. Levi's fashion jeans — in reality, then only a single garment offered in a variety of fabrics — stopped selling. Imports from the Far East, where cheap labor made patchwork denim and elaborate stitching economical, swept the market.

"What it forced us to do as a company," Pete Jacobi recalled, "was make some basic changes in the attitude of production people. They resisted change in the production lines." The longer a garment ran, the fewer problems they had; the higher their output, the lower the rejection rate. The Jeans Division, founded on the unchanging, unchangeable 501, had become fossilized.

Responding to the marketplace, the division sought to turn its factories around more than once a year — considered an impossibility — to produce more fashionable garments. "When finally faced with a situation where if you don't make the change and produce this garment or garments on a regular-type basis, we're going to shut you down, it's amazing what the production people were capable of doing," Jacobi commented wryly. Turnaround time plunged to six weeks in some plants.

McDermott, Cowan, Kasten, and Jacobi, with Fantus watching close at hand, rid the division of what the boss, Al Sanguinetti, called "the dinosaur in the tar pit" mentality. Levi Strauss's fashion jeans line could more closely follow the sales trends. "Some accounts say we're still a year behind, but our sales force thinks we're half a season to a season behind the trend-setters. That's as close as I want to get," Jacobi insisted.

It is Susan Fantus's responsibility to keep Levi Strauss's

$140 million fashion jeans line close to the market. She will produce four lines each year, major ones for spring and fall, smaller "sweeteners" for summer and the Christmas season. She works approximately nine months ahead of the first deliveries of her product to retail stores. (Shipments of a fall line are actually in some outlets early in March; the spring, in mid-August. This means that Fantus may not see models she is currently designing worn by customers for some sixteen months.) Mills, yarn-, and dye-makers will be three to six months farther ahead of her, preparing the fabrics and colors they will promote.

American fashion has no single source; the salons of Continental haute couture no longer dominate. Mills and manufacturers exchange ideas about appropriate colors and materials, each influencing the other. A fad in Atlanta or Tokyo or Amsterdam may be transformed into next year's fashion. The ideas come from everywhere and meld into the offerings of a handful of pacesetting manufacturers selling limited quantities to a select number of "trendy" shops. Not all of these will be successful; pacesetters are frequent bankrupts.

Four times a year, with twenty to thirty models, Susan Fantus attempts to capture that fashion and translate it into a garment for mass America. She travels to New York, examining piece goods and shopping boutiques. She visits retail accounts — Bloomingdale's in New York City is a personal favorite, "probably one of the more fashion-forward department stores," ironically not one "to carry a lot of my stuff and not a typical Levi's account by any means. But I'm shopping for ideas that are going to be on the market in six months or a year from now."

She also visits Montreal, "a very subtle market, interpreting European fashions for this continent." These she may attempt to retranslate for her eighteen-to-twenty-five-year-old American customer, who seeks a bit of styling flair but is not aggressively at the forefront of fashion.

Whatever trends she spots, *her* pants must have two back pockets, because her customer does not carry a purse. (Actually, a significant number of Fantus's pants are purchased by women who prefer to shop in young men's departments because of fit or styling. She may put in smaller sizes of a model she thinks will appeal to women, but the young male is her primary target.) Fantus's designs must have two front pockets, because the American man likes to put his hands in his pockets. It must have belt loops, because for the most part her customer feels insecure without a belt to keep his pants up.

Even more constricting, she cannot compromise on quality to reduce the retail price, a device of many fashion-oriented manufacturers who do not expect a garment to be worn very long. "Fashion jeans are not made less substantially than basic jeans. No, no." She shook her head rapidly, as if to brush away the evil thought. "I feel very strongly about this: put a Levi's tab on a garment, it's going to wear. Put out a garment and it's going to be a quality garment."

Searching for ideas about the cut, detailing, and color she must incorporate into her designs, Fantus scouts the fashionable shops of Beverly Hills. "Again, Beverly Hills is ridiculous." She laughs. "It has nothing to do with Levi's but ideas and feelings."

Retailers offer their ideas. There are regional differences to be considered. Los Angeles and New York seem to be fashion leaders, six months to a year in front of the rest of the nation. Atlanta is fashion-oriented but, like Dallas, prefers a flashier garment. Boston and the Northeast, San Francisco and the Northwest, are more conservative. Still more conservative is the great American Midwest, an area on which corporate executives intend to concentrate marketing efforts. Salesmen from all these areas must be convinced that there is something in the line for them and their accounts.

Any fashion jeans she designs must have validity in more than one area of the country. "It's not worth it if I can only sell fifty thousand units of a model. At a minimum, I must be able to support a ten thousand–unit line for six months, or two hundred and fifty thousand garments."

The numbers come easily for this young executive. "I

can't afford to do any speculative garments. If they failed, that would mean turning a factory too quickly.

"If a model is successful, I can support a line that's over thirty thousand units a week." She has done it, her most successful model run at the rate of 60,000 units a week to saturate the market.

Whatever the design, she must be conscious of what the industry calls "price points." Her bosses do not come to her with instructions to make a $9.95 garment. "If that need is out there, I better pick it up and find out how to do it. Coming up with a nice style is good, but I've got to be able to cost it where I think it will sell." That isn't always possible; after all, her initial competition relies on cheap labor and favorable import quotas.

Styling is the exciting part of her job — and the smallest. Jacobi estimates that a "merchandiser probably spends ninety-eight percent of his day keeping people working, the production facilities in fabric, solving quality problems, dealing with the distribution people. Two percent is on style, and that's usually after regular work hours."

It is then Fantus plans her major spring and fall lines and their 200 production codes — thirteen models in three fabrics, one of which is denim or brushed denim, the other two offered in an average of five colors. While she insists "there is a lot you can do" with even so mundane a garment, Fantus admits she is sometimes bored or satiated. Her own tastes in clothing are more basic. "I don't go in for the gimmicks and all that. I like wearing my Five-o-one, or the corduroy jean. But I'm an objective observer of the market. It's never what *I* don't like, or *I* wouldn't wear that. My tastes are very much different from my customer's."

She glances at her watch, frankly worried about an appointment with a mill representative showing a new fabric. He is not one of those who kissed her cheek, but a younger man more accustomed to dealing with women in executive positions.

Susan Fantus's success is measured in the number of models she can sustain for more than one season. Most of the first season is spent recouping the capital investment in equipment and operators' time lost during the production turnaround.

"Change a model, and you have to break all the mechanical habits of sewing a straight seam instead of a curved, or turning left instead of turning right," Jacobi explained.

"We protect the operators' wages. We're very conscious of average earnings. That's why it's very difficult making conversions from one model to another, why you want to continue to produce the same model as long as you possibly can." Turnaround times factored in, it costs from three to five times as much in labor costs to produce fashion jeans as basic jeans.

"Production is what makes fashion jeans happen," Fantus acknowledged. "It's not me sitting here saying we've got to do this or that. There's a tremendous amount of cooperation necessary if we're going to compete in fashions."

The second movement of a harpsichord concerto oozing around the edges of her conversation, Fantus admitted, "I have the last word. It's really my responsibility whether something goes into the line or doesn't, whether a factory is converted or not, whether we run ten thousand or twenty thousand a week of a garment.

"You make a decision that's wrong by three weeks, and they're grinding them out at twenty thousand a week, it's a pretty heavy decision." Wrong by a week, and a minimum of $100,000 in slow merchandise is shipped to the distribution centers, to be marked down drastically later in the year at crippling losses. If she should pick the wrong material or the wrong color, the $7 million in cloth for thirteen weeks' production of a single line may be lost.

One hundred and forty million dollars can be a heady responsibility. "If I stop to think about it, being larger than the Gals or Sportswear divisions, it's kind of frightening. 'Oh my God! I'm responsible for this huge department,' or 'Gee, I'm the most prominent woman here.'

"I don't even think about that. I know what I'm doing. I

know what the job is, and I try to keep all this within the realm of reality, and not some glory trip.

"The struggle to keep a sense of humor is very real — especially when Pete comes running down the hall, screaming about something. There are times I go home eating my stomach out, I'm so pissed or upset or confused. That's when I know I'm really struggling." She smiled faintly. There have been more than a few days like that this past year for the product manager of fashion jeans.

The job has inevitably influenced her private life. Fantus lives in a late-Victorian house of newels and knobs in San Francisco's Eureka Valley. She purchased it herself, almost to her surprise. "It's a perfect house, and buying it was very important to me." Her "roommate" — "I hate 'boy friend' and 'old man' " — confronts all the problems of the businessman's wife: jealousy, lack of attention, a fear of rejection.

A lawyer who has chosen to become a jazz pianist, he can be resentful of the hours Fantus spends at work. "I'm not home very much. I'm tired. Or I have a business dinner until midnight. My roommate wonders what I'm doing out that late, what there is to talk about."

Fantus and her roommate have worked out a mutually agreeable pact, each caring for him or herself. "There are shared responsibilities. I'm not in a position where I can depend upon him, nor do I want to be, nor do I want to put him in that role, dealing with household responsibilities because I work."

For all the groping, the competition, the problems both private and professional, there are worthwhile rewards. "I've made really important gains as a person. I feel better about myself in this job. I feel I've learned how to be a manager, which means not being a worker, but being able to delegate, motivate, transfer the pressure from my immediate boss to people who work for me. I've learned how to deal with division policies that come down that I may not necessarily believe in. I've learned how to fight for what I believe in."

Her success has led directly to Jacobi's decision not to scrap the small Fresh Produce line the Jeans Division had used as a test-market for its most advanced or forward-looking designs, those that attempt to compete head-to-head with the imported fashion leaders.

Its pocket tab carrying an embroidered carrot rather than the company name, Fresh Produce was sold to a select number of accounts when it was inaugurated in 1973. Its production runs were small, just 10,000 or 15,000 units; three former merchandisers had been unsuccessful with it.

A confident Fantus moved to open the line to all accounts, gambling that they would support the ten-to-twelve-thousand-a-week lines for three or four months. Fresh Produce would still be the fashion pioneer for the company, though "a lot of people would say we're not in fashion at all, but producing clothes for peer-group acceptance people, for people who need to see it for a while before buying it themselves."

Fresh Produce under her cultivation has flourished. "I think it is important because it gives us, our accounts, a jean that is a little more fashion-forward with that little carrot tab. It gives salesmen entrée to those accounts looking for something a little more radical."

But a line such as Fresh Produce, which deliberately attempts to follow hard on the heels of the instant fashions of the 1970s, increases the risks.

"Anybody who goes into merchandising, responsible for a large number of product codes such as Susan is, who thinks their creative ability and taste are so great they will never make a mistake; and their models all will be well accepted by the consumer whoses tastes vary, are fickle, and sometimes irrational, is absolutely crazy. You're bound to make mistakes," the spring-loaded Tom Kasten, vice-president of marketing for the Jeans Division, insisted. The quick-talking Kasten appears methodical, precise; even his carefully trimmed mustache and Vandyke enhance the efficiency embodied in the old-fashioned desk calculator on the hutch behind him.

"The thing that separates good from bad merchandisers is the ability to know where to take risks, and the ability, once a mistake is recognized by the failure, to book up to potential, to minimize the loss."

Kasten's reputation, *his* career in the company, is dependent on Fantus's performance to some extent; he selected her for "the cherry job" others desired. A former merchandiser, he can be tolerant — to a point — for he himself has brought out "losers and dogs," he admitted with a rueful smile. "And they performed exactly as you would expect. Like losers and dogs." The image of the corporate overachiever softens. There is something more to him than Plossl and White's *Production Control,* lying on the hutch within easy reach. On top of that textbook lay a collection of humorous essays by S. J. Perelman.

Fantus, too, will sponsor losers and dogs. Too many, and Susan Fantus, Kasten's protégée, will become an ex-merchandiser. Neither Kasten nor Jacobi could protect her or covertly take on her job. Both are overcommitted already.

Fantus recognizes the possible consequences; as they say in the garment trade, "It comes with the territory." This is the territory she chose, and she is confident of her ability. "People want things black and white. The fashion market is very volatile, and you can't be wrong," she explained.

The appearance of certainty even when decisions are not clear-cut, and no fashion decision is, marks the successful executive. Kasten exudes it in the quick answers to difficult questions; Jacobi has it, too. These young men are winners, and they expect to go on winning. With Fantus.

Merchandisers alone can judge merchandisers. Kasten was guarded, awaiting the "numbers" for the forthcoming spring season. "Susan's very intelligent and aggressive. She grew into the job very well. Overall, she has a good feeling for the market. Her merchandising acumen allowed her to concentrate on other areas, and Susan's smart enough to know when to ask for help and where to go. It was on-the-job training, but she's a fast learner."

Sanguinetti, who might be expected to be more critical, is actually more enthusiastic. "She has good disciplines in inventory control and production. It's tough to introduce these into fashion. I've seen too many guys in this company not look at this, and face tremendous write-downs. She has the savvy to keep abreast of the young men's market and what it's going to be." He smiles broadly; his gamble paid off.

"She has the confidence of the salespeople and has been instrumental in multiplying the breadth and size of the line." For the entrepreneurial Al Sanguinetti, that is important.

"It's been tough for her, competing against the imports. Forty-cent labor versus three-dollar-and-thirty-cent labor. Our markup is fifty percent. The import stuff starts at, *starts at,* fifty-six percent to sixty percent. It's very attractive to a retailer."

What they speak of as "the downside" is modest. "Our closeouts have gone from five percent to seven percent, but in the fashion business, seven percent isn't bad. It's been successful as far as I'm concerned."

Fantus herself is more cautious. "I'm waiting for the numbers. How the numbers come out means you meet plan or don't meet plan."

She shook her head suddenly. "No. It's more than how the numbers come out. It's what people think of me. Do people respect me? Can I deal with a certain amount of authority and get things done?"

Merchandising can be crushing. Young recruits to the company have shunned it for the more lucrative sales, staff, and production jobs. Traditionally underpaid — though the wage is being adjusted — merchandisers at Levi Strauss have had to work long hours for half the salesmen's $40,000 annual salary.

The survivors are the most hardened veterans and those most likely to be promoted in this merchandising-oriented company. Susan Fantus, at twenty-eight, is content where she is for the moment.

"I guess I don't see myself rising in the corporation. The next move I make is a very serious decision, because what I have done and done well is pull together models and make them real, make them happen. To go further in the company is to become more involved in administration, more involved in planning, financial figures, things like that.

"Part of my responsibility is to make the department profitable, so I can cope with financial sheets. But I am not divorced from the product. If it's a good line, I get credit for it. If it's a bad line, I get — " she paused — "credit for it."

Susan Fantus laughed that outrageous laugh, a moment's counterpoint to the Mozart string quartet.

Chapter XII

Lean and Mean

PETER THIGPEN was in over his head. He knew it; his wife, Judy, knew it, too. During the sleepless nights, after their sons were asleep, they would lie in bed talking about it, Judy shoring up his sagging ego, assuring him that whatever happened, they would make out all right; Pete would not be out of a job for long, he was too good.

Maybe he was, but at thirty-two Pete Thigpen wasn't good enough to manage Levi Strauss International's $100-million-a-year business in Europe. It had grown too fast, over 400 percent in just four years. It was too big, too sprawling, for one man to manage. Twenty-three people in thirteen countries reported directly to him — too many, too many. Seven local production plants with their supply lines stretched around the world. My God, he thought, it took them nine months to get product. No wonder the inventory was out of control.

Perhaps if Ed Combs were alive, they could have pulled it out. But Combs had died in the crash of his twin-engine Beechcraft on the small landing strip near Visalia. And Pete Thigpen, for the first time in his short business career, was facing a crisis without Combs's guidance.

Thigpen went to work for Levi Strauss International in June 1967, fresh out of Stanford Business School, as Combs's assistant. Combs himself was one of the major reasons Thigpen had accepted the job; Combs and the company's reputation. Combs was dynamic, a financial wizard, at thirty-three general manager of the company's entire foreign operation. Hired away from Time-Life International, since 1964 he had built Levi's overseas from an $8 million to a $228 million enterprise scattered across the globe. Their success had varied from country to country, but Ed Combs had delivered, first on the bottom line, profits, and then, as the jeans boom swept the world, on the top line, gross sales.

For eighteen months, Thigpen had been a part of it, at Combs's side, watching him open up new markets, expand production and distribution around the world, transform Levi Strauss into a multinational corporation. Then Combs kept his promise to send Thigpen overseas; at the age of thirty, Pete Thigpen moved to Brussels to become general merchandise manager for all of Europe.

In retrospect, Thigpen realized just how green he was. The only merchandising experience he had had was in dealings with the old Jeans Department for Combs. He had never had responsibility for buying piece goods or scheduling production. Now he had to do it, overcoming all the problems of low productivity — no one was as productive as the American worker, he had learned — and the barriers of language and customs, not just in Europe but as far away as Hong Kong and Mexico, where some of their piece goods and finished garments were produced. Quality control was a joke; Levi Strauss's garments in Europe and the Far East were too often poorly made, with fabric domestic divisions would have rejected out of hand.

Still, he had survived, buoyed by the phenomenal jeans boom. Denim, corduroy, basic jeans, fashion jeans, jackets — everything they marketed sold. The boom continued through Thigpen's ten months as marketing director, then for most of his first year as general manager for Europe. Not until September 1972 did he get his first glimmer that something was wrong.

The company had taken over all but one of its European distributors at Combs's direction, buying out the locals and dealing directly with retailers, as was company practice in the United States and Canada. It had been a mistake, he realized, explaining to Judy, "Maybe those guys were doing a pretty good job, and maybe they knew a lot about the market we didn't." Combs and the young entrepreneurs he gathered about him had been too cocksure, too certain they would be able to duplicate the American experience in Europe. Now they needed those local distributors. Badly.

After the years of growth, after reaching $100 million in sales, the market had suddenly matured. The upward curve of Levi Strauss sales had flattened. It caught highflying Pete Thigpen and Levi Strauss with huge inventories for the new year and more on the way. Compounding the problem, most of their pants were straight-legged, and the volatile European market had taken a fancy to flared bottoms and to bell bottoms of all sizes and silhouettes.

Until that time, Thigpen believed he had done the best job possible. Looking back, he saw the overseas divisions had committed almost as many mistakes as his business school textbooks had warned about. Levi Strauss's present predicament would make a great case study for graduate school, he thought wryly.

The company had outrun its management resources, literally run out of trained managers, and then compounded the situation by buying up the foreign distributors and opening new manufacturing plants. That was mostly an inherited problem, Thigpen realized; not his fault, but he had exacerbated it. "Trying to be all things to all people, selling jeans, sportswear, womens' wear, shirts, I failed to bore in on the blue jeans market and build myself a stake there. It was a classic business mistake, failing to define what business we were in." International was spread too thin, too eager to raise the flag and beat out competitors. Worse, the managers simply lacked control over the whole business.

By the spring of 1973, Thigpen recognized that his European Division was in grave trouble. There were too many goods on hand and too much on the way, considering that sales had slackened. There would be write-downs, he knew; large ones.

Hoping to salvage something, Thigpen had started to flush the slow movers from the inventory but again made a mistake an old-timer would not have. He sold off the easiest ones first, not the toughest.

He was working longer and longer hours and accomplishing less and less. San Francisco had dispatched a team to shore up the European staff, a half-dozen men with experience in inventory control, finance, distribution, merchandising, and marketing to help him. Some would remain for eighteen months; all would be rewarded with big promotions for their efforts. Mel Bacharach, named executive vice-president at Combs's death, pushed aside everything — including the chain of retail shops he was opening — to work on the dead-inventory problem. It was the first substantial influx of trained managers into the European Division, and it was coming too late.

Initially, the team believed the inventory could be sold off for a loss of perhaps $5 million. Ed Pera, sent to Europe as assistant corporate controller, kept revising the figures. "We frankly didn't know what the hell we had in inventory. In May, June nineteen seventy-three, we'd have one figure, and two hours later another, fifty percent higher." Even as Pera tabulated the columns, the inventory piled up when new shipments, ordered nine months earlier, continued to arrive. Goods accumulated on the docks, were inadvertently left to the elements, discovered, and dealt off for pennies on the dollar.

Thigpen was determined to end the plunge that year, no matter how great the loss on the inventory. It was better in a business sense to write it off entirely, to take the loss at one time, than to have it reported over two or more quarters. Even if it cost him his job.

"It's very subjective," he said later. "You look at a pair of green pants and say that's worth four dollars or it's not worth much more than a dollar twenty-five. I wanted to make sure I wasn't overvaluing anything."

The team in Europe tried dumping the pants in secondary markets — Africa, the Soviet Union, in other eastern European countries where the company was not established. Distributors there were hard-bargainers, and the price fell farther. Five years later, it would still bother Ed Pera. "I didn't predict the loss properly. The minute I hit Europe in April of seventy-three I said we have a five-million-dollar loss. But no one knew the magnitude of the inventory, that garments would go from a sell of ten dollars to a sell of fifty cents. That's never happened in the history of the apparel business. We just had too much to move."

The European crisis, a "debacle," according to Wall Street analysts, resulted in a vast house-cleaning. Out of eleven general managers, each jealously responsible for an individual country, nine were let go. Pera "cleaned out twenty financial people in the space of six months, almost all of the financial people. From middle to top management, between fifty and seventy-five, out of ninety, were fired."

On November 1, 1973, success-conditioned Levi Strauss & Co. announced that it expected a fourth-quarter loss, the first losing quarter since the Depression. The stock, which a year before had reached a high of $59.75 per share, plummeted to $16.62.

The effect on morale within the company was equally devastating. "The European disaster," Peter Haas, Sr., said ruefully, "burst the bubble. Our pride was hurt."

Walter, Jr., agreed. "It was one of the worst six months of my life, very bad, not so much for the monetary loss, but for the pride. It was a reflection on our management. A big part of it was that so many little people here were let down. We were terribly distressed about the stock because we had made a point of setting aside shares for our own employees when we went public. They were unsophisticated investors, and this debacle, coupled with the huge drop in the stock market generally — " Haas's voice faltered, the disappointment still keen, five years later.

"We always felt, it can happen to the other guy, it can't happen to us. And it caused us to reflect an awful lot on what we had done wrong.

"We were so proud of the image of Levi Strauss as successful and well managed." He paused. "I'm not saying it very well." He sighed. "It was traumatic, that's all."

Shortly after the fourth-quarter loss of $12 million was announced publicly, the stock plunging and his employees suffering severe financial setbacks, Walter Haas sat in the Brussels office of the young manager responsible for the trauma.

Pete Thigpen had matured during the year, no longer cocky, a good deal more humble. A tough year such as he had weathered constituted five times the experience of an easy year.

While Thigpen cleared his desk of the day's work, the chairman of the board of directors waited in a chair opposite him, hidden behind the international edition of the *Herald Tribune*.

Tentatively, the young man asked, "Walter, let me ask you a question, if you don't mind. Why didn't you fire me?"

There was a pause. The paper rattled, then Haas lowered it. "That's a very interesting question."

"Let me tell you why I asked. If you did fire me, it would relieve you of some of the tremendous heat you must be taking from the financial community, the shareholders, the board of directors, and so on, to be able to say, 'We know we have a problem in Europe, but we are making a major management change.' Why keep the same guy?"

Haas pursed his lips, nodded, then answered. "Well, we paid a lot of tuition, and we want to get a return on the tuition we paid."

Levi Strauss is not a "quick-knife" company, as one international manager put it. Thigpen stayed, though other companies had offered him jobs during the worst of the crisis, always with the assurance, "We know you're getting a hell of an education." Still, he realized the taint would follow him, and Thigpen was stubborn enough to want to recoup at Levi's. He managed to break even in the first quarter of 1974.

It would take the young manager three and a half years before he felt he had repaid the $12 million tuition. First, he was demoted.

In May 1974, the company reorganized its European Division into three parts. Thigpen was placed in charge of a southern bloc of countries including Switzerland, Italy, Spain, and France. Central and northern Europe each had autonomous managers, and all three reported directly to San Francisco. By the end of 1975, all of Gaul having been divided into three parts, Thigpen was given responsibility for both the southern and central portions.

"My career has been like a wild roller-coaster ride." On March 1, 1977, he was again named divisional president in Europe, "which means I got the whole thing back again." Europe was twice as large, with $200 million in annual sales, when Thigpen regained the presidency lost three years before.

It was a much different organization by then. The European collapse — people at the San Francisco home office tend to agree with Wall Street's harsh evaluation of the affair — was a sobering experience. "It was a shattering blow to the psyche of the company," Thigpen acknowledged. "The company took a tremendous battering. In retrospect we'll probably look at it as a plus, because we learned we're not infallible, that the label won't burn through all the mistakes. It made us in Europe a lot more lean and mean, a lot more professional."

It was not quite a debacle, Walter said later. "We're a better company for it." Peter agreed. "It was a good thing for the long term. It made us realize the top line wasn't important; it was the bottom line. Sales for sales' sake didn't mean anything. It certainly made us think about Dad's philosophy, which has essentially been more conservative. I remember in years past he said, 'How big do you want to grow? Do you have to keep running that fast?' " *

Though the company rebounded, its stock did not. Frank

* In its errors as well as its successes, the company maintained uncommon candor. An article by editor Elaine Ratner in the house organ, *Saddleman's Review,* for Spring 1975, noted: "Levi Strauss International ran into serious problems with high, hard to move inventories, and its meteoric rise abruptly turned into a nosedive that cost the division, and the company, $12 million and had a profoundly sobering effect on Levi's exuberant approach to international business. *Fortune* magazine, in an article that still makes a lot of people wince, declared that 'Levi Strauss burst its britches.' The phrase, unfortunately, was apt."

Brann, moved from the presidency of the expanding Boyswear Division to head the central European area, would see
a backlash from the investment community. It was less than
two years prior to the collapse that Levi Strauss had gone
public, its shares sold in an afternoon, its price rising dramatically. Then Wall Street was stung; a bad quarterly report undercut analysts' glowing recommendations. Levi
Strauss was just another cyclic apparel firm, despite its size.
"The investment community had gotten on the bandwagon,"
Brann recalled, "and recommended us, a funny little San
Francisco apparel firm. I guess they felt had. Therefore they
came down on us like a ton of bricks, and we're still suffering from that in terms of the way they couch their positive comments about the company." Despite new sales and
profit records, Levi Strauss & Co. stock would maunder for
two years between $12.50 and $22.00 per share.

It was precisely because Levi Strauss was a "funny" apparel firm that the company recruited the man who would
make it both lean and mean.

Robert Grohman was a forty-nine-year-old easterner who
had grown weary after more than thirty years in the apparel
business, including stints as head of International Playtex's
overseas operations and later as president of B.V.D. Co.
Something was missing; the opportunistic companies of Seventh Avenue seemed to have lost sight of the human values
Grohman believed important.

Late in 1973, Grohman told his wife, Betty, after a particularly discouraging day, that he was considering leaving the
industry. "There's only one company in this business I'd
consider working for."

"What's that?"

"Levi Strauss."

"Why?"

"First of all, because I'm fundamentally interested in a
branded company, and they're supreme in the industry, and
second, what I know about the company's sensitivity to people. That's something that's getting more and more difficult
to hold on to in large companies."

Two weeks later, shortly after Christmas, Grohman related, "I had this call; it was almost like Divine Providence."

The caller was one of those specialists disparagingly referred to in business circles as a "headhunter," a person who ferrets out high-ranking managers willing to change corporations.

In sixty seconds, Grohman recounted, the headhunter delivered his pitch. Levi Strauss was looking for someone to head up its international operations. The search had narrowed to three or four; Grohman headed the list. "Levi Strauss is in serious difficulty overseas, made some serious mistakes, needs someone with your background and experience to fix it, and that someone has to have credentials and potential to achieve even higher stature in the organization in a short period of time. The company is extremely embarrassed, extremely hurt about what happened to it overnight, wants to correct it as soon as possible, and wants to restore the integrity of management to the shareholders and, most important, to its employees, who really never had tasted adversity."

Intrigued, Grohman met with the recruiter in a motel room in Virginia. (Such executive searches are generally conducted in great secrecy.) Above all else, the job would be challenging, and Grohman enjoyed restoring corporations, like B.V.D., which had fallen on hard times. Now the largest apparel company in the world — and the most celebrated — was bidding for his healing powers. If nothing else, it was flattering.

A week later, Walter Haas, Jr., called from San Francisco, offering to fly to New York and meet with the restless Grohman. Haas was the first person from Levi Strauss whom Grohman had ever met. They spent two hours together, Haas candidly explaining the company's European embarrassment, then discussing their mutual business philosophies.

If there were significant differences between the two men, they lay in the amount of freedom individual managers were to be given. The Haas brothers had allowed their managers virtually free rein. (Harry Cohn, for example, had chosen to rename his division "Panatela," so as to avoid the blue denim image conjured by calling it "Levi's Sportswear"; Walter was opposed, but acceded. "I'm not omniscient. They're closer to the market. How could I hold whoever was responsible for results until I went along with his marketing philosophy?" Even when that philosophy discarded one of the company's strongest assets, the very name "Levi's.") In contrast, Grohman advocated tightly controlled operations with strict accountability. A personally friendly man, Grohman was neither rigid nor closed to fresh ideas; managers, however, would not be permitted to venture forth on their own. Those who did discovered that Grohman's affability vanished.

For all the success of Levi Strauss under the Haases' laissez-faire philosophy, Walter had come to realize that a $653-million-a-year corporation with 29,000 employees was too large, too diversified, to be managed effectively by personalities rather than policies.

At the end of the meeting, Haas asked Grohman if he would be willing to fly to San Francisco to discuss the move further. Despite the fact that his proposed compensation would be less than he earned at B.V.D., Grohman agreed, and Haas promised to call in a week or ten days.

"I left Walter and walked back to my office, a fifteen- to twenty-minute walk. About ten minutes after I got there, the phone rang, and Walter wanted to know if I could go to San Francisco the next day with my wife. 'I just couldn't wait for a week or ten days. I want you to come out now.' "

Grohman spent three days in San Francisco, privately meeting at his request with twelve of Levi Strauss's senior executives. "There was a lot of apprehension, a fair amount of defensiveness, a desire to tell me that this was a good company, that they knew what they were doing, and it was the young managers in the international area who got the rest into trouble.

"Feelings toward International were sharp, severe, and negative. They came through from just about everyone who remembered that a lot of employees were stockholders, and people were hurt personally as well as the company they were a part of."

Grohman was aware of a mixed reception. "I was being tested by everyone in terms of my knowledge, my experience, my ability. These were managers of the most successful company in the industry, managers who felt they didn't need anyone else. Levi Strauss was a company that had the record of bringing most people in through the stockroom and having them grow up to the levels they were capable of, a company that was extremely proud, a company built on a lot of integrity."

Levi Strauss was inbred, and Grohman an outsider. "It was like a heart transplant. Would the body reject it, even though in rejecting it the body might stop functioning?"

Grohman's immediate problem would be Europe. Beyond that, he would be charged with bringing order to the entire international organization. Its operations in more than twenty countries were uncoordinated; sales, erratic. In Japan, theoretically a lucrative market, it was doing poorly; Japanese firms early on had pre-empted the field by passing themselves off as American companies, even going so far as to shoot television commercials, using white actors, in the United States. Australia was fertile ground; New Zealand, underdeveloped. Argentina was well run, but the manager of the new Brazilian operation had hired a designer whose line included sequined brassières. Each country seemingly chose its own products, attempting to blanket the market with clothing for men, women, teen-agers, and children. The potential for future "Europes" was enormous.

There had been merit in Combs's never clearly articulated concept of rushing into markets and staking out a claim; it was easier to be first than to dislodge competitors. But the "General Patton" philosophy, of taking the high ground and securing the rear later, could prove risky. There were no controls, the organization's supply lines had been stretched to breaking, and the lack of experienced managers became apparent once the boom slowed.

"The fundamental thing in this business," Grohman said in a later interview, "is the changing value of merchandise because of consumer choice. The great trick is to keep your merchandise current and to recognize when it's becoming obsolete. That's why many companies in this industry are heroes for eleven months and bums for the twelfth, why many companies go Chapter Eleven [bankrupt] after their best season."

Grohman confronted the European situation first. "Each general manager in Europe's thirteen countries was doing his own thing, and making his own decisions on merchandise, contracting work, jealous of his prerogatives. L-E-V-I-S was being put on garbage, on products that were not worthy of the name. There was a total fragmentation of effort."

Five days after his arrival in San Francisco, Grohman left for Europe. He stayed for five weeks, picking up from Mel Bacharach, reshaping the entire division. He later estimated that the $12 million loss at the end of 1973 in Europe could have been tripled worldwide if there had not been quick action.

Ultimately, Grohman charged a handful of area managers with the responsibility of merchandising. He eliminated all women's wear from those lines, cut back on boys' wear, and reduced stock-keeping units by one-half. The emphasis was placed on men's basic jeans, rather than on fashion items, permitting longer production runs and greater efficiency. Each region was organized to be nearly self-sufficient, with its own factories locally producing the much narrower lines of clothing. The managers drastically trimmed the number of accounts selling Levi's, reducing sales costs while limiting themselves only to those stores willing to provide customer service.

Finally, he gathered together another $12 million of slow-moving merchandise and arranged to deal it off in secondary markets outside Europe, where the "garbage" would not further tarnish Levi's image.

Over this organization Grohman instituted controls — of production, of inventory, of planning, of merchandising — controls that had been ignored in the hectic rush to capture the lion's share of the market.

"I don't think it was an 'old management did it wrong and

a new management did it right' thing," Grohman explained in a far-ranging discussion. "It was a case of previous management having had normal objectives, racing to achieve them, and failing to recognize exposures being created. On the other side, that same management called for corrective action; the people responsible for the problem were responsible, too, for the turnaround."

Some of the more entrepreneurial-minded resisted Grohman's constricting pressure. The one-time Levi's salesman who opened Levi Strauss Canada and built it into a $50-million-a-year enterprise could not bend his traditional attitudes, declined a job offer in the home office, and left the company. Two ranking executives shunted aside in the reorganization of the International Group left Levi's for other companies. Both had been hired by Combs from outside Levi Strauss for international positions, were relative newcomers, and went on to more entrepreneurial companies.

(Grohman was resented in San Francisco as well. Given expanded authority later over the highflying domestic divisions, Grohman moved to institute the same kind of checks. One division president challenged Grohman to show him a single control not then in effect that "would add to the bottom line." Another manager, angered by what he felt was undue credit accorded Grohman for the European recovery, went to some lengths to make it clear that Mel Bacharach had stopped the flow of red ink before Grohman joined the company, in March 1974. A senior member of the staff snarled when Grohman's name was mentioned, complaining about "easterners who come in here without understanding Levi's and our values." Not until December 1977 did Grohman himself feel he had overcome the animus and had both domestic and international groups cooperating; diplomatically, he pointed out that the redirection and reorganization of Levi Strauss "has been accomplished with essentially the same management before and after.")

The 1974 annual report validated Grohman's efforts. They had averted further international disasters, confining the decline to a one-quarter lapse. Despite the worldwide recession caused by the Arab oil boycott, Levi Strauss sales increased more than one-third, to $987.6 million. It was the largest increase, both in dollars and as a percentage, in corporate history. More important, profits that had skidded to $11.8 million with the European loss of 1973 ballooned to $34.8 million.

The following year, insistence on controlled growth taking hold, the company still broke through the billion-dollar sales mark. Thirty years before, at the very beginning of the baby boom that was to propel it to international prominence, the "funny San Francisco apparel house" had sold $3.1 million worth of Double X waist overalls. In 1975, with literally thousands of styles, models, and colors of pants, slacks, vests, jackets, shirts, and sweaters in the lines, it had surpassed $1.01 billion. The profits of $117.5 million were larger than all corporate sales had been just eleven years earlier.

To celebrate the billion-dollar sales year, Levi Strauss awarded each of its more than 29,000 employees with more than six months' service either shares of stock or a $50 cash bonus. Some 2700 divided 23,000 shares worth about $1 million on the basis of job grade and seniority. Levi Strauss paid all income taxes on these awards, bringing the total cost of the celebration to over $2.1 million. Milton Grunbaum, long retired to an honorary director's chair, had lived to see the concept of his $5.00 Christmas bonus magnified a thousandfold.

At the same time, the Haas brothers repaid a self-imposed moral debt to the employees of the company who had retired during the two years when corporate stocks had sunk as low as $12 a share. Because profit-sharing was tied to the price of the stock, those who had retired between 1973 and the end of 1975, and had cashed in on their participation, received less than they might have had the European disaster not ravaged the market value. For those employees, Levi Strauss & Co. recalculated the benefits in terms of the revived market price, and gratuitously paid out from profits an additional $1 million to them.

Grohman, meanwhile, was hammering out a management

charter for his International Group, a series of documents he insisted "is not there for window dressing, or to have something to show to people and say we're do-gooders."

The charter codifies Levi Strauss's obligations as a multinational corporation; numbered and receipted copies are distributed to all international managers, who are held to the letter of corporate law. "We've fired managers as recently as nineteen seventy-seven for indiscretions. It doesn't matter in terms of magnitude — sixty dollars or six hundred or sixty thousand. That's not the criterion. The criterion is if the charter is knowingly violated," Grohman stressed.

Grappling with the major issues on which multinational corporations have been faulted, among other points, Levi Strauss's charter stipulates:

> The company is committed to operating well above the minimum legal standard such that its conduct and intentions are above question . . .

> The company recognizes the influence it possesses by virtue of its size. It also recognizes its responsibility to ensure that this influence is not brought to bear on any partisan political activities within any country . . .

> The company will use to as great an extent as possible local sources of management, labor, raw material, and service when price, quality, and service are competitive . . .

> The company subscribes to a single global philosophy of fair treatment of employees that is also consistent with local laws and practices . . .

> The company applauds the laws of all countries which prohibit restraints of trade, unfair practices, or abuse of economic power and will itself avoid such practices in areas of the world where laws do not prohibit them . . .

Recognizing an international social responsibility, Levi Strauss's charter attempts to export its domestic philosophy: "The company will employ people without discrimination, ensure that they are properly trained, sufficiently motivated, and fairly paid, and ensure both job safety and the safety of its products." Beyond that, "the company pledges to assume a position of leadership and involvement, and encourages its employees to do the same on an individual basis, in an effort to support and develop matters of non-partisan public service."

The statement concludes with an enforcement clause: "Any employee who may have knowledge of, or reason to suspect, a breach of the preceding principles is obligated to immediately inform his or her immediate superior not involved in the breach of principle. Any such employee may, at his or her sole discretion, inform a higher level of management, including the office of the president."

Despite such implied mandates in the past, Levi Strauss was sorely embarrassed twice in 1976, the first time when it announced publicly that an unnamed foreign subsidiary had made "improper payments" of $75,000, to local officials; the second time when a thorough management audit revealed three additional under-the-table payoffs, totaling $70,000. In all four cases, Levi Strauss asserted, the payments were made by local managers without the knowledge of San Francisco — certainly without its consent — "seemingly for a continuation of good relations without anything specific tied to them."

The company that prided itself on its civic virtue had feet of clay. Realistically, the $145,000 passed in four foreign countries during 1974 and 1975 had little impact on either international sales or profits, but the disclosure left Levi Strauss red-faced.

To prevent reoccurrences, Grohman created a dual responsibility for the disbursement of funds overseas. Normally relaxed, the chief operating officer became increasingly intense, his words more clipped. "We are extremely rigid and very firm that if any manager anywhere in the world takes an action that's in violation of that code, he is in severe trouble. As a minimum we tell him that if there's an action that violates the code — not your country's laws — you re-

quire a partner. Go to the next level of management, the
area manager, and if he concurs, he's taking upon himself
the responsibility for action. He, in turn, has every right
and is urged to go to his division president, and the division
president to me. *You're going to get in trouble if you take
the action on your own.*"

Further, local controllers had a separate responsibility to
report questionable disbursements to San Francisco. "Those
controllers can be in severe trouble just by being party to
something, even if they did not initiate it."

Both controllers and managers are likely to be nationals of
the countries in which they are employed by Levi Strauss.
Fewer than 10 percent of the overseas managers are United
States citizens.

For the corporation, the question remains: Will a national
blow the whistle on another national? Grohman was less
than convincing. "The very essence of a multinational corporation is to develop a management code and philosophy
that can be administered ignoring national origins."

Striving to maintain its posture as Caesar's wife, Levi
Strauss International has abandoned its own sales operations
in Indonesia, a potentially valuable market of 111 million
people, of whom 60 percent are under thirty, the corporation's prime sales target. "We really can't operate down
there because of the ethics policy," a well-placed company
executive conceded. "In Indonesia, you can't get anything
done without bribing somebody. We sell to a distributor
down there whom we hold to sticking to our standards of
ethics. Well —" He was doubtful. "I'm sure if we knew
about it we'd stop it immediately, if anything's going on, but
the whole nature of life there is keeping things secret."

Thus, Levi Strauss International has shifted the burden to
an Indonesian distributor — forgoing the middleman's profits it enjoys elsewhere in the world, in order to keep its own
slate clean. The reduced profit is a small price to pay to protect its trademarks in that nation of islands. The company
bends its ostensibly rigid code; the alternative would be to
abandon the market entirely, knowing that Taiwanese and

Hong Kong manufacturers, willing to counterfeit Levi's, stand ready to bribe greedy officials as well.*

Despite the problems inherent in the operation of a multi-national corporation, international sales are the company's immediate growth area. Selling almost $500 million worth of goods overseas, for the balance of the 1970s, the corporation will focus attention on its foreign operations.

Levi Strauss International starts from a huge base. Putting its emphasis on basic jeans — corduroy pants and preshrunk versions of the Double X pant are the strongest sellers — restoring fashion garments and sportswear to the international lines only as the company reaches saturation in the basic jeans business, Levi Strauss has vast areas yet to explore.

The nations of eastern Europe, where Levi's jeans still black-market at prices four and five times the American cost; the Middle East and especially Turkey; Africa and the Indian subcontinent; and, mammoth market beyond all markets, the People's Republic of China — all are virgin territory.

Europe, despite its well-developed status, offers the greatest market potential. According to Pat Manning, market researcher for the far-flung international organization, "Jeans are not found everywhere in Europe. They are in major metropolitan centers, but not in the countryside. In France, for example, jeans are sold in Paris and on the south coast, and that's it." Scandinavia has a fledgling sales organization; it is one of those areas, according to Manning, "where we're

* The counterfeiting of Levi's, down to the last trademark and stitch, plagues the company. Ersatz 501s and its zippered kin, the most frequently copied, have turned up in twenty-four countries. In Italy, Levi's were the number one–selling jean, and counterfeit Levi's the number two — until company security officers, in 1975, helped local authorities close two plants turning out the faked Levi's. In August 1977, Swiss and Dutch police seized 52,000 pairs of imitation Levi's worth an estimated $800,000, and arrested four people for manufacturing the garments in South Korea for resale in eastern Europe. The following month, the company filed a civil action in federal court seeking damages of more than $5 million against four people who allegedly conspired to manufacture bogus Levi's in Taiwan for sale in Continental Europe.

in business not because we did a market-feasibility study and said, 'That's a good fit; let's go in.' We're there because Levi's were being black-marketed, or brought in through the back door from a U.S. dealer who sold overseas at three times the domestic price."

The company's first serious penetration in eastern Europe was negotiated by Mel Bacharach in early 1977, when he signed a contract with a Hungarian manufacturer to produce Levi's denim pants. Under terms of the agreement, Levi Strauss will ship yardage into Hungary, then export a portion of the plant's output for sale in jeans-short western Europe. The balance will be sold in Hungary and other eastern satellite nations.

The agreement is typical of the complicated arrangements multinational corporations must adopt to do business across international frontiers. The Hungarian government restricts the outward flow of its currency. Levi Strauss, by accepting its profits on the sale of pants in that nation in the form of finished goods, meets the government's regulation and still has needed garments for western European sales. It is not quite the unfettered free trade that Levi Strauss advocates, but it is practical.

Canada and Latin America are less likely growth areas, the one because of a relatively small population, the other because of minimal per capita income. Levi Strauss and its wholly owned subsidiary, GWG, already hold 40 percent of the jeans market north of the border; a larger share is possible if the company can increase its sales in the eastern provinces. Brazil, finally rid of its sequined brassières, and Argentina can provide the other nations of South America for the foreseeable future; Chile is likely to be the next country to be opened. Production in Mexico, once intended for Europe, will be sold entirely in Central America. (While Mexico is close enough to provide the United States with garments, as a matter of corporate policy Levi Strauss intends to manufacture and sell its garments within the same market. The company imports for sale in the United States only a limited number of shirts and sweaters made in the Far East, so as to be competitive with other American clothing houses.)

The Far East, according to one well-placed corporate source, remains "a disaster area. Grohman was a hero in Europe, and attempted to do the same thing in Japan, but was not successful." There were more than 100 Japanese manufacturers already producing denim pants when Levi Strauss opened for business in that country in 1970. A significant number of Japanese consumers believes that the locally owned, best-selling Big John is actually the original blue denim pant. Belatedly into that market — which Manning considers the most fashion-conscious in the world — the company initially assumed that the label alone would carry the firm to success. Then poorly made goods, badly sized for the smaller Japanese, were imported from Hong Kong and the Philippines, and sales lagged further. Unaccustomed to the severe competition, manned by people with scant garment experience, bewildered by constant, instant fashion changes, the company could not push sales beyond 5 percent of that $400 million market.

Grohman and the restructured international group confronts this potential market in a stronger position than ever before. The scattered baronies of twenty-five individual countries have been regrouped, their managerial staffs remanned, largely with experienced nationals operating on familiar turf. Each geographic division produces about 85 percent of the garments it sells; no longer do supply conduits stretch across continents and long periods of time. More manageable product lines have been narrowed to the level occupied by the domestic Levi Strauss of the early 1960s. Advertising will be coordinated, as it never has been, centering on the themes that made Levi Strauss successful in the United States — leisure and durability. Gradually, the corporation is becoming a marketing-oriented company — one that must compete with worthy rivals — rather than a merchandising-oriented firm that could not produce fast enough to satisfy the demand for its products.

Through the middle years of the 1970s, overseas sales accounted for one third of Levi Strauss's total revenues, somewhat less than one third of the profits. By the end of the decade, both figures will approach one-half, as overseas markets gain the "jeans maturity" Manning has postulated — the psychological freedom for anyone to wear blue denim in almost any situation.

For Levi Strauss, that is the best of all possible worlds.

Chapter XIII

The Behemoth, the Kharma, and the Crown Prince

THE NUMBERS ARE TOO LARGE to grasp, like government budgets, so big they are meaningless, the chairman of the board of directors confessed. The year he began in business, Levi Strauss sales reached $4 million; the corporation now billed that much and more every day of the year.

Once, Walter Haas, Jr., had dreamed of annual sales of $50 million. It seemed possible, but a long way off, near the end of his career, maybe. "One hundred million? Unreal! One hundred million dollars is unreal to me today," he said, shaking his head. "Now that we're one and a half billion, our responsibilities don't seem any tougher than when we were one hundred million. You grow with it. It's like chips in a poker game. After a while, you just add more zeros on them."

Adding zeros, Levi Strauss has become the largest apparel manufacturer in the world, with 32,000 employees in seventy countries. In 1977, it made and sold over 150 million garments, enough to put a pair of pants, a shirt, a jacket, or a sweater on every single person living in the nineteen largest cities of the world. In the United States, the company produces one of every three pairs of jeans sold, one of every ten pairs of men's slacks, one of every ten women's jeans. It is the world's largest sport coat manufacturer; the largest manufacturer of brand-name boys' wear, more than twice the size of its leading competitor. In just five years, it has become one of the four largest shirt-makers in the United States, and has yet to manufacture its first dress shirt.

The world's largest consumer of denim, corduroy, and hop-sacking, Levi Strauss bought more than 250 million yards of fabric, enough to wrap a cummerbund of cloth six times around the equator. To produce more than fifty million denim garments in 1977 alone, the company's fifty-one domestic and twenty-seven overseas plants used nearly 100 million yards of heavyweight denim and 8.4 million miles of orange thread — sufficient to spin a line from the earth to the moon and back eighteen times. Into those denim pants went 200 million rivets, seventy million buttons, and, of course, fifty million orange or red tabs peeping from the seam on the right rear pocket.

Its 1000 salesmen call on 46,000 stores around the world, the company claiming the widest distribution of all clothing manufacturers. Over 111 stores or chains in the United States billed more than $1 million with the firm during 1977; department stores that once shunned Levi's altogether, or only grudgingly stocked the workaday 501s in the basement, were responsible for half of Levi Strauss's domestic sales, and that share is rising. Another 25 percent of the company's production went to 1300 pants stores or LOSs.

Though the 501, which started it all, contributed a declining percentage of garments the company manufactured, it was nevertheless responsible for five million units in 1977. Fashions came, fashions went, and year after year the Double X denim waist overall continued to sell. The firm estimated it had produced more than one billion pairs of heavyweight denim pants since Jacob W. Davis cut his first pair for the Reno woodchopper with dropsy.

The numbers continue to grow, beyond comprehension.

A single share of the company's original issue in 1890 — there were 18,000 shares priced at $100 each — would have mitotically multiplied to 900 with a total market value of $2340 at the end of 1977, corporation treasurer Robert Kern calculated. (Actually, the rise is more dramatic, since employees bought that nominal $100 stock at big discounts. Milton Grunbaum, still rosy-cheeked at eighty-five, estimated that he paid an average price of "pennies" for the shares that made him a millionaire many times over.)

From sheer size has come complexity, and from complexity problems that neither Walter nor Peter Haas could have foreseen in those modestly ambitious years after World War II. The company of old, paternalistic, friendly, caring, is in jeopardy.

"We know that the company has grown so much that we've lost humanistic values. I used to know everybody by name," said Daniel Koshland, the retired president, hardly bothering to mask the wistful nostalgia for quieter years. "Now I go up in the elevator and I don't know anybody. I bow, say hello to everybody, but I don't know them by name.

"The atmosphere is changing. We're doing the best we can to preserve it, but it's inevitable: the bigger we grow, the less personal touch there is."

The sense of loss grew as the business grew, and became keen when Levi Strauss, after 108 years on Battery Street, crowded beyond endurance, moved to a new corporate headquarters in 1974.

The thirty-two-story building — of which the corporation would lease fourteen floors — offered vast space, a far more pleasant working environment, and 360-degree views of the city and the bay. Nonetheless, Walter, Jr., remembered, "That last day in the old building, it was a terrible day."

His secretary, Rita Guiney, suggested they get champagne for everybody. "I went down and tried to shake hands with everybody; I just wanted to make a tour. I don't know why. It was just a major change in relationships, I guess, and the closeness we all felt. I didn't know what to say. I patted people on the back and said, 'See you next Monday,' and 'Gosh, won't it be great to get out of these lousy elevators?' I guess I had a lump in my throat when I went out of that building."

Their new headquarters was part of an urban redevelopment built on landfill that had swallowed up San Francisco's Commercial Street wharf over a century before. Though Levi Strauss himself had attended ship auctions in 1853 on virtually this same spot, the company he founded was of necessity making a sharp break with that past.

"Certainly the move to this building didn't help us keep the old feeling," a senior executive lamented in his office on the twenty-eighth floor. "Up to this time we've avoided the syndrome of the eastern-establishment kind of company. I fear for it, between you and me," he said, clucking disapproval.

"We're introducing too many outside executives who look upon the company as part of *Fortune*'s Five Hundred, and something to be controlled by computers and Wall Street, the financial aspects." Fresh in his mind was the ranking announcement that Levi Strauss was moving a distribution center from San Jose, California, to Henderson, Nevada. The financial benefits to the corporation were tangible; his objection was to what he considered the crass treatment of the 225 employees at the distribution center. Only those with ten or more years' service were likely to be offered jobs in the Bay Area. The company would help the balance find other employment locally, but the gesture appeared a token; their loyalty would be "sacrificed" in the name of profits. This was not the way Levi Strauss, which had kept its people working in the depths of the Depression, traditionally treated employees.

The changes are apparent even to those with relatively few years at Levi Strauss. John Wyek, the corporation's lanky market analyst for seven years, said without sarcasm, "I get a warm and squishy feeling because the company I work for gives a damn about the human environment."

Towering even while seated at his desk, the former University of Wisconsin basketball player toyed with a pencil. "There are a lot of forces pulling Levi Strauss toward the plastic-and-chrome organization, but, down deep, it's still a family-run business, and everybody in it is part of the family.

"I'm disturbed by the pull, but maybe it's a natural tendency of organizations to calcify and lose a lot of the sensitivities toward people — not only the people in the company, but the people who buy the products, and just the people around us affected by the existence of Levi Strauss and Company. In order to make a billion-and-a-half corporation run, you've got to move away from the familial and into a more impersonal, more structured, more formal organization.

"But I'm pleased by the extent to which we've maintained the 'peopleness' we have. You've got a helluva task to be that big, that structured, and still give a damn about people. It's all too easy to get swept away in running this behemoth we call 'the company.'"

For Barbara Clemens-Pitre, feeling the responsibility of a $10 million product line in Womenswear, the plastic-and-chrome corporation is at hand. "Most people working here need the family-type atmosphere. You need to feel involved. But now I feel like Standard Oil or General Motors. I don't feel like I really belong to a whole. 'You're on your own, baby. Sink or swim.'"

Perhaps the most powerful black woman in American industry, Clemens-Pitre is frustrated. Womenswear has not prospered as she would have wished. "In the last five years, I've done more giving than I've gotten, and you just get to the point where you feel you're drained." There were tears in her eyes. "I've just lost five years out of my life, and I just feel cheated.

"I can give more," she said, smiling through the tears. It was a promise to herself. Barbara Clemens-Pitre sometimes dreams of being the first woman employee to be elected to the corporation's board of directors.

Parceled out on fourteen floors of the new structure, with some departments still scattered in nearby office buildings, Levi Strauss lost some of the cohesiveness that had marked the "store" on Battery Street. "Eight years ago, when I came to work as a temporary employee — " Kit Durgin broke off, surprised. "Eight years! *That's* a statement about the company. I've never done *anything* for eight years." She laughed. "I was introduced to every executive in the building, so if they called, I'd know who they were and they'd know who I was. I met Walter and Peter Haas the second day I was here. Today, you don't even know all the people on your own floor."

Durgin, at thirty-three secretary of the Levi Strauss Foundation and assistant secretary of the corporation, paused. "Those days are gone, but I think Walter and Peter hope they aren't, and still try to operate in that way. Maybe they're a little bit naïve in that. We have more high-powered executives than we had in those days, men who are more political and maybe take advantage.

"It all happened so fast. I'm not sure Walter and Peter have a real hold on it. Not that they don't know what's going on, but in terms of how they're going to handle this growth."

In an interview shortly before his retirement in 1977, Paul Glasgow agreed. "The thing is, we don't have as many people dedicated to what I call unselfish desires as we formerly had. There's a real feeling that we're losing something."

Unlike many, Glasgow was optimistic. "I think eventually the esprit de corps" — in his Missouri drawl it sounded like "speer decor" — "will come back. We're going to have to have training programs that really encompass these things, and we're going to have to sell, sell, sell. We can't just do it once.

"Probably the biggest problem we've got is between floors here at Two Embarcadero. The divisions are profit-making, and they probably don't have the feeling they once had of helping this division over here."

The lack of communication between competitive divisions can have an effect on performance. Acknowledging that she was competing with the Womenswear Division "for some segment of the market," fashion jeans product manager Susan Fantus commented, "If I came out with a jean that women bought, I probably wouldn't suggest it to Gals because those channels of communication really aren't that available." Unaware that Womenswear under McDermott, the former jeans merchandising manager for whom she worked, could turn a factory in six weeks, Fantus added, "The timing would be off."

What assistant corporation counsel Cassandra Flipper called "the kharma" is changing. Throughout the home office, the sense of loss is acute.

"Levi Strauss is a classic example of the old-line, paternalistic company coming of age in the impersonal, modern world," Ernest Griffes, manager of Employee Benefits, explained. "The family's desire to relate to the good old days is like two people trying to pull a horse through a knothole."

In an effort to keep some sense of the traditional family presence, Walter and Peter made a conscious effort to maintain contact with the rank and file. The two visited various floors of the building for coffee *klatches,* inviting employees to visit with them.

But the gap was too wide. The workers felt the effort superficial. "They're not looking for Walter and Peter caring, but for caring by their immediate boss. The employees' perception of what's happening — the Haases' attitude as opposed to that of their boss — leads to sarcasm and skepticism toward management."

And further erodes the kharma that the Haases seek to foster. Still, Griffes is cautiously optimistic. "Walter and Peter's tenacity has preserved it so far and will get us through a few more years. Paternalism won't survive, but a sense of personally caring will."

Walter and Peter Haas are keenly aware of the loss to the corporation and within the corporation. To preserve their concept of corporate humanism, they have attempted to institutionalize the sense of caring through the community relations program. In the factories across the United States, it has apparently helped imbue some employees with a larger sense of responsibility. Ironically, in the home office such feelings wane.

"I'm not sure I can give you precise methods to mitigate the loss of family feeling," Peter said, "except to do our best through influence and example, and try to explain our philosophy toward people."

In addition, he said in a second interview, "you hire the people who seem to fit your mold. You don't hire the ruthless professional, the man who takes an ax to clean up a situation that needs cleaning up. It's a self-perpetuating sort of thing, a way of life." He chuckled. "There's just got to be the right chemistry with the people you hire."

But the chemistry required a catalyst, Walter and Peter learned. A study of the corporation's future organization by outside consultants indicated widespread sentiment that the continued presence of the family was important to the employees, more vital than either the employees or the Haases had imagined.

"It was they who came to us and said a lot of people are concerned that the family presence will be lost, and your sons, Bob and Peter, Junior, have the qualities and are well thought of, and they should be put on a fast track. It was only at that point, when we felt it was coming from an objective source, it was — Hallelujah!" Walter grinned.

"This made us think maybe we were doing the company a disservice in bending over backward not to give our sons special preference, to let them move ahead at the proper pace, as we would anyone else. We began to think we ought to put them on a faster track, because if the family feeling is important to people, let's get some signals out, and make sure as we bow out that there's someone else to take over."

Five years before, the Haas brothers had been openly doubtful that a family member would be president of the corporation in the future. By 1977, two proud parents, the chairman of the board and the president, have changed their minds. "Nothing makes Peter and me feel better than that a Haas will continue as chief executive officer," Walter happily admitted.

The sense of relief is palpable throughout the company. Even the senior vice-president for corporate policy and planning, who at forty might be considered the most likely to succeed to the presidency if the Haases should retire, was pleased with the decision to accelerate the career of the two sons.

"The Haases just didn't feel comfortable treating Bob and Peter, Junior, differently, talking to them about the business problems, the issues, the major concerns. They certainly didn't talk to these guys' colleagues about such things, so it wouldn't be fair," Frank Brann said.

"Bob Grohman told them, 'You're wrong. The history of the company, your philosophy, needs continuation. It's absolutely required that you develop Bob and Peter, Junior, to the greatest degree possible.' And I think that was a helluva good answer."

Robert D. Haas, the older of the two, became the crown prince.

Like his uncle before him and his younger cousin Peter, Bob had shunned the family business until he proved to himself "that no matter what the environment, I could stand on my own two feet, be productive, and be recognized as competent."

The oldest of Walter and Evelyn Haas's three children, Bob was determinedly independent. When, at twenty, Bob grew a beard, his father's suppressed discontent welled up finally, Walter pointing out beards were not common and might not be becoming.

"Think of all the great men in history who wore beards: Abraham Lincoln, Jesus Christ," the junior at the University of California answered.

Walter looked at his son a moment. "Levi Strauss also had a beard, and he died a bachelor."

Haas kept his beard for the while, and his independence.* The young English major graduated as valedictorian in 1964, then joined the Peace Corps. He spent two years in the Ivory Coast, teaching English as a second language and physical education, "which was a joke; I'm a real stumble-fall."

---

* By no means is this sense of independence handed down unilaterally. Evelyn Haas, "a hothouse flower from New York," according to her trout-fishing husband, Walter, took up the sport and wrote a book on fly-casting for women. In late 1977, it was offered to publishers under Mrs. Haas's maiden name.

Haas elected to attend the Harvard Graduate School of Business Administration, again like his uncle, a Baker Scholar. "My thought was, I'd probably end up in some sort of administrative job, not necessarily business, and a business education would prepare me for anything: hospital administration, government, whatever."

After a year as a White House Fellow, then a stint managing political campaigns, including a portion of Eugene McCarthy's abortive presidential effort, Haas returned to San Francisco. He took a job with a management-consulting firm, finally deciding he wanted neither to be a consultant nor to work for the kinds of firms to which he had been exposed.

At thirty-one, he began to consider Levi Strauss as a potential employer, "attracted to the things which attract a lot of people today: the social responsibility, the fact that it's a popular product, and one that generally isn't polluting or exploitative or represents hazards."

Haas first told his father, "which made him very happy. As much as he secretly wanted me to come to the company, he wisely never urged it. He always urged me to make up my own mind."

Walter, Sr., on the other hand, felt strongly about the role of the family and that "it was his right to say whatever was on his mind — which was true — because he might not have an opportunity to say it again."

The grandson invited himself to lunch with his grandfather. "I told him over the first course that, with his permission, I would like to be considered for a job in Levi's. And his eyes misted over and then twinkled. It was a very moving moment. Suddenly this floodgate of reminiscences and stories about the business burst open, not the reminiscences of an old man, but of a person who was so overjoyed emotionally and excited by the prospect of my coming into the firm." Bob Haas paused. "I know I'll never forget that."

His career at Levi Strauss began in inventory management, improving deliveries and vendor relations in 1973. Then he spent two years in the Jeans Division. "Recognizing my natural inability to judge fashion trends, they gave me a couple of the more stable items which were doing extremely well. Then came the trend for a more dress-up jean, and I managed to run what was a very profitable series of lines pretty well into the ground."

Meanwhile, Haas met and married Colleen Gershon, an attractive attorney working in the office of Charles Garry, counsel for the Black Panther Party.

Transferred to Levi Strauss International, where he rose to assistant general manager of the Far East Division, his primary responsibility was to manage supplies of heavyweight denim in the Orient. Piece goods being in tight supply, Haas spent the greater portion of his time in the "degrading lifestyle of the international business executive, traveling around the world in search of the demon bitch denim." The responsibility of negotiating with suppliers for greater quantities and quality was heavy, but he discovered that "the Haas name did lend a credibility to our insistence on things being done correctly."

Though he laughingly protested his career at Levi Strauss was not quite so well managed as some believed, Haas was on a fast track. On November 22, 1977, he was elected a vice-president of the corporation, the first member of the fifth generation to become an officer.

Haas's ascension to the presidency is not immediately assured. Both his father and uncle are determined that he prove himself, and Bob Haas himself insists his rise must be based on his contributions, not solely on his blood lines. "Otherwise I could be very happy teaching Chaucer."

Grohman having assigned Haas high marks for his performance so far, it is doubtful that the young man will ever grace a university faculty.

Haas has accepted the role of heir apparent at Levi Strauss with marked grace. "Sure the name's a burden, but anybody who's going to lead a major corporation has that burden, name or not. It's a terrible responsibility to have the livelihood of thirty-two thousand people dependent upon the quality of your decisions and foresight."

But he has prepared, probably as have few others who will head major American business enterprises. He is satisfied that he proved his worth outside the nurturing womb of Levi Strauss. "I'm glad that I taught and was in politics and involved in government service and a range of other kinds of businesses. A lot of ideas that make Levi's unique come from places completely outside the corporate environment."

Many of those ideas, however, do come from within the family tradition, culturally Jewish though attendance at Temple Emanu-El is limited to the High Holy Days. "When I was young, the dinner table conversation did not revolve around business. After friends and the day's adventures, we'd talk about pride in being able to help somebody, or how a person of rather low rank in the company came in to talk to my dad about a personal problem, and my dad's pleasure that that person would reach out to him and feel comfortable about coming in and talking about that."

The sense of family tradition evolved from the mandatory contribution of a portion of his allowance to charities — a requirement earlier demanded of the young Dan Koshland by his parents before the turn of the century. It came from the example of his father's being at work by 8:00 A.M. It came in the examples, set by all the Haases of, a lack of ostentation. "Most members of the family I know have never felt the trappings of wealth are that desirable. There seems to be a male characteristic in this family: absolutely no interest in clothes." Suddenly conscious of the obviously expensive suit he was wearing, he quipped, "I'm my wife's Barbie doll."

Haas is aware of the gap that name, title, and wealth create between him and co-workers. The higher he rises, the greater the distance he must span. It is a corollary of the careers of Bob and Peter Haas, Jr.

This fifth generation faces a greater challenge than did its predecessors. By virtue of its very size, Levi Strauss & Co. can no longer be personally managed by a small group of like-minded men. (Its status as a publicly held corporation has no great effect in this regard. Members of the Haas and Koshland families, and their private foundations, own a majority of Levi Strauss stock; closely allied board members reinforce those holdings substantially.)

"People would like to think that because there is family involvement the depth of feeling we had in the past can be continued." Bob Haas frowned, then shook his head. "The philosophy can continue, the sense of fairness and justice can continue, but there's no way that any individual, no matter what his position, is going to be able to touch people in the way that's been done in past generations.

"Right now we have a number of units in the company that are as large as or larger than the whole company was ten, fifteen years ago. And these are headed by individuals who knew the family environment of old. Many have recreated this feeling, and maybe that will spawn further feeling.

"In the future, it will be the division managers, the regional sales managers, the departmental managers — all with their own little organizations — who must maintain the 'family' feeling, and make it a better environment."

But Haas is critical. "I don't believe we encourage these managers enough. There's no reward for divisional presidents or department heads who create a good environment — developing, training, and motivating people and preparing them for more challenging responsibilities. I think we've got to find ways to make individual managers responsible for the working environment, because that's the only way to have this feeling work down through the corporation."

The responsibility is not entirely that of ranking managers, however. The corporation itself must continue to foster an attitude of concern for the employees' welfare, maintaining or improving benefits and providing job opportunities. It was with just such a concern in mind that, in December 1977, the company announced an unusual, and probably largest of its kind, stock disbursal.

Levi Strauss would supplement the perfunctory service pins with shares of stock, one for each year of work with the company. All employees, with the exception of officers, directors, and division presidents, will each receive five shares on every fifth anniversary of his or her employment.

More than 8800 sewing-machine operators, salesmen, truckdrivers, clerk-typists, computer programmers divided 60,000 shares with a market value of $1.7 million in the first year. Ernest Griffes estimated that at present employment levels, each year an additional 2000 employees will mark their first quintennial anniversaries and divide 10,000 shares.

The program must inevitably grow. Levi Strauss & Co. is adding an average of 2000 employees annually, and that figure is likely to increase as the firm diversifies.

According to Walter Haas, Jr., Levi Strauss can double its $1.56 billion annual sales before 1987, on the base the company presently has, adding a handful of related lines, such as outerwear, ski wear, and golf clothes. Most of the growth will come through expansion of the company's share of the market, at least in the near future. International sales provide the greatest virgin market for basic jeans, and in selected countries sportswear items trimmed from the line during Grohman's 1974 retrenchment will be reinstated.

Domestically, the Boyswear Division, already the corporation's fastest-growing, has been renamed Youthwear and will add infants' and girls' clothing to its catalogue. Panatela, reassuming its maiden name, Sportswear, and Levi's for Gals, renamed Womenswear, have the largest potential markets. As leisure time expands, and with an increasingly older median age of the population caused by declining birth rates, Levi Strauss will necessarily broaden its major target group from the narrow teen-age market it sought to capture. Women's leisure wear is a $3-billion-a-year industry; no single firm dominates. Levi Strauss, selling approximately $62 million in women's garments and already ranking itself fifth or sixth in size among firms scrambling in that fast-changing market, can increase its volume tenfold within the next six years, according to Jim McDermott. Barbara Clemens-Pitre, who remembers when the $171 million Youthwear Division was only a single line of double-knee jeans managed by her new boss, McDermott, will be delighted.

Similarly, the $108 million Sportswear Division will focus its efforts on the aging postwar baby crop. As their purchases built the Jeans Division over the last two decades, so these twenty-five-to-thirty-five-year-olds will increase Sportswear to $250 million by the early years of the 1980s, Harry Cohn predicts. The division ranks second in sales nationally to competitor Haggar, but there is no pressure from within Levi Strauss to overtake the leader. It isn't necessary, Sportswear vice-president Robert Siegel said, only half-joking. "We create our own pressure. Personally, I cannot be satisfied with being number two."

The Jeans Division faces the toughest test. The population group to which the division has most appealed will constitute a smaller percentage of the future population of the United States. John Wyek predicts 15 percent fewer people by 1990 between the ages of fourteen and twenty-four, the company's largest traditional market.

As division president, Al Sanguinetti "kept his elbows out," to use Walter Haas's phrase. The fashion jeans line, already larger than the entire Sportswear Division, sought the same customers as Harry Cohn's minions — jeans graduates looking for a somewhat more dressy, tailored garment. Sanguinetti also staked a claim on new products, notably outerwear; the freebooter in him would never permit Al Sanguinetti to preside over a gradual deterioration of the Jeans Division he so cherishes.

But named to the additional post of executive vice-president of the United States Group, with overall responsibility for both the Jeans and the Youthwear divisions, Sanguinetti must take a broader view. His horizon is no longer bounded by the fourth floor at Two Embarcadero, but extends to the corporation as a whole. According to Bob Grohman, who adroitly managed the restructuring, Sanguinetti's new vision makes feasible a realignment of some product lines, which obviates intramural competition. (In the offing is an amalgamation of the four present shirt lines into a single division.)

The United States, which still accounts for two thirds of

all Levi Strauss sales, is undergoing a subtle but measureable shift in lifestyles. Automobiles and large suburban homes have lost some of their luster as status symbols for many, and have become too costly for many more. Money once spent for these major purchases is being diverted to clothing, to leisure activities, especially hobbies and vacations, and to household furnishings.

The birth rate, declining steadily since 1971, according to the United States Bureau of the Census, will not have a measureable impact on company sales in the immediate future. Oddly, families spend about the same percentage of their income on children's clothes regardless of the number of offspring. For the long run, though, the decrease in the number of young people threatens the volume of business.

Offsetting this trend are major changes in urban lifestyles. Young people are delaying marriage, and single people spend more for clothing than do married. More women are working, and working women generally have larger wardrobes than do housewives. Each year a smaller percentage of American workers holds blue-collar or laboring jobs; though this may slow the sale of blue denim work garments, greater numbers of employers are permitting white-collar workers to wear casual or leisure garments on the job. (In a November 1976 memo, Wyek noted, "Of 300 business organizations, 98 percent permit sportcoats, 79 percent permit leisure suits, 65 percent permit turtlenecks [or] open-collar shirts, 24 percent permit blue jeans." The relaxation of clothing standards, that is, the blurring of the boundaries between work and leisure garments, is so pervasive in California that the most conservative of business institutions, including banks, permit women to wear denim pants, men to wear sport shirts at work.)

To take advantage of these trends, Levi Strauss as a corportation will place more emphasis on leisure wear and the twenty-five-to-thirty-five age group. Wyek's predictions for the future, he concluded, "are not particularly rosy. Maintaining traditional Levi Strauss & Co. growth rates will require massive brand share increases, expansion beyond our traditionally strong consumer groups and our traditionally strong products. The positive factors may help a little, but we're facing a very stiff task."

Within the corporation's higher echelons there is general agreement that Levi Strauss cannot sustain its current growth rate, doubling in size every five years or less. (Public relations director Bud Johns wryly notes, "We said the same thing when we went public, which shows what poor forecasters we are.") Even so, the company in 1977 began an intensified advertising campaign, at a cost of $5 million in the first year, to promote the tag line: "At Levi's it doesn't have to be blue, it just has to be good." Frank Brann told New York reporters, "Our goal is to demonstrate that we've moved away from being purely a jeans manufacturer to a leisure wear manufacturer for the entire family. We want to acquire a greater share in every product category."

Despite the new campaign, and the parallel $8 million purchase of 123 television commercials to be shown during the 1980 Olympic Games, there are paradoxical hints that sheer sales growth, the single measure of success in the world of business, is not enough.

Almost reluctantly, Peter Haas, Sr., conceded, "I think we have to continue to grow to provide opportunities and to attract good people, because if we don't grow, they won't come to us.

"There's a success factor to it, too," he added with a laugh. "Present rules require that you have to beat last year's figures all the time. I suppose there's a continual need to prove yourself, to do something well. Maybe that's a better way of putting it.

"But I think we like to measure ourselves not only by growth, but by some of those other things: good relations with our people, a good record in the community. That's part of doing well, too."

Those criteria might be overlooked in the pressure for ever-increasing bottom lines. "The company has become extremely profit-oriented," one successful middle-manager complained. "People today can't afford the luxury — this is a very tender subject — of time and money to develop social programs, to do a favor for someone, to hire someone who may not be right. You can hire minorities all day long, and the EEO [Equal Employment Opportunity] people are very happy, but it's costing you money because they're not performing. Management is in the position where it can't hire people just for the sake of hiring people. They have to carry their weight, whether black, red, female, whatever.

"Increased profitability feeds upon itself. And the person who says why don't we stop growing and consolidate our operation and make it more efficient — This is almost heresy."

There is, beyond increased efficiency and larger market shares, a third way for profits to increase: through the acquisition of other companies.

One logical area of expansion the company has already ruled out: retail stores. In 1971, Mel Bacharach, with the tacit agreement of the Haases, created a dummy corporation as the owner of the company's first retail store. Anomalous Inc. was to be the initial stage in vertically integrating Levi Strauss, from production to consumer, and the dummy corporation was to mask actual ownership.

Bacharach opened the first store, christened by the manager "It's," in Knoxville, Tennessee, an area in which the company had poor market penetration and low per capital sales.

There were drawbacks. Other retailers disliked the vigorous competition; company salesmen resented the implied criticism of a Levi's-owned store in their lagging territory; and even though treated as a regular customer, It's helped use up the availability of scarce denim. Further, as each of the It's stores opened, competitive pants stores followed, thereby achieving full market penetration for the company and obviating the original need.

Before the adventure ended three years later, thirteen additional It's outlets were operating in the Southeast. Those first-quality stores, carrying not only Levi's but competitors' products as well, are to be sold off, leaving only twenty-five frankly named "Goofs" and four Canadian "Boo Boos" outlets selling factory seconds under the Anomalous banner.

Goofs and Boo Boos absorb the great bulk of Levi's irregulars, "but our irregulars are not seconds in the industry sense since we have such high standards," said Tom Austin, president of the Diversified Products Division and overseer of the retail operation. Labels and tabs are stripped from the garments, but the trademarked arcuate stitching remains on the irregulars. Most customers are aware of the manufacturer, and are shopping for bargains, enough so that Anomalous is one of the corporation's larger accounts.

Vertical integration closed off as a matter of policy, the problem Brann confronts in exploring future acquisitions is what direction to take. "Once you're the largest apparel company, you can then become only a larger largest apparel company unless you diversify. We may have to make some acquisitions outside the apparel industry, to move a portion of our earnings into dynamic growth areas such as energy or leisure."

Neither Brann nor, more important, Walter and Peter Haas believe Levi Strauss will become a conglomerate, that is, will buy firms in unrelated fields and let those acquisitions run themselves.

"I don't think any of us wants a conglomerate-type thing," Walter Haas said in as firm a voice as he musters. "We're not going to try to buy a chewing gum company or a real estate company. But if I were to guess what's going to come out of Frank's study, he'll suggest we build on our strengths, starting with the name and what it connotes."

Levi Strauss bubble gum or Levi Strauss condominiums are jarring concepts. But Levi Strauss backpacking equipment and sleeping bags fit well in the corporate image. The company's most valuable asset, its name, can be comfortably stretched over leisure, recreation, and sporting goods lines.

"The only trouble I have with that," Walter said, "is that most firms in those fields are relatively small compared to a two-billion or two-and-a-half-billion-dollar company. We had an opportunity to acquire a manufacturer of outdoor equipment with one hundred and thirty million dollars' annual sales. What was that going to accomplish?''

The notion of turning away from the purchase of a corporation of that size suddenly amused the chairman of the board. "I'm running out of ideas, and new ideas are something I've always prided myself on. Maybe it's good I'm getting near retirement age."

Acquisitions within the garment business appear foreclosed. Though Levi Strauss is dominant only in the jeans and slacks business, it is the largest of the nation's 22,000 apparel firms. Acquiring even a noncompetitive firm, perhaps a manufacturer of outerwear, would undoubtedly draw the jaundiced eye of the Department of Justice's Antitrust Division.*

Short of acquisitions, Levi Strauss has found one way to expand into related markets: by licensing other manufacturers to use the coveted Levi's label. The small-scale efforts of Now! Designs and Ghettos Enterprises have been succeeded by a multimillion-dollar arrangement with the na-

---

* Levi Strauss has already felt the ire of the Federal Trade Commission, to the delight of the nation's discount houses, with which the company had steadfastly refused to trade. On May 7, 1976, the FTC began administrative proceedings, charging the company with price-fixing and restraint of trade because it declined to deal with retailers who would not agree to maintain the suggested retail prices. (Six years earlier, the federal agency had approved that same policy.) Evidence submitted at the subsequent hearing established that some company salesmen had threatened retailers with discontinuance if they did cut prices or resold garments to other stores unable to buy from the company. Levi Strauss offered a consent agreement, according to which the company would abandon the use of printed price tags or suggested resale prices, but would retain the sole right to choose its customers. At first rejected by the government, the agreement was accepted in October 1977, ten months after Levi Strauss voluntarily gave up suggesting list prices. To the dismay of those major discount houses declining to offer the customer service that Levi Strauss demands of its accounts, the company remained free to select its outlets. Predictably, for the first time in the company's history, retail stores across the country began a savage price-cutting war on 501s and the two other best-selling pants. The ironic result was that Levi's, without reducing its wholesale prices, increased its share of the jeans market to an estimated 40 percent, as customers rushed to buy $15.00 pants for as little as $8.99. (See FTC Docket No. 9081, and File No. 7510001.)

tion's largest shoe manufacturer, Brown Group Inc. Within a year of introducing the Levi's for Feet line of thirty casual boots and shoes, Brown sold one million pairs, each with its own Levi's label. (A similar agreement with Burlington Mills, signed in 1977, brought Levi's socks into the marketplace.)

Levi Strauss played a major role in the introduction of the shoe line, selecting Brown after twenty other manufacturers had previously sought to market "Levi's" shoes. According to Gerald O'Shea, Levi Strauss's vice-president for domestic marketing, the corporation tapped Brown because "the two companies have the same kind of people, ethics, and quality standards." The Levi's image was to be transferred from pants to shoes.

Beyond the profits, the introduction of Levi's for Feet generated considerable excitement among retailers. The line turned over from self-selling display racks in stores as often as six times a year; traditionally, a shoe store turns over its stock twice a year. Such figures impress retail merchants; the Levi's label might magically sell anything.

Or almost anything. Tom Austin, who heads a $34-million-a-year division, is responsible for screening suggestions for new products that come in off the street. He has turned down, among others, proposals for a Levi's tab embedded in plastic for a zipper-fly pull, a denim-covered mousetrap, and a ceramic, buttocks-shaped planter with a red tab.

Austin did accept one suggestion brought in by a customer — that the company market a line of ski wear. The idea came from Maryann Buxton, an erstwhile designer then clerking in a ski shop. The notion intrigued Austin, a former Buffalo Bills football player and quite as fervid a buccaneer as his most outspoken opponent, Al Sanguinetti. For years, Levi's jeans and cords had served on the slopes, irreverently dubbed "Mexican Bogners" by young skiers more concerned with practicality than fashion.

Austin retained Buxton as a consultant, and adroitly lobbied the company's first formal sally into athletic clothing through corporate management. Together the pair launched "the oldest new name in ski wear." As Bud Johns sardonically stated, "The world's largest manufacturer of ski wear now makes ski wear."

Buxton designed the test line, modeled it for advertising photos, sold it to retail stores, then supervised its manufacture. The first test-marketing of 8000 padded overalls and parkas, in the winter of 1976–1977, sold out. The following year, a second test of 60,000 units, worth $2.5 million, also sold out.

Convinced by that success, Grohman approved the incorporation of ski wear as the first product of a new marketing division, Activewear. Into that agency will go all sports-oriented garments made by other divisions, including jogging outfits and parkas, as well as new lines of tennis clothes and athletic shoes. Austin maintaining that, like the pressed-into-service Mexican Bogners, Levi's "is probably the oldest manufacturer of golf clothes," a formal golfing line may also be assigned to the new division.

By the end of 1977, Grohman had shaped a marketing plan to spread the umbrella of the corporate image and accompany consumer loyalty over new lines and products in six divisions: Jeans, Sportswear, Womenswear, Activewear, Youthwear, and Accessories. (The company owns two belt manufacturers, and licenses others to make luggage, wallets, and related items.)

The Levi's tab implies not only high quality but a rare status devolving from that quality and the unassuming nature of the corporation's most famous product, the 501 Double X denim waist overall. A century after its creation, that garment remains the fundamental asset of the corporation. It is the one item discount houses want most, the one Levi Strauss product most frequently bootlegged, counterfeited, and even highjacked. According to Michael Gibbons, the Jeans Division regional sales manager in Atlanta, "Law enforcement officials claim Levi's are among the top three highjacking targets, along with cigarettes and liquor."

The 501 has stirred an enduring affection among consumers, an affection that leads them to patch, stitch, and repair pants they cannot bring themselves to discard. The company regularly receives tattered garments from customers who ask that Levi Strauss give them proper burial because the saddened owner did not have the heart to throw them out. A few of the choicest make their way to the Levi Strauss Museum for preservation in the company's archives.*

Over time, frugal patches gave way to fanciful repairs, and those embroidered scraps to elaborately decorated denim pants and jackets fashioned to express the owner's individuality. Responding to the esthetic quality, the company sponsored a nationwide denim art contest in 1974, drew more than 2000 entries, and finally dispatched the studded, appliquéd, and embroidered winners on an eighteen-month museum tour. The mundane workingman's garment of an earlier age had become an art object.

Having risen above its humble origins, the garment surmounted class distinctions, as well. On June 1, 1977, the President of the United States told a White House gathering that Levi Strauss & Co. was a favorite business of his. "I am one of their best customers," Jimmy Carter added. "I just don't have time to wear out my blue jeans as much as I used to."

Characteristically, the company will not use that testimonial in its advertising or publicity.

At Levi Strauss, the products must speak for themselves.

---

* The company does not solicit letters — such a common business practice would be too self-serving for the Haases — but does maintain a "Letters to Levi's" file. That collection contains dozens of testimonials, proffered by patients and doctors, that the strength of the garments saved the owners from more serious injuries after traffic accidents, in mountain falls, or construction mishaps. One man wrote that his Sta-Prest pants retained their crease after he was immersed in the ocean for eighteen hours; another, that his survived twenty-two months in Vietnam, including seven of daily wear in a Viet Cong prison. Yet another prisoner wore his 109 days straight in a Havana prison, writing that the "slacks are as good as new" after the ordeal.

Epilogue

By ones and twos they walked slowly in the bright sun, hesitating at the foot of the stairs leading to the doorway of the Italian-American Social Club off Mission Street. At sixty-five and seventy, they took stairs slowly, cautiously.

For a few moments they stood in the entryway of the club, awkward in their best dresses, looking around the room, sniffing the musk of yesterday's cappuchino and Chianti.

There was what's-her-name from shirts, the one who married the handsome Irish mechanic in — heavens, was it that long ago? — 1921? And there were Julius Phillips's two sisters, Lydia and Paula, who came by every month for a visit. And Little Joe Corrieri with his ukulele; try to keep him away from these annual affairs.

Familiar faces, more lined since the last luncheon the company gave for its retirees, but friends. The uncertainty disappeared, and they smiled tentatively.

The oldest found chairs along the wall, sighing as they sat down. Shoes and girdles pinched. The younger ones, or the more spry, moved about — a handshake, a kiss, a hug — the laughter and friendly teasing growing louder.

The shyness rushed back as the three men walked slowly into the lobby, Dan Koshland leaning on his cane, Walter Haas deferring to his brother-in-law at the doorway. Behind them came young Peter, here this year as he had been all the other years. He was nearing sixty himself, but he would always be "young Peter" to these women who had taught him how to sew a pair of pants and men who had shown the boss's son how to cut fifty-four layers of fabric or repair a broken machine.

In moments, Walter was surrounded by the retired cutters and mechanics who had worked at Valencia Street through the years. Walter grinned as they teased him about his thinning hair, promising to try their guaranteed remedies, but it was hard to find good Chianti in Atherton.

More shy, the elderly women from North Beach and Chinatown hung back. Peter moved from chair to chair, beaming, animated, a man once again with old friends.

Slowly, carefully, eighty-five-year-old Dan Koshland eased himself into a folding chair and looked around the room. Koshland did not know the birdlike woman seated next to him. He introduced himself. The woman blushed, stammered a few words in Spanish, and fell silent.

Across the room Koshland spotted Hortense Thomson, sitting quietly, almost primly. Carefully, he placed the cane in front of himself, leaned on it a moment, then levered himself to his feet to pick his way carefully through the crowd and pay his respects.

Hortense Thomson reached toward Koshland. Holding hands, the multimillionaire and the retired button-machine operator silently looked at each other for a long moment.

Then they smiled. Big smiles.

They were friends. And co-workers.

Acknowledgments
Notes
Index

Acknowledgments

IT SAYS A GREAT DEAL about the people of Levi Strauss & Co.
that I can acknowledge with no little gratitude their utter
candor, their sense of integrity, and their appreciation of
the value of history for its own sake. Though this book is
an unsponsored history, I was given the run of the company,
free to compile the information I wanted and to draw such
conclusions as I felt warranted.

I pored through financial records at will — surely the first
outsider permitted to view those once closely guarded family secrets. I talked to whomever I chose, skipping about
without regard to chains of command, protocols (there seem
to be very few at Two Embarcadero), or egos. I talked with
more than 100 people, from a retired chairman of the board
to a button-machine operator living on social security.
Many times I probed various sensitive areas, often pried
into personal feelings. As a reporter, I was secretly delighted
when Walter Haas, Sr., a man of stunning intelligence, said,
"You're asking me about things I've never thought about,"
and his son, Peter, later said with a laugh, "You want to put
me on the couch." To all of these people who so freely
gave of their time, whether they appear in this book by
name or not, my thanks.

Anyone who attempts historical research in San Francisco quickly learns of the impact of the earthquake and
fire of 1906. Only skilled librarians can help fill the gap

created when that tragedy destroyed three quarters of the paper in the city. I took shameless advantage of the knowledge of such experts as Mrs. Gladys Hansen, city archivist, San Francisco Public Library; Ms. Debby Ginsberg, of the Society of California Pioneers, San Francisco; Ms. Joan Salz, of the Wells-Fargo History Room, San Francisco; Ms. Judy Cohen, of the California Historical Society, San Francisco; and of Mrs. Mary Weinstein, of the California State Library, Sacramento.

Others helped as well: Ms. Elaine Ratner; Mrs. Nancy Arndt Finken, who provided goodly material about her maternal great-grandfather, Jacob W. Davis; and Douglas E. Goldman, the grandson of Walter A. Haas, Sr., and the sometime family genealogist.

Finally, a word about the most professional of public relations staffs I have encountered, and Bud Johns, its director, a man of Menckenian proportions without that Baltimore irascible's ill humors. Mrs. Joyce Bustinduy, Ms. Linden Farrar, Ms. Barbara Powell, Ms. Pat Gerber, and especially Ms. Mary Anne Easley did innumerable good services in my aid. Indeed, Ms. Easley helped well beyond my wildest expectations.

— E. C.

Notes

All quotations in the text are from the author's interviews, conducted in 1977, unless otherwise credited in these notes. Tape recordings of most of those interviews have been deposited in the Levi Strauss Museum, San Francisco, California.

CHAPTER I
The Founder (*pages 1–15*)

Page

1 Norton B. Stern, editor of the *Western States Jewish Historical Quarterly*, identified Abraham Gunst in a conversation with the author.

8 seclusion of Gentiles: Harriet Lane Levy, *920 O'Farrell Street* (New York, 1947), p. 67.

13 in sudden fury: Rockwell D. Hunt, ed., *California and Californians*, Vol. II (Chicago, 1930), p. 475.

14 A large portion: "Dr. John T. McLean and the Israelites," an undated pamphlet in the UCLA Research Library, Department of Special Collections.

15 He is a professional man: Ibid.

CHAPTER II
A Credit to His Race (*pages 16–43*)

18 The conversation is quoted in J. W. Davis's interrogatory of June 17, 1874, in *Levi Strauss et al* v. *A. B. Elfelt et al*, United

Page

States Circuit Court, District of California, No. 1211. Other details concerning Davis's career and the invention of the riveted garment are in *Levi Strauss & Co.* v. *The King Co.*, United States Circuit Court, Southern District of New York, No. 276, 1877.

18–19   Davis quotes: Ibid.

20–21   Davis letter: Courtesy of the Levi Strauss Museum. I have retained the idiosyncratic spelling while slightly amending the punctuation to aid the reader.

21   Patent application: Courtesy of the Levi Strauss Museum.

25   If these gentlemen: "Thanking James Lick," a clip in the Levi Strauss Museum marked "Post, June, 1874."

27   These goods: *Pacific Rural Press*, March 24, 1877.

28   Such an institution: *The Commerce and Industries of the Pacific Coast of North America* (San Francisco, 1882).

33   excellently adapted: *Industries of San Francisco* (San Francisco, 1899), pp. 51–52, courtesy Levi Strauss & Co. It is a pity: Jacob Stern to Dear Friends, July 25, 1881. This is one of the very few documents to survive the 1906 earthquake and fire; a copy is in the Levi Strauss Museum.

34   the poorest clothing man: Ibid.

37   From time to time: *The Bay of San Francisco, Its Cities and Their Suburbs* (Chicago, 1892), p. 337.

40   I am a bachelor: C. M. Older, "Does Wealth Bring Happiness?" San Francisco *Bulletin*, October 12, 1895, p. 13. This newspaper story — actually an attack on Leland Stanford, one of the Big Four, by a partisan editor — contains the only known interview with Levi Strauss. Earlier, he had shunned publicity.

42   Mr. Strauss, how do you feel: San Francisco *Bulletin*, September 28, 1972.

42   pioneer merchant and philanthropist: San Francisco *Call*, September 28, 1902, p. 1. At his death, Levi Strauss had apparently amassed the largest fortune held by an Israelite in San

Page

Francisco. The largest estates probated until 1904 were those of Charles Crocker, one of the Big Four, $24.1 million; Mark Hopkins, the second of the Big Four, $20.6 million; and Leland Stanford, the third of that railroad quartet, $17.7 million. By comparison, mining tycoon and United States Senator George Hearst, the father of playful Willie, left $8.8 million. After Strauss, the most wealthy Hebrew was Adolph Sutro, a Comstock mining engineer and promoter who later came to own as much as one twelfth of San Francisco's land area and served a term as mayor. Sutro, however, gave much of his fortune away during his lifetime; his estate totaled $2.7 million. A multiplier of ten will convert these turn-of-the-century fortunes into 1977 dollars. See R. E. Renaud, "San Francisco Great Estates That Have Passed through the Probate Court," San Francisco *Bulletin*, May 28, 1904, p. 1.

42 Voorsanger quote: San Francisco *Bulletin*, September 29, 1902, p. 6.

43 We must not forget: San Francisco *Bulletin*, October 2, 1902, p. 6.

CHAPTER III
The Koveralls Complement (*pages 44–58*)

53 The Kind of Klose: undated advertisement courtesy of Mrs. Nancy Davis Arndt Finken, deposited in the Levi Strauss Museum. Mrs. Finken is the granddaughter of Simon Davis.

55 Oh! Was I proud: Author's interview, March 3, 1977; also an interview with Grunbaum conducted by Steve Murdock, August 13, 1969, a tape recording of which is in the Levi Strauss archives.

CHAPTER IV
The New Company (*pages 59–78*)

60 Why go back: Walter A. Haas, Sr., "Levi Strauss and Company: Tailors to the World," with an introduction by E. T. Grether, an interview by Harriet Nathan, Regional Oral History Office, the Bancroft Library, University of California,

Page

Berkeley, 1976, p. 1. Quoted by permission of the Director, the Bancroft Library.

61 caused overwhelming trouble: Interview with Walter A. Haas, Sr., conducted by Steve Murdock, August 8, 1969, a copy of which is in the company archives.

62 Has your town: Carey McWilliams, *Southern California: An Island in the Sun,* reprint edition (Santa Barbara and Salt Lake City, 1973), p. 121.

64 It was the first year: Undated interview with Mrs. Walter A. Haas, Sr., a tape recording of which is in the company archives.

65 I think that Beronio: Walter A. Haas, Sr., memorandum, dated February 22, 1919.

67 We had a ship: "Levi Strauss and Company," p. 4.

72 a fair-haired young Lochinvar: Daniel E. Koshland, Sr., "The Principle of Sharing," with an introduction by John R. May, an interview by Harriet Nathan, Regional Oral History Office, the Bancroft Library, University of California, Berkeley, c. 1971, p. 93. Quoted by permission of the Director, the Bancroft Library.

76 Mr. Haas felt: Interview with Milton Grunbaum, conducted by Steve Murdock, August 13, 1969, a copy of which is in the company archives.

78 first significant step: Author's interview with Daniel Koshland, Sr., March 9, 1977. He added, with a laugh, "Each year there was a demonstration, but a little more subdued. And by the time the fifth year passed, I believe we would have had a strike if we hadn't given it."

CHAPTER V
The Apotheosis (*pages 79–97*)

80 Negroes and Okies: Carey McWilliams in Studs Terkel, *Hard Times* (New York, 1971), p. 280. Information on the Depression was drawn from Irving Bernstein, *The Lean Years* (Boston, 1960); and Arthur Schlesinger, Junior, *The Crisis of the Old Order* (Boston, 1957).

Page

82 We needed to find: Grunbaum to Murdock, August 13, 1969.

83 It was painful: Koshland to Murdock, August 5, 1969.

85 We made a mistake: Grunbaum to Murdock, August 13, 1969.

91 The Campbell letter is quoted courtesy of the Levi Strauss Museum.

91 The English letter is quoted courtesy of the Levi Strauss Museum.

CHAPTER VI
Transition (*pages 98–119*)

101 I want you to see: Interview with William Lagoria, conducted by Steve Murdock, August 1969, a copy of which is in the company archives.

106 We had these Christmas parties: Peter Haas in "Levi Strauss and Company," p. 8.

106 It's in the genes: Walter Haas, Jr., to Elaine Ratner, March 1, 1977, a tape recording courtesy of Levi Strauss & Co.

106–107 It starts way back: Peter Haas to Elaine Ratner, March 2, 1977, a tape recording courtesy of Levi Strauss & Co.

112 I learned more: Walter Haas, Sr., in "Levi Strauss and Company," p. 20.

116 We found that in a jobbing department: Walter Haas, Sr., Ibid., p. 18.

CHAPTER VII
With Utmost Confidence (*pages 120–139*)

127 Details of the Blackstone integration effort were drawn from the author's interviews as well as the interviews conducted by Elaine Ratner of Walter Haas, Jr., March 1, 1977; and Peter Haas, March 2, 1977, courtesy of Levi Strauss & Co.

136–137 I knew a lot more: Walter Haas, Jr., in "Levi Strauss and Company," p. 56.

CHAPTER VIII
A Period of Strain (*pages 140–159*)

Page

153　It was just a crescendo: Peter Haas in "Levi Strauss and Company," p. 16.

155　I kind of gulped: Ibid., p. 17.

CHAPTER IX
Far Too Little Competition (*pages 160–180*)

Though not specifically quoted, Mss. Kit Durgin, Cassandra Flipper, Donna Goya, Rity Guiney, Karin Håkanson, Daret Morgan, and Kris Schaeffer contributed greatly to my understanding of Levi Strauss & Co.'s, concept of social responsibility.

160–161　It wouldn't be effective otherwise: Walter Haas, Jr., to Ratner, March 1, 1977.

162　I wrote 'em: *Business Week,* November 1, 1969.

162–163　The Ghettos Enterprise, Inc., history is detailed in a case study prepared in 1971 by Peter Haas, Jr., for a class at Harvard Business School.

163　A lot of things don't work: Walter Haas, Jr., to Ratner, March 1, 1977, and Peter Haas to Ratner, March 2, 1977.

164–165　The Pera committee report dated August 21, 1970, is courtesy of Ed Pera, Levi Strauss & Co.

167　Details of the Stern trust are in Walter Haas's oral history, "Levi Strauss and Company."

179　The absenteeism figures are from "Searching for a Better Way to Work," *Saddleman's Review,* published by Levi Strauss & Co., Summer 1975, p. 5.

179n　Sweatshops: "Levi Strauss Legs It Toward Automation," *Business Week,* July 21, 1973, p. 62.

179n　Ms. Arrington's letter: *Northern Neck News* (Warsaw, Virginia), September 22, 1977.

CHAPTER XII
Lean and Mean (*pages 214–234*)

This chapter was based substantially on interviews with Frank Brann, Ed Gibson, Robert Grohman, Robert Haas, Ms. Pat Manning, Ted Michel, Ed Pera, Will Pilcher, and Peter Thigpen. In addition, Ms. Manning made available various market studies prepared by and for her office; and I had access to "Levi Strauss International Group Management Charter" and its Code of International Business-Principles, as well as to the frank, confidential minutes of the international group's operating board.

CHAPTER XIII
The Behemoth, the Kharma, and the Crown Prince (*pages 235–251*)

Page

250 Wyek memorandum, "Possible Impact of Future Trends," was prepared for the United States Group's Jerry O'Shea, November 12, 1976.

255 the two companies have: *Business Week*, November 10, 1975.

Index